Approaches to Teaching Baraka's *Dutchman*

Approaches to Teaching Baraka's *Dutchman*

Edited by

Matthew Calihman

and

Gerald Early

The Modern Language Association of America

New York 2018

Printed in the United States of America

Library of Congress Cataloging-in-Publication Data

Names: Calihman, Matthew, 1971– editor. | Early, Gerald Lyn, editor.
Title: Approaches to teaching Baraka's Dutchman / edited
by Matthew Calihman and Gerald Early
Description: New York : The Modern Language Association of America, 2018. |
Series: Approaches to teaching world literature ; 153 |
Includes bibliographical references and index.
Identifiers: LCCN 2018009903| ISBN 9781603293549 (hardback) |
ISBN 9781603293556 (paper)
Subjects: LCSH: Baraka, Amiri, 1934-2014. Dutchman. | Baraka, Amiri,
1934–2014—Study and teaching. | BISAC: Language Arts and Disciplines /
Study and Teaching. | Literary Criticism / American / African American. |
Literary Criticism / Drama
Classification: LCC PS3552.A583 D834 2018 | DDC 812/.54—dc23
LC record available at https://lccn.loc.gov/2018009903

Approaches to Teaching World Literature 153
ISSN 1059–1133

Cover illustration of the paperback and electronic editions: Joan Iaconetti,
6 LCL Blue, 2011, watercolor. © Joan Iaconetti.

Published by The Modern Language Association of America
85 Broad Street, suite 500, New York, New York 10004–2434
www.mla.org

CONTENTS

PREFACE

This book is a guide to teaching *Dutchman*, the most widely studied work of the writer-activist Amiri Baraka (1934–2014). In 1964, the play premiered at Greenwich Village's Cherry Lane Theatre, then one of the centers of the international avant-garde. A year later, *Dutchman* was produced in Harlem by Baraka's new Black Arts Repertory Theatre/School (BARTS), which was both a local cultural institution and a national laboratory for black radical aesthetics. With these productions, *Dutchman* began two sometimes parallel, sometimes intersecting lives: it became both a major work of postwar American experimental theater and a crucial achievement of the (then emergent) black arts movement.

Today *Dutchman* appears in a number of widely read anthologies and is frequently taught in African American literature, American literature, and theater courses. But even many well-informed readers are unfamiliar with the play's social and cultural contexts. It is now more difficult to see, for example, that the play's characters belong to the multiracial, multiethnic bohemian world of downtown Manhattan, circa 1964. Similarly, it is now harder to grasp the play's complicated relation to the era's civil rights and black liberation struggles. It may even be more difficult to recognize *Dutchman* as an avant-garde experiment—a break from the realist and naturalist aesthetics to which many readers are most accustomed and which many expect to find in black-authored texts.

A central aim of *Approaches to Teaching Baraka's* Dutchman is to help instructors make these dimensions of the play accessible to students. Toward this end, we begin with a brief intellectual biography of Baraka. We hope to describe his thinking about how, where, and on whose behalf he might function as an intellectual and to reconstruct in broad outlines the historical struggles, ideological and aesthetic, through which he arrived at *Dutchman*.

In 1964, the year *Dutchman* first appeared, President Lyndon Johnson announced the beginning of the War on Poverty; Cassius Clay (soon to become Muhammad Ali) beat Sonny Liston to win the Heavyweight Championship of the World; Malcolm X and the Nation of Islam parted ways, with Malcolm resolving to bring the fight against white supremacy to mainstream political and social institutions; Nina Simone released an album, *In Concert*, featuring the civil rights protest songs "Old Jim Crow," "Go Limp," and "Mississippi Goddam"; civil rights organizers James Chaney, Andrew Goodman, and Michael Schwerner were murdered in Mississippi; the 1964 Civil Rights Act was signed into law; a six-day race riot broke out in Harlem and Bedford-Stuyvesant after an off-duty white police officer shot and killed a black male teen; Congress passed the Gulf of Tonkin Resolution; the Berkeley free speech movement began; Martin Luther King, Jr., won the Nobel Peace Prize; Ralph Ellison published *Shadow and Act*, his first book of essays; and Richard Hofstadter's *Anti-Intellectualism in American Life* (1963) won the Pulitzer Prize for General Nonfiction.

Bound up in various ways with these events was a mid-century public discourse about the social status, responsibilities, and community and institutional affiliations of American intellectuals.[1] Baraka was a participant in this conversation, which engaged many writers, social scientists, historians, public officials, and others. A year or so before *Dutchman*'s appearance, he told the poet Edward Dorn that he was reading *Power, Politics and People* (1963), a collection of essays by the sociologist C. Wright Mills. During the 1960s and 1970s, Mills's work inspired a wide range of radicals, including Baraka's sometime collaborator Harold Cruse, another major contributor to the debate about the intellectual. Writing to Dorn about Mills, Baraka said, "you shd get [the book] for definite." He quoted Mills's assertion that "it is our own personal style of life and reflection we are thinking about when we think about politics" and said that such notions "make the book swing, and very very useful" (Baraka and Dorn 78). Mills's line comes from the essay "The Social Role of the Intellectual" (1944). Here Mills urged the "*intellectual worker*," whose labor ought to reveal the real world and the possibilities for action in it, to reappropriate the "*means of effective communication*" (297). Mills also argued that, in order to resist the bureaucratic administration of intellectual labor, writers, artists, scholars, magazine editors, and the like needed to bring their lived particularity to their work. They needed to think of their "own personal style[s] of life and reflection" when they thought about politics. Similarly, they needed to "know [their] own social position[s]" (299).

It is not hard to imagine why Baraka found Mills's work compelling and "very very useful." From the beginning of Baraka's career, he had measured the radical potential of intellectual labor. He had often thought of the intellectual as an alembic through which others' feeling, knowledge, and power moved. However, Baraka's "personal style of life and reflection" and "social position" were by no means unitary and fixed; they shifted and multiplied under the force of inwardly felt social conflicts. Like W. E. B. Du Bois, whom he greatly admired, Baraka pondered the possibility of becoming "a co-worker in the kingdom of culture" (Du Bois 4). But could a black writer, even in the final days of de jure Jim Crow, really become a coworker in an American "kingdom of culture"? If so, which roads led to the kingdom? What were the costs of traveling them? These are some of the questions that Baraka asked in *Dutchman*, which, seen from one vantage point, is a play about the identity, place, and role of the African American intellectual ten years after *Brown v. Board of Education*.

These questions trouble not only Clay and all the unnamed black intellectuals whom he ritually embodies but also the author's personal history. When *Dutchman* appeared, Baraka, then known as LeRoi Jones, lived and worked astride contradiction. In some respects, even by his own account, he was a bourgeois. Born Everett Leroy Jones in Newark, New Jersey, in 1934, Baraka grew up black lower middle class among other blacks and the children of European immigrants. His father was a post office supervisor; his mother was a social worker. But Baraka seems to have been always at odds with the conformism, philistinism, and quietism that he saw in middle-class life. He also seems to have discovered early that racism limited the black bourgeoisie's access to the real benefits of middle-class life. In 1957, after stints at Rutgers University, Newark, and Howard University and another in the Air Force, he moved to New York City and quickly became a prominent figure in the bohemian, avant-garde arts scenes in downtown Manhattan, the site of more than a century of cultural and political radicalism. He wrote poetry (*Preface to a Twenty Volume Suicide Note* [1961], *The Dead Lecturer: Poems* [1964], and *Black Magic: Collected Poetry, 1961–1967* [1969]), fiction (*The System of Dante's Hell* [1965] and *Tales* [1967]), criticism (*Blues People: Negro Music in White America* [1963], *Home: Social Essays* [1966], and *Black Music* [1967]), and, of course, drama (*The Eighth Ditch* [1961], Dutchman *and* The Slave [1964], and The Baptism *and* The Toilet [1967]).[2] In 1964, *The Baptism, Dutchman, The Slave*, and *The Toilet* premiered in New York, and *The Eighth Ditch* was revived there. The plays received a great deal of critical attention, much of it laudatory. Baraka was also well known, and esteemed by many, for his pathbreaking music criticism and experimental poetry.

In addition, he was recognized as a prolific and purposeful institution builder. Baraka was not so disaffiliated as to be categorically opposed to institutions, and he wanted to establish outside of the mainstream a cultural infrastructure that would represent the various modes of dissent and radicalism expressed by the avant-garde artists of the day. He cofounded the Totem Press and the magazine *Yūgen* (1958–62) with his first wife, Hettie Jones, who is white and Jewish. Among Totem's publications were two anthologies of poetry, *Jan. 1st 1959: Fidel Castro* (1959) and *Four Young Lady Poets* (Bergé et al.); Baraka also edited Corinth Press's *The Moderns: An Anthology of New Writing in America* (1963). From 1961 to 1963, he coedited with the poet Diane di Prima *The Floating Bear: A Newsletter* (1961–69). She and Baraka were among the founders of the New York Poets Theatre. These venues featured work by such postwar experimental writers as John Ashbery, William S. Burroughs, Robert Creeley, Dorn, Allen Ginsberg, Bobb Hamilton, Jack Kerouac, Denise Levertov, Frank O'Hara, Charles Olson, John Rechy, A. B. Spellman, and Diane Wakoski, along with Baraka and di Prima themselves. Few earlier black intellectuals had achieved Baraka's level of prominence in an interracial intellectual community (though his position was certainly comparable to Richard Wright's on the radical Left in the 1930s and early 1940s and Ralph Ellison's among the New York intellectuals in the postwar period).

But Baraka had growing doubts about what his work downtown accomplished for black people, and he feared that bohemia, like the mainstream, could recognize and countenance only its own peculiar images of African American culture and the black intellectual. In his music writing, he argued that the jazz avant-garde, with which he ardently identified, was rooted in a traditional African American culture that few, if any, whites could apprehend (even if they, too, embraced the music). For Baraka, the work of innovators like Ornette Coleman, John Coltrane, Archie Shepp, and Cecil Taylor was a radical aesthetic refusal of a middle-class, assimilationist ethos that obscured black racial subordination. This refusal, said Baraka, sprang from a creative rediscovery of the blues tradition, and many of his own aesthetic experiments likewise emerged from confrontations with black vernacular culture.

Yet Baraka's intellectual agency was not confined to purely literary and critical work. In what some now consider a major event in twentieth-century intellectual history, he traveled to Cuba in 1960 as a member of an unofficial delegation of black writers, artists, and activists invited there by the new revolutionary government. Baraka came back to New York a vocal defender of Cuban self-determination and an influential proponent of a Third World politics in which African Americans figured as a colonized people. More generally, he came back as a writer eager to live in the world of acts. In 1961, Baraka participated in a protest at the United Nations following the assassination of Patrice Lumumba, the Congolese independence leader and prime minister. Soon after the demonstration, Baraka joined Cruse, Tom Dent, Calvin Hicks, Shepp, Spellman, Sarah Wright, and others in a new organization called On Guard for Freedom, which articulated a variety of positions in black nationalist and radical aesthetics and politics. Baraka and other On Guard members also took part in the struggle to vindicate the black civil rights leader and self-defense advocate Robert F. Williams, who faced charges of kidnapping and unlawful interstate flight. In both his organizational work and his writing, Baraka challenged the mainstream civil rights movement's absolute commitment to nonviolence, and he sometimes urged blacks to use systematic social violence—to withdraw their labor, on a mass scale, from the United States economy. He also imagined various pluralist and nationalist alternatives to the assimilationist ideology that, he thought, went hand in hand with the movement's nonviolent praxis.

Winning considerable national acclaim during *Dutchman*'s first run did not make Baraka more sanguine about black people's chances, or the black intellectual's effectuality, in American society. The assassination of Malcolm X in February 1965 made Baraka feel that his bohemian life was a kind of race treason. Soon he would depart downtown Manhattan and his marriage to Hettie Jones for a life in Harlem as a black nationalist writer-activist. But, even before *Dutchman* closed, Baraka began seeking financial support for BARTS. The ambitious aims of this project, which quickly became a model for black cultural institutions in other cities, were to cultivate black artists and arts audiences, to involve a large black community in a self-conscious experience of black culture and nationhood, and so to ready the community for a future of revolutionary cultural and political practice. During its brief and sometimes tumultuous existence, BARTS presented many theater, music, dance, and poetry performances, including stagings of *Dutchman* and *The Toilet*, as well as Baraka's *Experimental Death Unit #1* (staged in 1965; published in 1966) and *Jello* (staged in 1965; published in 1970). The institution also offered courses in the arts, humanities, and social sciences, along with remedial education classes. A BARTS devotee could see a production of Charles Patterson's *Black-Ice* (1965), attend a panel discussion titled "The Black Artist and the Revolution," study visual art with the painter Joe Overstreet, join a parade led by Sun Ra and his Myth Science Arkestra, listen to a benefit performance by Dionne Warwick, and take a class like The History of the Afro-American Presence as a Culture within a Culture with the critic-social theorist Harold Cruse.[3]

In late 1965, as a result of internal conflicts and outside pressures (some of which are discussed in the "Materials" essay), BARTS began to come undone. Baraka left the group and Harlem at the end of the year and returned to Newark, where he would live for the rest of his life. Through his past work with BARTS, his ongoing work as a writer, his work on editorial projects like *Black Fire: An Anthology of Afro-American Writing* (1968; coedited with Larry Neal), and his future work with such institutions and organizations as Newark's Spirit House, Maulana Karenga's US, and the Congress of African People, Baraka became a leading figure in the black arts and black power movements of the late 1960s and early 1970s. It was during this period that LeRoi Jones took "the Bantuized Muslim name Imamu ('spiritual leader,' later dropped) Ameer (later Amiri, 'Prince') Baraka ('blessed')" (Harris, "Chronology" xxxii) in an effort to describe his evolving identity as a black leader. He would remain closely identified with black nationalism for nearly a decade, until 1974, when he embraced internationalist Marxism, a politics with which he had grappled for many years.

NOTES

[1] Among the major contributions to this debate were *America and the Intellectuals: A Symposium* (1953); Merle Curti's *American Paradox: The Conflict of Thought and Action* (1956); Jacques Barzun's *The House of Intellect* (1959); Mills's *Power, Politics and People* (1963); Hofstadter's *Anti-Intellectualism in American Life* (1963); Christopher Lasch's *The New Radicalism in America, 1889–1963: The Intellectual as a Social Type* (1965); Lewis Coser's *Men of Ideas: A Sociologist's View* (1965); and Cruse's *The Crisis of the Negro Intellectual* (1967).

[2] These books were either in print or in progress in 1964.

[3] Some of BARTS's promotional materials, including those that advertise the events listed here, can be found in Lorenzo Thomas's "Black Art/Handbills" (1978) and *The Black Power Movement, Part 1: Amiri Baraka from Black Arts to Black Radicalism*, edited by Komozi Woodard et al. (2000).

Part One

MATERIALS

Biographical and Autobiographical Materials

Because the study of *Dutchman* (1964) and Amiri Baraka's other work has relied heavily on narratives of the author's own life as a black intellectual, the preface to this volume provides one such narrative. For others, see, in particular, Kimberly W. Benston's *Baraka: The Renegade and the Mask* (1976), Werner Sollors's *Amiri Baraka/LeRoi Jones: The Quest for a "Populist Modernism"* (1978), William J. Harris's *The Poetry and Poetics of Amiri Baraka: The Jazz Aesthetic* (1985), and Jerry Gafio Watts's *Amiri Baraka: The Politics and Art of a Black Intellectual* (2001). Harris's introduction to *The LeRoi Jones/Amiri Baraka Reader* (1991; rev. ed. 1999) is especially useful as a teaching resource. Gerald Early's "The Case of LeRoi Jones/Amiri Baraka" (1986) is an estimate of Baraka's first quarter century as a public intellectual. Baraka's own account was published as *The Autobiography of LeRoi Jones* (1984; rev. ed., 1997).[1] Also see *Conversations with Amiri Baraka* (ed. Charlie Reilly; 1994), a collection of interviews dating from the early 1960s to the early 1990s. A number of documentary films—for example, Woodie King's *Black Theatre: The Making of a Movement* (1978), St. Clair Bourne's *In Motion: Amiri Baraka* (1983), Lewis MacAdams and John Dorr's *Amiri Baraka* (1991), and *Sounds of Poetry with Bill Moyers: Amiri Baraka* (1999)—portray parts of Baraka's complex story.

Book-Length Studies, Edited Collections, and Special Issues

The list of books devoted entirely to analysis of Baraka's artistic and political work includes Theodore R. Hudson's *From LeRoi Jones to Amiri Baraka: The Literary Works* (1973), Benston's *Baraka*, Sollors's *Amiri Baraka*, Lloyd W. Brown's *Amiri Baraka* (1980), Henry C. Lacey's *To Raise, Destroy, and Create: The Poetry, Drama, and Fiction of Imamu Amiri Baraka (Le Roi Jones)* (1981), Harris's *Poetry*, Komozi Woodard's *A Nation within a Nation: Amiri Baraka (LeRoi Jones) and Black Power Politics* (1999), Watts's *Amiri Baraka*, and Michael Simanga's *Amiri Baraka and the Congress of African People: History and Memory* (2015). The most widely cited of these books are probably those by Benston, Sollors, Harris, and Watts.

Two edited volumes, *Imamu Amiri Baraka (LeRoi Jones): A Collection of Critical Essays* (ed. Benston; 1978) and *Amiri Baraka: The Kaleidoscopic Torch* (ed. James B. Gwynne; 1985), collect essays about Baraka's work in various genres. Several journal issues have been devoted solely or largely to essays on Baraka: *Boundary 2*, vol. 6, no. 2, 1978; *African American Review*, vol. 37, no. 2–3, 2003; *Callaloo*, vol. 37, no. 3, 2014; and *Transition*, vol. 114, 2014.

Early Productions

Some instructors teach *Dutchman* alongside critical responses to productions of the play, and some students may be interested in doing research projects that work with reviews. Using Letitia Dace's *LeRoi Jones (Imamu Amiri Baraka): A Checklist of Works by and about Him* (1971), *Google*, library databases like *JSTOR*, and the periodical collections at a college library or large public library, a student could go far in collecting critical responses to the early productions of *Dutchman*. These research tools would also help one locate responses to more recent stagings.

Until *Dutchman*'s premiere, Baraka was known mainly as a poet and a music critic, but he had begun writing plays several years earlier—in the hope, he later said, of writing an "action literature" (*Autobiography* [Lawrence Hill] 275). During this period, he became a member of New York's Playwrights Unit workshops, whose history David A. Crespy recounts in "A Paradigm for New Play Development: The Albee-Barr-Wilder Playwrights Unit" (2006). Organized by Edward Albee, Richard Barr, and Clinton Wilder's theatrical production company, the workshops developed plays by such experimental dramatists as Adrienne Kennedy, Sam Shepard, and Jean-Claude van Itallie. By Baraka's account, it was not long after joining the workshop group that he "sat up all night and wrote a play [he] called *Dutchman*" (*Autobiography* [Lawrence Hill] 275). On 12 January 1964, the Playwrights Unit did a workshop performance of the script off-off-Broadway at the Village South Theater,[2] and then Albee, Barr, and Wilder produced the play off-Broadway at Greenwich Village's Cherry Lane Theatre, "[t]hat temple of the avant garde" (Thompson). Edward Parone directed, and Robert Hooks and Jennifer West played the lead roles. Between 24 March 1964 and 6 February 1965, the play was performed 366 times (Willis 156). It opened on a triple bill with Fernando Arrabal's *The Two Executioners* (1958) and Samuel Beckett's *Play* (1963). Later in the run, *Dutchman* appeared with Albee's *The American Dream* (1961) and, later still, Baraka's play shared a billing with Albee's *The Zoo Story* (1959). *Dutchman* won the *Village Voice*'s Obie ("Off-Broadway") Award. The selection committee, whose members were prominent figures in the theater, gave *Dutchman* the nod for the best American play of the year. Among the other Obie winners that year were Beckett's *Play*, Adrienne Kennedy's *Funnyhouse of a Negro* (1964), and the Living Theatre's production of Kenneth H. Brown's *The Brig* (1963).

The Obie notwithstanding, many reviewers and other playgoers did not see *Dutchman* as avant-garde theater. Many instead saw the work as an especially provocative addition to the quickly growing list of plays about blacks. The previous decade had seen the beginnings of a loosely defined postwar black theater movement in such plays as Louis Peterson's *Take a Giant Step* (1953), which was made into a film in 1959; James Baldwin's *The Amen Corner* (1955); Lorraine Hansberry's *A Raisin in the Sun* (1959), made into a film in 1961; and Ossie

Davis's *Purlie Victorious* (1961), adapted for the screen in 1963 and for the musical stage in 1970; as well as the all-black 1961 to 1964 production of Jean Genet's *The Blacks* (1958). Among the plays performed in New York during the 1963 to 1964 and 1964 to 1965 seasons were Baraka's *Dutchman*, *The Toilet* (1963), *The Baptism* (1964), *The Slave* (1964), and *The Eighth Ditch* (1961) and the following new scripts, adaptations, and revivals: Baldwin's *Blues for Mister Charlie*, Irving Burgie and Loften Mitchell's *Ballad for Bimshire*, Vinnette Carroll and James Weldon Johnson's *Trumpets of the Lord*, Martin B. Duberman's *In White America*, Athol Fugard's *Blood Knot*, Genet's *The Blacks*, William Hairston's *Walk in Darkness*, William Hanley's *Slow Dance on the Killing Ground*, Hansberry's *The Sign in Sidney Brustein's Window*, Langston Hughes's *Tambourines to Glory* and *Jerico-Jim Crow*, Kennedy's *Funnyhouse of a Negro*, Robert Lowell's *Benito Cereno*, Alan Paton and Krishna Shah's *Sponono*, and Vernon Duke, Lynn Root, and John Latouche's *Cabin in the Sky*. *Dutchman* was often directly compared to *Blues for Mister Charlie*, which likewise posed questions about the lure of interracial sexuality, the psychopathology of American culture, the rise of black militancy, and the agony of the black artist-intellectual. Critics also compared *Dutchman* to Baraka's *The Toilet* and *The Slave*. *The Toilet*, set in a high school boys' restroom, glimpses same-sex intimacy behind the color line and across it. In *The Slave*, a black revolutionary leader, formerly a bohemian intellectual, visits the home of his white ex-wife and her new white husband during an American race war, a conflict that may bring an end to white supremacy and, with it, interracialism.

"[T]he year of the Negro," as *Playboy* described the 1964 to 1965 off-Broadway theater season ("Theater"), was one in which *Dutchman* was worried over, scorned, and canonized, often all at once. The play's anger was a central concern in many early reviews. Was LeRoi Jones angrier than James Baldwin? Did blacks really feel as angry toward whites as Clay seems to feel? Was his anger somehow intended to gratify white liberals' masochistic desires? Or, if real, might this sort of anger soon radicalize black intellectuals or all blacks? Did this anger thus presage the end of the interracial liberal coalition and perhaps predict some even greater social transformation? "If this is the way the Negroes really feel about the white world around them," wrote *New York Times* critic Howard Taubman, "there's more rancor buried in the breasts of colored conformists than anyone can imagine. If this is the way even one Negro feels, there is ample cause for guilt as well as alarm, and for a hastening of change" (46).

Related to this critical discussion of *Dutchman*'s emotional violence was a discussion of the play's aesthetic radicalism. Many critics identified *Dutchman* with the work of Albee, Beckett, Genet, Eugène Ionesco, and other major figures in postwar avant-garde theater. *Dutchman* was often likened (though not always aptly) to Albee's *The Zoo Story*, a play about the violence of conformity, and of what Baraka might call "luxury," in postwar America. More generally, perceptive critics saw that *Dutchman* was breaking from the long realist-naturalist tradition. Articulating a mid-century modernist argument that would appear, in various forms, in a wide range of critical responses to Baraka's work, *Newsweek* praised *Dutchman*'s "mythic dimension" and "complex poetic texture" for raising the play "far above sociology" ("Underground Fury"). Observations like this one linked the play less to absurdism than to the symbolist and expressionist tendencies that first appeared in the late nineteenth century and early twentieth century in the work of August Strindberg and Frank Wedekind.

Black critics' and playgoers' responses to the first production deserve some special attention because they anticipate the black arts discourse that would soon develop around *Dutchman*. After the *Village Voice* critic Michael Smith reported that Clay's long penultimate speech terrified whites and "moved [blacks] to cheers," Blanche M. Jackson, a black Brooklynite, wrote to the paper to say that many blacks were not as burdened as Clay is by black bourgeois neurosis and by the need to throw it off violently (M. Smith 17; Jackson 6). Jackson was moved by the play, but she felt that Clay—"the type of person who totally surrenders himself to a button-down world for which he has little respect"—was not representative of blacks as a group (6).[3] Others thought that *Dutchman*'s diagnosis of the problem, and treatment of it, were astute. According to Robert Hooks, who played Clay at the Cherry Lane, *Dutchman* revealed that "even the black bourgeoisie is hip to the man when you get right down to it" (qtd. in C. Russell 11). For both Hooks and Jackson, *Dutchman* was an occasion on which to imagine the black subject beyond bourgeois class consciousness. During the next decade, as the "Contexts" section below makes clear, *Dutchman* would be a crucial object lesson in many black arts movement manifestoes, which envisioned a black culture unencumbered by white aesthetic norms and white supremacist ideological impositions.

One of the cultural moments in which this discourse developed was the 1965 production of *Dutchman* at Harlem's Black Arts Repertory Theatre/School (BARTS), which Baraka had cofounded that year. At the time, few accounts of the production were published (for critics were hardly the group's principal audience), and the subsequent scholarship on the play provides few details about this staging. Still, there is a fragmentary published record of it. The critic Hoyt W. Fuller's *Negro Digest* profile on BARTS featured a photograph accompanied by this caption: "Rehearsing Mr. Jones' one-act play, *Dutchman*, actors Norman Bush and Kelly Marie Berry get instructions from the author himself" (50). Reviewing the 27 June preview performance for the *Amsterdam News*, the playwright-critic Loften Mitchell likewise named Bush, among a number of other actors. Missing from Mitchell's and Fuller's lists, though, is Baraka's sister, Sondra Lee Jones (later Kimako Baraka), who, according to Baraka, "directed and did the lead role in *Dutchman*" (Baraka, "Black Arts Movement" 501).

Although the show that Mitchell saw was performed at BARTS's West 130th Street brownstone, where *Dutchman* was to be staged again on 10 and 11 July, it seems as if the play was also brought even more directly to Harlemites. BARTS plays were performed in a variety of spaces—at the group's own theater, at downtown theaters (for a few benefit productions), and on improvised stages in public places in Harlem:

> For eight weeks [during the summer of 1965], we brought Drama, Poetry, Painting, Music, Dance, night after night all across Harlem. We had a fleet of five trucks and stages created with banquet tables. And each night our five units would go out in playgrounds, street corners, vacant lots, play streets, parks, bringing Black Art directly to the people.
>
> (Baraka, "Black Arts Movement" 501)

It seems that *Dutchman* appeared in one or several of these latter kinds of spaces, which likely created meanings distinct from those produced in the downtown theater context. Two decades later, Baraka said of BARTS's black populist project, "We had huge audiences, really mass audiences, and though what we brought was supposed to be avant and super-new, most of it the people dug" (*Autobiography* [Lawrence Hill] 308).

Others responded differently. In 1970, Baraka told an interviewer that "[w]hen we performed *Dutchman* downtown, the white people gave it the Obie award. When we put it out on the street and showed it to black people, it suddenly became 'anti-white' and they pulled the money" (*Conversations* 75–76). That money was the financial support that BARTS received from HARYOU-ACT (Harlem Youth Opportunities Unlimited–Associated Community Teams), a youth-development coalition that was in turn funded by the federal Office of Economic Opportunity at the beginning of the War on Poverty. Although *Dutchman* was not the only BARTS play that outraged public officials and the press, the relationship between the group and HARYOU-ACT did become very controversial (perhaps predictably), and one outcome was the termination of BARTS's funding.

BARTS's production of *Dutchman* was distinct from the Cherry Lane's not only because BARTS brought the play directly to a black community—at the price of ninety-nine cents per ticket—but also because the Harlem production had an all-black cast. "In a bold experiment," Mitchell wrote, "the company's whites are played by black actors in 'white face.' And the experiment works. The June 27 preview audience responded enthusiastically, often leaping up, applauding vigorously." Indeed, the performance was evidence that "a brilliant, vital theatre movement [was] going on" in Harlem. There is also the question of whether any whites were in attendance at the BARTS performances of *Dutchman*, for the company sometimes refused to admit whites. If this ban was in effect at these performances, the absence of whites may have been yet another factor in the reception of the Harlem production.

A number of studies offer accounts of the organizational and institutional contexts of Baraka's black arts–era theater work. See, especially, Harold Cruse's *The Crisis of the Negro Intellectual* (1967), Harry J. Elam's *Taking It to the*

Streets: The Social Protest Theater of Luis Valdez and Amiri Baraka (1997), Woodard's *A Nation within a Nation*, Watts's *Amiri Baraka*, Errol Hill and James V. Hatch's *A History of African American Theatre* (2003), James Edward Smethurst's *The Black Arts Movement: Literary Nationalism in the 1960s and 1970s* (2005), Daniel Matlin's *On the Corner: African American Intellectuals and the Urban Crisis* (2013), and William J. Maxwell's *F.B. Eyes: How J. Edgar Hoover's Ghostreaders Framed African American Literature* (2015).

Among the many post-BARTS iterations of *Dutchman* is Anthony Harvey's film adaptation (1966), which starred Al Freeman, Jr., and Shirley Knight.[4] Some instructors use Harvey's *Dutchman* (either the complete film or clips from it) in their units on the play. In a course that is not confined to American materials, an instructor might also teach Jean-Luc Godard's film *Masculin Féminin* (1966), which features a scene that interprets *Dutchman*.

Contexts

Dutchman, *Bohemia, and the Avant-Garde*

During *Dutchman*'s first run, Baraka reported that he was at work on a book entitled "The Black Bohemians: A Study of the Contemporary Negro Intellectual" ("LeRoi Jones to Give a Course"), which was "really about myself and some black boys I know on the lower East Side" (qtd. in Eberstadt 14). Although he never published anything under this title, his work from the late 1950s and 1960s is often preoccupied with this subject. In the poem "Short Speech to My Friends" (1963), for example, Baraka's speaker recalls his "many years of trying to enter their kingdoms" (29)—perhaps alluding to W. E. B. Du Bois's aspiration to become a "co-worker in the kingdom of culture" (4). One might go further and say that Baraka had even sought to create his own cosmopolitan "kingdom of culture." Allen Ginsberg remembered in a 1970 interview that, in the late 1950s, Baraka "became a sort of intellectual arbiter and energy setter in New York City." Baraka "had the grand 'salon,'" Ginsberg said in a later interview (*Spontaneous Mind* 277, 507).

Many instructors attend to *Dutchman*'s representation of the black intellectual's perilous romance with bohemian interracialism—a putative alternative to life in the white supremacist, middle-class mainstream (if one could really find one's way into it) and to life in the black middle class. Baraka's critique of the latter was shaped by his personal experience, including his reading, listening, and so on. Especially important in this regard was the sociologist E. Franklin Frazier's *Bourgeoisie Noire* (1955; *Black Bourgeoisie* ([1957]). Frazier despaired over the black middle class's estrangement from both "the white world" and "the Negro world" (though he granted that other ethnic minority groups also faced this sort of predicament). Baraka, too, grieved the black bourgeoisie's alienation from everyday blacks. He shared Frazier's sense that the members of the black middle class were "in the process of becoming NOBODY" (Frazier 26).

Readers interested in further contextualizing *Dutchman*'s black bohemian might look next at Baraka's "The Beat Generation" (1958), a reply to Norman Podhoretz's "The Know-Nothing Bohemians" (1958); "How You Sound??" (1960); *Preface to a Twenty Volume Suicide Note* (1961); the introduction to *The Moderns* (1963); *The Dead Lecturer* (1964); *Home* (1966); "Philistinism and the Negro Writer" (1966); *The Autobiography of LeRoi Jones* (1984; rev. ed. 1997); and *Amiri Baraka and Edward Dorn: The Collected Letters* (2013). In many ways, these texts represent Baraka's early commitment to both bohemian life and avant-garde aesthetics, for his personal assaults on white-supremacist, middle-class society can be only partially distinguished from the aesthetic violence that he perpetrated against it. When Baraka declared that art is not the preservation of lifeless forms—just as "hunting is *not* those heads on the wall"—he was describing an avant-garde anti-aesthetic (Baraka, "Hunting" 176). But the same words could have described his bohemian personal ethic.

Many of Baraka's contemporaries and associates have written portraits of the downtown bohemian, avant-garde arts scenes of the late 1950s and early 1960s. See, for example, Fred W. McDarrah's *Greenwich Village* (1963); Isabel Eberstadt's "King of the East Village" (1964); Cruse's *The Crisis of the Negro Intellectual*; Tom Dent's "Umbra Days" (1980); Ronald Sukenick's *Down and In: Life in the Underground* (1987); John Gruen's *The New Bohemia* (1990); Hettie Jones's *How I Became Hettie Jones* (1990); Dan Wakefield's *New York in the Fifties* (1992); Lorenzo Thomas's *Extraordinary Measures: Afrocentric Modernism and Twentieth-Century American Poetry* (2000); Diane di Prima's *Recollections of My Life as a Woman, the New York Years: A Memoir* (2001); and Allen Ginsberg's *Spontaneous Mind: Selected Interviews, 1958–1996* (ed. David Carter; 2001).

Readers interested in archival approaches could explore the period's bohemian, avant-garde periodical culture, over which Baraka loomed large. For introductions to this subject, see Elliott Anderson and Mary Kinzie's *The Little Magazine in America: A Modern Documentary History* (1978); Edward E. Chielens's *American Literary Magazines: The Twentieth Century* (1992); Steven Clay and Rodney Phillips's *A Secret Location on the Lower East Side: Adventures in Writing, 1960–1980: A Sourcebook of Information* (1998); and volume 2 of Peter Brooker and Andrew Thacker's *Oxford Critical and Cultural History of Modernist Magazines* (2012). *Yūgen*, a literary magazine Baraka edited with Hettie Jones, can be found in the collections of several dozen United States libraries. *Kulchur*, another magazine to which he contributed frequently and for which he served as music editor, is also held by dozens of libraries. The full run of *The Floating Bear*, which Baraka coedited with di Prima, has been published in a single volume, *The Floating Bear: A Newsletter* (1973).

Among the aforementioned scholars, those who give significant attention to the bohemian and avant-garde contexts of Baraka's early work are Benston, Harris, Sollors, Thomas (who writes as a former participant in downtown aesthetics and politics but also as a scholar), and Watts. No less important are the chapters on Baraka's poetry and fiction in Aldon Lynn Nielsen's *Writing between the Lines: Race and Intertextuality* (1994), *Black Chant: Languages of African-American Postmodernism* (1997), and *Integral Music: Languages of African American Innovation* (2004). Also see Stuart W. Little's *Off-Broadway: The Prophetic Theater* (1972); Leslie Catherine Sanders's *The Development of Black Theater in America: From Shadows to Selves* (1988); Sally Banes's *Greenwich Village 1963: Avant-Garde Performance and the Effervescent Body* (1993); Nathaniel Mackey's *Discrepant Engagement: Dissonance, Cross-Culturality, and Experimental Writing* (1993); Jon Panish's *The Color of Jazz: Race and Representation in Postwar American Culture* (1997); Benston's *Performing Blackness: Enactments of African-American Modernism* (2000); Daniel Kane's *All Poets Welcome: The Lower East Side Poetry Scene in the 1960s* (2003); Fred Moten's *In the Break: The Aesthetics of the Black Radical Tradition* (2003); Scott Saul's *Freedom Is, Freedom Ain't: Jazz and the Making of the Sixties* (2003); Stephen J. Bottoms's *Playing Underground: A Critical History of the 1960s Off-Off-Broadway Movement* (2004); Mike Sell's *Avant-Garde Performance and the Limits of Criticism: Approaching the Living Theatre, Happenings/Fluxus, and the Black Arts Movement* (2005); Smethurst's *The Black Arts Movement*; Crespy's "A Paradigm for New Play Development"; Andrew Epstein's *Beautiful Enemies: Friendship and Postwar American Poetry* (2006); John Gennari's *Blowin' Hot and Cool: Jazz and Its Critics* (2006); Matthew Calihman's "'Where Are the Italian Anarchists?': Amiri Baraka and the Usable Pasts of the Immigrant Left" (2007); Alex Houen's *Powers of Possibility: Experimental American Writing since the 1960s* (2012); Lisa Siraganian's *Modernism's Other Work: The Art Object's Political Life* (2012); and Crespy's *Richard Barr: The Playwright's Producer* (2013).

Throughout the 1950s and early 1960s, one impulse animating Baraka's bohemianism and avant-gardism was ethnic identification. Baraka, the cultural radical, was also a cultural conservator. In the essay "Philistinism and the Negro Writer," published in 1966 but presented as a lecture two years earlier, Baraka recalled his aims as coeditor of *Yūgen* and described them in cultural pluralist terms. He had sought to publish "those white and black people who were talking about a side of America that was more valuable because it hadn't been talked about." The writers whom he named, Allen Ginsberg and A. B. Spellman, represented traditional ethnic modes of dissent—in these cases, Jewishness and blackness. He also mentioned "the Italian thing," Italian immigrant dissent (60–61). However, as Baraka fully realized by the time this essay was published, dissent presupposes a basic commitment to that from which one is dissenting. By the summer of 1965, when *Dutchman* played in Harlem, Baraka no longer thought of redeeming an American society to which blacks were only tenuously connected. *Dutchman*'s move uptown followed Baraka's movement beyond dissent and beyond a pluralist understanding of black ethnic identification.

Dutchman *and the Black Arts Movement*

The BARTS production of *Dutchman* was among Baraka and the black arts movement's early efforts to galvanize an autonomous, black culture-community, the subject of black national liberation. The play also became a central exemplum in black arts aesthetic theory. One of the earliest theoretical texts that treated the play as such was Baraka's manifesto, "The Revolutionary Theatre" (1965), which he published in movement magazines and *Home* and also delivered as a speech. Throughout 1964, Malcolm X had repeatedly told audiences that he was "not an American" but instead "one of the 22 million black people who are the victims of Americanism" ("Ballot" 26). By 1965, Baraka was saying the same. In "The Revolutionary Theatre," he declared that the word "*Fascist*, and with it, *Fascism*, has been made obsolete by the words *America*, and *Americanism*" (Baraka, *Home* [Morrow] 214). He also described *Dutchman*, *The Toilet*, and *The Slave* as plays through which blacks might discover their identity as "victims," their absolute alterity and subordination in American society (211). And, although Baraka had rejected bohemian interracialism and generally distanced himself from Western art and artists, he remained, in many ways, committed to avant-garde aesthetics, which he regarded as anything but essentially white. It would be through a black avant-garde theater of myth, ritual, and emancipatory violence that blacks would feel not only their victimhood but also "the strength in their minds and their bodies" (211). Antonin Artaud's theater of cruelty provided one point of reference for this praxis, but Baraka came very close to saying that genuinely radical theater was a field open to only blacks and other Third World peoples.[5] "Most white Western artists do not need to be 'political,'" he wrote, "since usually, whether they know it or not, they are in complete sympathy with the most repressive social forces in the world today" (214). Here "The Revolutionary Theatre" anticipated such later black arts manifestoes as Ed Bullins's "The So-Called Western Avant-Garde Drama" (1967) and Larry Neal's "The Black Arts Movement" (1968).

Some instructors include "The Revolutionary Theatre" in course units on *Dutchman*. A possible alternative to assigning the manifesto, or to excerpting from it, is to play for students a sound recording of Baraka reading the text (Baraka, "Amiri Baraka"). Among the other black arts aesthetic statements in which *Dutchman* figures are Neal's "The Black Arts Movement," Toni Cade Bambara's "Black Theater" (1969), Clayton Riley's "On Black Theater" (1971), Lance Jeffers's "Afroamerican Literature: The Conscience of Man" (1972), Paul Carter Harrison's *The Drama of Nommo* (1972), and Sherley Anne Williams's *Give Birth to Brightness: A Thematic Study in Neo-Black Literature* (1972). All these writers agreed that *Dutchman* was revolutionary theater, but Williams was among those who felt that Clay's transformation was incomplete. Even after Clay has vented his anger, the relationship between Baraka's black bourgeois-bohemian intellectual and "the streetman [*sic*] is, at best, tenuous" (116). Riley, by contrast, was among those who saw the play as a vanguard expression of everyday blacks' inner lives:

> For the middle sixties, *Dutchman*'s language was a shocking display—the most bluntly communicative and blackest outpouring of a vibrant heart. It was a language steeped in the purest traditionalism of America's original bandit population—nigger words, a crackling brush fire of secret native intelligence and total description. (316)

Furthermore, Riley was among those who viewed Clay's black consciousness as an anticolonial consciousness, just as Clay himself does when he counts blacks as one of the world's "subject peoples" (36). Riley's description of Clay as "well-spoken, well-mannered issue of a colonized tribal group" (317) suggests the possibility of teaching *Dutchman*, and the black arts more generally, as contributions to the international anticolonial discourse of the postwar era. Instructors interested in such an approach might teach the play with Frantz Fanon's *The Wretched of the Earth* (1961), which Greenwich Village's Grove Press brought out in translation in 1963.

To go further in reconstructing the black arts culture to which *Dutchman* belonged during the late 1960s and early 1970s, students might explore some of the movement's periodicals: for example, *Black Dialogue*, *Black Theatre*, *The Journal of Black Poetry*, *Liberator*, *Negro Digest/Black World*, and *Soulbook*. Of these magazines, *Negro Digest/Black World* is by far the most widely available. It can be found at many large libraries, and many of its issues now appear in full-text, searchable form on *Google Books*. Students interested in doing this sort of research should also see *The Black Power Movement, Part 1: Amiri Baraka from Black Arts to Black Radicalism* (eds. Woodard et al.; 2000), a microfilm resource held at several dozen college libraries and some major public libraries. For scholarly histories of black arts periodicals, see Abby Arthur Johnson and Ronald Maberry Johnson's *Propaganda and Aesthetics: The Literary Politics of Afro-American Magazines in the Twentieth-Century* (1979) and Howard Rambsy's *The Black Arts Enterprise and the Production of African American Poetry* (2011). Textual discourse around black arts writing was not, however, confined to black arts periodicals. *The Drama Review*'s Summer 1968 "Black Theatre" issue (vol. 12, no. 4) represents one important engagement between the black arts movement and what one might call "the avant-garde establishment," and Baraka's plays were the topics of essays in such academic venues as *Educational Theatre Journal*.

To explore the periodical culture around *Dutchman* is to be reminded that the play was one of countless black arts texts and that Baraka was one of a great many writers engaged in a collective black arts struggle. The movement's literary anthologies offer similar reminders. See, for example, *Black Fire: An Anthology of Afro-American Writing* (eds. Baraka and Neal; 1968), *New Plays from the Black Theatre: An Anthology* (ed. Bullins; 1969), *Black Expression* (ed. Addison Gayle, Jr.; 1969), *The New Black Poetry* (ed. Clarence Major; 1969), *A Black Quartet: Four New Black Plays* (1970), *The Black Aesthetic* (ed. Gayle; 1971), and *Understanding the New Black Poetry: Black Speech and Black Music as Poetic References* (ed. Stephen E. Henderson; 1973). A recently published anthology, *SOS—Calling All Black People: A Black Arts Movement Reader* (eds. John H. Bracey, Jr., et al.; 2014), offers a large and varied sampling of black arts movement writing, including manifestos and organizational statements of purpose, along with new introductions to this material. Another useful collection of movement texts can be found in *The Dictionary of Literary Biography*'s documentary volume entitled *The Black Aesthetic Movement* (ed. Jeffrey Louis Decker; 1991).

Some of the scholarly studies that place *Dutchman* in the context of either the black arts movement or its immediate prehistory are Benston's *Baraka*; Sollors's *Amiri Baraka*; Geneviève Fabre's *Drumbeats, Masks, and Metaphor: Contemporary Afro-American Theatre* (1983); Mance Williams's *Black Theatre in the 1960s and 1970s: A Historical-Critical Analysis of the Movement* (1985); Sanders's *The Development of Black Theater in America*; David Lionel Smith's "What Is Black Culture?" (1997); Benston's *Performing Blackness*; Marlon B. Ross's "Camping the Dirty Dozens: The Queer Resources of Black Nationalist Invective" (2000); Watts's *Amiri Baraka*; Matthew Rebhorn's "Flaying Dutchman: Masochism, Minstrelsy, and the Gender Politics of Amiri Baraka's *Dutchman*" (2003); Nita N. Kumar's "The Logic of Retribution: Amiri Baraka's *Dutchman*" (2003); Lotta M. Löfgren's "Clay and Clara: Baraka's *Dutchman*, Kennedy's *The Owl Answers*, and the Black Arts Movement" (2003); Sell's "The Drama of the Black Arts Movement" (2004) and *Avant-Garde Performance and the Limits of Criticism*; Smethurst's *The Black Arts Movement*; Amy Abugo Ongiri's *Spectacular Blackness: The Cultural Politics of the Black Power Movement and the Search for a Black Aesthetic* (2010); Houen's *Powers of Possibility*; Matlin's *On the Corner*; Aimee Zygmonski's "Amiri Baraka and the Black Arts Movement" (2013); and Elam's "Post–World War II African American Theatre" (2014). Also see *The Theatre of Black Americans: A Collection of Critical Essays* (ed. Hill; 1980); *A Sourcebook of African-American Performance: Plays, People, Movements* (ed. Annemarie Bean; 1999); *African-American Performance and Theater History: A Critical Reader* (eds. Harry J. Elam, Jr., and David Krasner; 2001); and *New Thoughts on the Black Arts Movement* (eds. Lisa Gail Collins and Margo Natalie Crawford; 2006).

Dutchman *and Its Intertexts*

An early black revolutionary drama of myth and ritual and a play that expands the symbolist and expressionist projects in avant-garde theater, *Dutchman* is the site of a bewildering variety of intertexts. Although it is a two-scene composition typically performed in less than an hour, *Dutchman* is also a kind of encyclopedic theater. Many instructors make much of the play's opening sentences, which describe its setting: "*In the flying underbelly of the city. Steaming hot, and summer on top, outside. Underground. The subway heaped in modern myth*" (Baraka, Dutchman *and* The Slave 3). And a lot of criticism focuses on the play's complex encounters with received religious, folkloric, literary, and historical plots. There are many studies devoted to *Dutchman*'s engagement with such transgression myths as the Flying Dutchman legend (e.g., Hugh Nelson's "LeRoi Jones' *Dutchman*: A Brief Ride on a Doomed Ship" [1968]), the story of Adam and Eve (e.g., Willene P. Taylor's "The Fall of Man Theme in Imamu Amiri Baraka's [LeRoi Jones'] *Dutchman*" [1973]), the Dance of Death allegory (e.g., George Knox's "The 'Mythology' of LeRoi Jones's *Dutchman*" [1975]), and the drama of Othello and Desdemona (e.g., James R. Andreas's "Othello's African American Progeny" [1992]). Other readings put *Dutchman* in conversation with earlier African American literature. In "Visions of Love and Manliness in a Blackening World: Dramas of Black Life since 1953" (1995), Darwin T. Turner challenges commonplace distinctions between pre-black-arts drama and black arts plays. Melvin Dixon's *Ride Out the Wilderness: Geography and Identity in Afro-American Literature* (1987) places *Dutchman* and Baraka's *The System of Dante's Hell* (1965) in a tradition of black underground plots that includes Richard Wright's "The Man Who Lived Underground" (1944) and *The Outsider* (1953) and Ralph Ellison's *Invisible Man* (1952). In "Non-Review: *Dutchman & The Slave*" (1964), Edward Dorn describes Baraka's plays as direct descendants of Chester Himes's novels, wherein, Dorn argues, black protagonists accomplish the speech of which Wright's Bigger Thomas was incapable. Dorn was also among the first to name the Jim Crow plot *Dutchman* engages from the outset. He decodes "modern myth" as "[w]hite woman, black boy" (4).

Editions

There are two published versions of the *Dutchman* playscript. One was collected in *New Theatre in America* (1965), an anthology edited by Edward Parone, the play's first director. The other first appeared in Dutchman *and* The Slave (1964), which is now published by HarperCollins.[6] The essays in *Approaches to Teaching Baraka's* Dutchman cite the HarperCollins edition, except where noted.

The HarperCollins version has long been the one that most readers encounter. Unlike Parone's collection, Dutchman *and* The Slave remains in print, and its version of *Dutchman* has been reprinted in such important anthologies as *Black Theatre U.S.A.* (eds. James V. Hatch and Ted Shine), *The Heath Anthology of*

American Literature (eds. Paul Lauter et al.), *The Norton Anthology of African American Literature* (eds. Henry Louis Gates, Jr., et al.), *The Wadsworth Anthology of Drama* (ed. W. B. Worthen), and *The LeRoi Jones/Amiri Baraka Reader*, all of which have been published in several editions. These anthologies include useful pedagogical tools—introductions to the author, annotations of the text, bibliographies, discussion questions, and so on.

Some instructors may find it worthwhile to ask students to compare the Parone and HarperCollins versions. They do not vary in many ways, but there are some striking differences. For example, the Parone version is somewhat less explicit when it comes to locating the young black intellectual in history. Absent from this script is the "old Negro conductor" who says "Hey, brother!" to the bookish "young Negro," Clay's double, at the very end of the HarperCollins version (37–38). The HarperCollins script thus does more than the Parone version to place the young black intellectual of the 1960s in an intergenerational drama.

Other Texts

As we and the other contributors assume throughout, students of *Dutchman* will benefit greatly from reading Baraka's other works. For a broad, chronologically organized sampling of his writing, one should turn first to *The LeRoi Jones/Amiri Baraka Reader*. One might turn next to *The Fiction of LeRoi Jones/Amiri Baraka* (2000) and *SOS: Poems, 1961–2013* (ed. Paul Vangelisti; 2014). There is no complete and up-to-date bibliography listing all of Baraka's publications, but Dace's *LeRoi Jones (Imamu Amiri Baraka)* is an indispensable resource for researchers.

Some research inquiries may take students to archives of Baraka's unpublished papers. Among the major repositories of this material are Columbia University's Rare Book and Manuscript Library Collections, Howard University's Moorland-Spingarn Research Center, Indiana University's Lilly Library, the New York Public Library's Schomburg Center for Research in Black Culture, and Syracuse University's Special Collections Research Center.

NOTES

[1] Some readers may find it helpful to know in advance that, in *Autobiography*, Baraka changes some of the names of people, magazines, etc. in the manner of the roman à clef. *Yūgen*, for example, becomes "*Zazen*" here.

[2] The Playwrights Unit workshop production of *Dutchman* featured Al Freeman, Jr., who later played Clay in Anthony Harvey's film adaptation of the play (1966), and

Jennifer West. Edward Parone staged the workshop production (Crespy, *Richard Barr* 126–27).

[3]We have not been able to find any additional information about Blanche M. Jackson.

[4]Another possibility is Paul Vangelisti's radio production of *Dutchman* (1982).

[5]Grove Press published a translation of Artaud's *The Theater and Its Double* (1938) in 1958. The theater of cruelty was a major influence on postwar American experimental theater. For a discussion of the Artaudian dimensions of Baraka's plays, see, e.g., Sanders.

[6]This edition was initially published by William Morrow, which has since become an imprint of HarperCollins.

Part Two

APPROACHES

Introduction

In 2011, a few years into the new postracialist discourse that followed the election of President Barack Obama, the sociologist Lawrence D. Bobo synthesized a large amount of social science data in an attempt to determine whether or not racial inequality persisted in the United States and to sketch the contours of whatever racial divide might remain. More specifically, Bobo wanted to see what happened to black-white racial inequality in the years since 1965, the peak of the civil rights movement. He found first that the biologistic racial ideology that legitimated the Jim Crow system of racial segregation, discrimination, and subordination had been steadily repudiated in the intervening half-century. However, new and more insidious forms of racist ideology seemed to have emerged, and they appeared to be influencing levels of support for social policy designed to ameliorate racial inequality. Looking at actual indicators of equality and inequality, Bobo charted some progress in the area of economics, for there had been "considerable expansion in the size, security, and, arguably, salience and influence of the black middle class" (19). But, in important ways, economic inequality in the United States was still racialized. The black poverty rate remained much higher than that of whites, and blacks had much less wealth. Contributing to economic inequality and representing problems in their own right were a much lower level of educational attainment among blacks and a much higher level of black incarceration. Residential segregation also continued, albeit at lower overall rates than in 1965. So, when Bobo pressed himself to sum up, he could speak of only the "nation's 'mixed' or ambiguous circumstance—suspended uncomfortably somewhere between the collapse of the Jim Crow social order and a postracial social order that has yet to be attained" (29).

Amiri Baraka's *Dutchman* (1964) prophesies the uncomfortable "'mixed' or ambiguous circumstance" in which Bobo finds contemporary American society. Although the play is not sociology, it captures perhaps the earliest moment in the narrative that Bobo constructs. Set a decade after *Brown v. Board of Education*, *Dutchman* enacts a long, intimate public exchange between a young, college-educated, middle-class black man and a young white woman. Yet, no less important, the play stages a society that has already wished away the fact of ongoing racial inequality. Today *Dutchman* reads as an early, forceful answer to postracialism (avant la lettre). The play is a tragedy for an era that has rushed to herald the end of race. Thus, when we teach *Dutchman*, we are not only asking students to explore the histories of bohemia, the avant-garde, and the black arts movement but also calling on students to think about their own working histories of race and nation in the US.

One focus of this thinking is likely to be American racial violence, past and present. In 2000, more than a decade before the current spate of high-profile police killings of blacks, the critic Greg Tate saw in a recent Hartford,

Connecticut, production of *Dutchman* a play that "confronts the cyclical and near-conspiratorial phenomenon of violence against African-American men" (44). Among the other works in which Baraka confronts such violence is "What Does Nonviolence Mean?" (1963), a polemic collected in his influential volume *Home: Social Essays* (1966). In this essay, as in *Dutchman*, nonviolence is figured as repetition, as the repeated rediscovery of black racial subordination: "in most parts of America the social system still hews to the intransigence of its beginnings and no real advance into [the] mainstream is really being offered" ([Morrow] 145). *Dutchman*'s action—a set of events that have happened already and that will happen again, perhaps ceaselessly—likewise "hews to the intransigence of its beginnings" and offers "no real advance." To end this national repetition compulsion, Baraka argued in the essay, blacks needed to embrace self-defense. Here Baraka echoed the Nation of Islam and Robert F. Williams, author of *Negroes with Guns* (1962), among other black radical organizations and leaders. Going a good deal further, Baraka also urged blacks to organize general strikes in American cities or to find some other means of doing "political and social violence to the existing system" (146).

Baraka's works also constitute a theory and practice of black cultural radicalism, and they prompt us to ask what culture has meant in the making of race and nation. Though nonviolence, by Baraka's account, offered blacks no real entry to channels of social power and economic opportunity, nonviolence was sold to blacks (by civil rights organizations, white liberals, and others) as a chance to enter American culture: "Nonviolence in the American context means, at its most honest evocation, a proposed immersion into the mainstream of a bankrupt American culture, and that's all" ("What" 149). For Baraka, then, submission to white violence went hand in hand with assimilation, which he defined as submission to white cultural hegemony.

And there is no more sustained and vivid record of the experience of assimilation—felt as loss—than the one that we find in Baraka's works of the 1960s and 1970s. Nor is there a postwar writer who has done more than Baraka did to vindicate ethnic cultural self-assertion in American letters. He was a key figure in the black arts movement and, more generally, a key figure in the making of contemporary cultural pluralism. In "Black Writing" (1964), another essay from *Home*, Baraka challenged a Cold War–era aesthetic ideology that embraced as universal all expressions of cultural particularity save those of black writers. He reproached the poet Gregory Corso for saying that "Black writers are stuck because they're always talking about their people." All of the most esteemed white writers, Baraka replied, were just as inclined to talk about their people: "What does anyone think [James Joyce's] Dubliners were—abstract literary categories?" ([Morrow] 163). Earlier in his career, however, Baraka often talked about his people only in the negative. His first volume of verse, *Preface to a Twenty Volume Suicide Note* (1961), includes a series of poems that rewrite the famous Harlem Renaissance–era "Africa" lyrics of Countee Cullen and Langston Hughes. Whereas the speaker of Cullen's "Heritage" (1925) finds himself *"three centuries removed"* from Africa yet still inwardly inhabiting a black continent (104), the speaker of Baraka's "Notes for a Speech" discovers that "Africa/is a foreign place" and that he is "as any other sad man here/american [*sic*]." Later, in "*An Agony. As Now.*," a poem from *The Dead Lecturer* (1964), Baraka gives voice not to an "american" but to a black captive. His address begins with the words "I am inside someone/who hates me" (15). The poem ends, though, with an intimation of an emancipatory aesthetic radicalism. The captor, who is really more of an unfeeling metal "enclosure," "burns the thing/inside it. And that thing/screams" (15, 16). In *Dutchman*, Clay occupies a similar enclosure, a New York City subway car, which finally resounds with his scream. Like many of Baraka's other works from the period, the play embodies on stage and page what Tate describes as a widely felt and persistent fear, among blacks, of "assimilation unto annihilation" (45).

Dutchman's confrontation with this fear gives teachers and students an opportunity to examine critically the concept of race itself. At moments, to be sure, the play seems to construct a racial taxonomy. In one such instance, Clay tells Lula that true blackness is nothing with which she is familiar but instead "dark places, with big hats and overcoats held up with one arm" (34). *Dutchman* here imagines a radically autonomous black culture, as does most subsequent black arts writing. But Baraka, his critique of assimilation notwithstanding, also challenged notions of racial purity. In a 1963 review of E. U. Essien-Udom's *Black Nationalism: A Search for an Identity in America* (1962), Baraka chided the author, a Nigerian scholar, for his reductive understanding of culture:

> "African Culture," as a contemporary phenomenon, is almost as much a diverse collection of socio-cultural elements as the culture of the American Negro. Only anthropologists and crackpots can formulate some kind of "pure" African culture, i.e., if they want to arrive at some mythical ethnic statement that has very little to do with actual human existence.
> ("Uncle Udom's Cabin" 88–89)

Baraka resumed this challenge in *Dutchman*, which is a metadrama of the writing and performance of race. The play resists the formulation of a "pure" African American culture when, for example, Lula scripts Clay as a black bourgeois upstart and archly reminds him that his grandfather was a slave. Clay answers, "My grandfather was a night watchman" (18). With this retort, Clay does not efface the history of slavery, nor does he dispute Lula's characterization of him as a middle-class striver ("night watchman" is a figure for a black junior steward of American society and culture), but he does refuse Lula's singular, reified plotting of the African American past. In this respect, Baraka may be closer than is often thought to Ralph Ellison, who was always alive to the moments in which black lives have gone off-script. Focusing on *Dutchman*'s challenges to the received racial script, the critic Nita N. Kumar contends that "[t]he charge of Baraka's propounding 'black essentialism' . . . needs further examination, since the polarization of white and black in his work may be more apparent and strategic than real" (271).

Indeed, neither a black/white binary nor a black/American binary comprehends all of *Dutchman*, and the play ultimately asks us to read and teach it as world literature. Like other avant-garde and black arts works, *Dutchman* must be located in both a national context and a transnational matrix. Captive though he is, Clay engages a world beyond the United States. We learn, for example, that he has cut a path through the history of the European avant-garde and the history of bohemianism: In college, Clay thought he was "Baudelaire" (19). One of his current personae is the colonial subject. Like contemporaneous texts by Malcolm X, Harold Cruse, and others, and like a great many black radical texts of the following decade, *Dutchman* identifies United States blacks with the anticolonial movements of the postwar period. Clay predicts the emergence of a black radical intelligentsia fully conversant in the culture of the West but also fully committed to bringing an end to its dominion over people of color:

> [M]aybe one day, you'll find they actually do understand exactly what you are talking about. . . . And on that day, . . . when you really believe you can "accept" them into your fold, as half-white trusties late of the subject peoples. With no more blues, except the very old ones, and not a watermelon in sight, the great missionary heart will have triumphed, and all of those ex-coons will be stand-up Western men, with eyes for clean hard useful lives, sober, pious and sane, and they'll murder you. (36)

It is therefore apt that Olga Barrios, Tejumola Olaniyan, and other critics have situated *Dutchman* and Baraka's other works within broad African and African diasporic frameworks and that Harry J. Elam, Jr., has written a comparative study of Baraka's black-arts-era theater and Luis Valdez's radical Chicana/o theater of the same period. It is also fitting that *Dutchman* has been produced around the world, from France to Brazil to the Netherlands to South Africa.

In order to grasp *Dutchman* as both an "American play" (the designation that the Obie Award committee used) and a work of world literature, students need to grasp several more specific contexts: mid-century avant-garde and bohemian culture; the civil rights, black power, and black arts movements; and the histories of slavery, Jim Crow, and the African American vernacular culture that developed during these epochs. Although it would be a dubious endeavor to try to make *Dutchman* agreeable to all students, all ought to find out where the play comes from, and all ought to discover ways of talking or writing about it. The aim of *Approaches to Teaching Baraka's* Dutchman is to help instructors either to create the conditions for this work or to lead students in these efforts.

The essays in "Performing Identities," the first of the three subsections that follow, focus on teaching *Dutchman* as theater and film art. Included here are contributions about using creative writing exercises in a course unit on the play, involving students in the play as performance, and teaching productions of *Dutchman*. The scholar-playwright Andrew Ade has his students write their way into the play. Among the creative writing assignments from which students may choose is one that asks the writer to script "a highly personal tirade that taps into [the student's] resentments and social anxieties." Jim Cocola is interested in performance and in placing *Dutchman* within multiethnic American and international theater traditions. His drama classes physically inhabit these traditions by producing Baraka's play and others "in the round" and by discussing, and writing about, their stagings. Katarzyna Jakubiak teaches *Dutchman* in Literary Research and Analysis, an undergraduate methodology course, and shares with the class her own research materials: an archive related to the 1969 Warsaw production of the play. What happens to the range of *Dutchman*'s possible significations, she and her students ask, when the work is moved from its presumed cultural coordinates in the United States to coordinates beyond the nation's borders, and how can students find information about international productions? William Thomas McBride's drama and film courses explore the British director Anthony Harvey's 1966 film adaptation of the play. Considering script, cinematography, music, and set and costume design, McBride's classes read Harvey's screen interpretation of Baraka's modernist myth-drama.

The essays in the second subsection, "Dramatic Histories," are about reading *Dutchman* within the various aesthetic traditions to which it belongs, comfortably or uncomfortably. Intent on addressing students who reflexively turn away from the play's "social and political implications," Meenakshi Ponnuswami places *Dutchman*'s provocations against a few historical backgrounds. Her classes read the play as an intervention in the black liberation struggles of the 1960s, the postwar European and American theaters of the absurd, and the work of "staging the black body." Daniel Morris's American literature students approach *Dutchman* as a postwar text that engages with a multiplicity of early- and mid-twentieth-century modernist aesthetics. He and his students ultimately focus on the play's appropriation of a high modernist mythopoesis, often associated with T. S. Eliot, which Baraka employs to portray "race, interracial desire, violence, and masculinity in urban America in the 1960s."

Several of our contributors place special emphasis on *Dutchman*'s arguments with the Euro-American avant-garde and even with aspects of Baraka's own radical theater aesthetic. Kurt Hemmer leads the students in his Beat Generation course in an exploration of the play's critique of bohemianism, a critique that discloses some of the racial ideology informing beat texts. Other contributors ask students to think about Baraka's conception of black art as a radical agency. *Dutchman* figures in Matthew Calihman's African American literature survey as a work of postwar modernism but one that challenges the avant-garde's absolute futurism. Calihman's class reads the play as an audacious act of historical witness that is itself a kind of black aesthetic radicalism. Deborah M. Mix teaches the play alongside Baraka's poetry, other black arts writing, and black popular music. Mix helps her students to see how Baraka and many of his contemporaries used art as "an alternative to—but not a substitute for—social violence." Teaching *Dutchman* with Baraka's manifesto "The Revolutionary Theatre" (1965), Koritha Mitchell reveals in these texts a discourse of love—love "for oppressed people," "for the American ideal of self-determination," and "for that which is spiritual and human and cannot be labeled *American*." While acknowledging Baraka's "masculinist Afrocentrism," Mitchell's classes also find in his work a love inspired by the art of blues women like Bessie Smith.

The essays in the final subsection, "Cultural Interplays," describe additional course units about *Dutchman*'s reckoning with the past. Andrew Sargent's classes look at the play's representation of the compulsive performance of racial myth. This repetition today unsettles the certainties of contemporary postracialism. Richard Schur's African American literature students learn that, for blacks, railroads were long identified with both modern mobility and segregation, and his classes consider how these pasts persist on Baraka's subway train, even though it moves within the boundaries of a northern city in the 1960s. Schur and his students view the play's interminable subway ride as a counterplot to civil rights–era progress myths. In another interdisciplinary project, Danny M. Hoey, Jr., places *Dutchman* against the background of American jurisprudence. Employing the conceptual framework and legal history elaborated in Randall Kennedy's *Race, Crime, and the Law* (1997), Hoey's class reads *Dutchman*'s symbolic enactment of the encounter between the law and the black male body.

In the same subsection are essays about teaching *Dutchman*'s engagement with popular culture and vernacular culture. Tess Chakkalakal's undergraduate seminar Reading *Uncle Tom's Cabin* in the Twenty-First Century includes a unit on *Dutchman*'s conversations with Stowe's novel (1852) and with stage revisions of it. The class seeks to understand the ideological and aesthetic function of the vernacular signifier "Uncle Tom" in Baraka's black radical text. Roland Leander Williams, Jr., pairs *Dutchman* with Lorraine Hansberry's *A Raisin in the Sun* (1959), another landmark in African American drama. Williams's African American literature classes examine the plays' revisions of the black character types of the minstrel theater. Jean-Philippe Marcoux draws on Baraka's *Blues People* (1963) and other critical works to give the students in his American drama course a grounding in the history of black vernacular culture. With this foundation in place, Marcoux and his students go on to explore *Dutchman*'s participation in the liberatory tradition sustained by black vernacular music. D. Quentin Miller's African American literature class looks broadly at the ways in which *Dutchman* and James Baldwin's *Blues for Mister Charlie* (1964) represent black cultural and political transformation in the mid-1960s. Then, working with *Blues People*, Baldwin's essay "The Uses of the Blues" (1964), and recorded music, the group focuses on the role of the blues in these dramas of black consciousness.

This attention to the vernacular raises questions about *Dutchman*'s discourses of cultural authenticity, and some of our contributors directly address such questions in their classroom work with the play. In Molly Hiro's African American literature survey, *Dutchman* is a representative black arts text insofar as it denies its readers and audience an identification with an authentic black self, which the movement envisioned not as an individual affirmation but as a collective intragroup articulation. In several of his courses, James D. Bloom puts *Dutchman* in dialogue with *The Human Stain* (2000), the novel by Baraka's contemporary and fellow Newarker Philip Roth. Bloom's classes encounter the two texts as passing plots for a post-*Brown* America in which identification with place increasingly functions as physical imposture once did. In an African American literature course that tracks the history of "arguments along the color line," Caleb Corkery, our final contributor, begins work on *Dutchman* by asking his students to screen and discuss *Chappelle's Show* (2003–2006) skits that stage race rhetoric as comedy. Corkery's group then turns its attention to the play's tragic staging of this rhetoric.

The essays in this volume can be read in any order. We encourage instructors who have only a general familiarity with Baraka, *Dutchman*, and the contexts in which it first appeared to begin with the preface, the materials essay, and the subsection entitled "Dramatic Histories." But there is no wrong place to start, and we anticipate that many readers will be guided by their particular interests and teaching objectives.

Teaching *Dutchman* through Creative Writing

Andrew Ade

That *Dutchman* remains an arresting and unsettling theater experience a half century after its off-Broadway premiere, as well as a perennial selection in drama anthologies, assures its stature as an essential dramatic text for investigation in our own time. The confluence of race, class, and gender issues in the play invariably compels modern audiences to reflect on America's tragic social history and to reassess the nation's progress in overcoming its persisting ideological antagonisms. To gauge a modern audience's willingness to confront such issues, Pittsburgh's Bricolage Production Company followed each performance of its 2012 production (directed by Mark Clayton Southers) with a series of public "talk-backs" titled "Between the Lines: Conversations about Race Relations in Pittsburgh." This series, led by artists, columnists, filmmakers, city philanthropic leaders, and community organizers, created a forum in which audience members could respond publicly to the play. The guest moderators' opening remarks bore such titles as "How Prejudiced Are You? Cultural Perceptions in Post Racial America," "White Supremacy: The First Step to Recovery Is Acceptance," and "How Do We Talk about What Makes Us Uncomfortable?" (Rawson). The post-show discussion—by turns cautious, heated, and revealing—often ran longer than the play performance itself.

Encountering *Dutchman* for the first time as a reading text in an academic setting can prove no less an assault on student expectations of plot, character relationships, and language. Because I feel a special responsibility to present as wide-ranging and challenging a reading list as I can, I have always given *Dutchman* a prominent place on my syllabus. My first experiences teaching the text to undergraduates, however, met with a certain level of resistance, despite my expressed enthusiasm for the work. At my small liberal arts college, many students come from rural areas that are predominantly white and lower middle class. These students are often unfamiliar with urban life, particularly as presented in the aggressive world of *Dutchman*. The play appeared to alienate a portion of the class, but I remained interested in teaching the play and set out to devise alternative means of presenting it to students.

The most successful of the strategies that I have implemented involves creative writing exercises, to be done as preparation before (or reflection after) the students read the play. The idea for this approach sprang naturally from my ancillary work as a creative writing instructor. Before teaching *Dutchman* for the first time, I had already established a practice of cross-pollinating my playwriting course with any dramatic literature course (e.g., Shakespeare, Modern British Drama, History of Dramatic Criticism) I might offer in the same semester. To satisfy an end-of-term requirement, each student in the literature class must serve as an actor in a staged reading of a new play by a student in the playwriting class: that is, the scholars enact and interpret the roles created by the dramatists. The performing students regularly remark that this fun, commingling event not only surprised them with their fellow students' writing ability but also further illuminated the craft at work in the canonical plays they had been analyzing all semester.

It was but a short step for me, as both a literature professor and a working playwright, to integrate the two skill sets into a single course. Asking students to write dramatically, in fact, dovetailed neatly with my department's principles of pedagogy. We theorize that students who are asked periodically to undertake the writing of poems, short fiction, nonfiction, and plays come to a more immediate appreciation of the quality of artistic product they investigate in our standard literature courses. Mindful of the wide range of artistic talent in the class, we weight this assignment lightly (five to ten percent) in relation to the rest of students' course requirements. Ultimately, the aggregation of these composition assignments prepares our majors to tackle the more ambitious creative writing component that complements the analytic research portion in the senior capstone thesis.

My research into the application of arts-education techniques to the general education curriculum, subsequent to designing and deploying my *Dutchman* exercise, confirmed that creative writing has become only more valuable and versatile in bettering people's lives. Because theater is a dynamic representation of life that moves from the individual writer's imagination to the cooperative social activity of live performance (by actors, for an audience), it consistently demonstrates an uncommon power to affect positively all involved. Psychologists have recognized the benefits of patient-authored plays to empower the marginalized and demoralized, as well as these works' therapeutic capacity to promote healing for victims of trauma. Recent articles such as "Raising Voices: Teaching Teen Girls to Speak Out" (Davidoff and Hunt), "Piloting PlayWrite: Feasibility and Efficacy of a Playwriting Intervention for At-Risk Adolescents" (Bernstein et al.), and "'Our Side of the Story': Moving Incarcerated Youth Voices from Margins to Center" (Winn), to name only a few, offer strong evidence of how scripting one's own life experience for performance can foster self-actualization and self-esteem.[1] Equally, for young people with underdeveloped reading and writing skills, playwriting can be an engaging, interactive means to raise literacy levels and promote personal ease in collaborative work. Educators in the United States and Canada (Amour; Chizhik; Perry et al.), as well as their counterparts in Britain and Australia (Woolland; Jester and Stoneman; Gardiner and Anderson), have successfully incorporated short-play compositions into primary and secondary school curricula to enhance student academic performance.

More sophisticated models enlist students to undertake playwriting projects that engender consciousness-expanding experiences on civic issues, social-identity controversies, and global citizenship. Mary Frances Buckley-Marudas and Joshua Block's "Putting Research on Stage: Playwriting in the English Classroom" documents the experience of a class of tenth-graders who researched a student-selected human rights issue and then scripted and performed it as a class play rather than writing separate reports.[2] Similarly, Jennifer S. Thom and David Blades report on an experiment in multicultural assessment in which selected university students were charged with sharing and transcribing the difficulties faced by their institution in honoring their mandate to welcome and accommodate a racially and culturally diverse student body. They converted their findings into a four-act play about three people whose understanding of others' needs evolved into a more respectful attitude toward campus culture. More interesting for my purposes here, Samuel Jaye Tanner's study "Accounting for Whiteness through Collaborative Fiction" prompted students at a mostly white high school to probe their own racial identities through a lens of critical race theory. The research resulted in a short play depicting how the students defined and articulated their understanding of whiteness.

As a pedagogical strategy to facilitate learning and self-reflection, creative writing has a wide range of applications, including, as in my own experiment, the means by which students can grapple with, and invest in, a provocative text like *Dutchman*. Analogous proposals have on occasion appeared in other Approaches to Teaching volumes. Ann E. Imbrie, for example, explains how she sets up her students' reading of *King Lear* with a presentation on archetypes, followed by a list of those in *Lear*. She then asks the students to construct a fairy tale out of *Lear*'s opening scene and, after reading the play, to compare their stories to Shakespeare's plot. In "Outlining Your Own Greek Drama: A Creative Project," Adele J. Haft lays out an activity to let students delve into the artistry of Euripides by writing and performing their own poetic tragedies. My approach, in the case of *Dutchman*, also defuses any feelings of trepidation or hostility toward Baraka's vision by having the students take up his artistic purpose and vantage point to express their own experience of oppression and social unrest. I have designed writing assignments to elicit the students' own apprehension of various social tensions in American culture while giving the students the power to control the representation of these tensions. Working as both social critic and dramatist, each student finds a protective way into the world Clay and Lula cohabit, and, in the compositional process, the student gains greater appreciation for Baraka's artistic imagination.

I offer here ten feasible creative writing exercises to facilitate student engagement with (and understanding of) *Dutchman*. Some of the exercises serve to prime students for the play by anticipating key plot points and character behavior, while others ask students to expand on, or depart from, Baraka's original text based on their reading and discussion of it. My grouping them as "pre-" and "post-" is only tentative; instructors may prefer, for instance, to assign the "pre-" exercises after the reading. I also recommend carving out class time for student volunteers to read aloud (with a scene partner) any exercises they may wish to share.

I find that, given the short length of these assignments (a minimum of three scripted pages, double-spaced), students do not need supplementary instruction in playwriting technique. They draw instinctively on previously read works as models for laying out a page of script, and they pick up easily enough where Baraka leaves off. They also tend to trust in my advice not to hold back in terms of offensive language or action. Perhaps most important, I ask them to devise scenarios of which they have firsthand knowledge; here, the axiom "write what you know" is key if the students are to attempt an honest exploration of their own feelings and judgments as a conduit to Baraka's vision.

Pre-Reading Assignments: Five Sample Writing Exercises

1. Write a scene in which two people stereotype each other—either wittingly or unwittingly. What observations does each make about the other? How might each character acknowledge, deny, or defend such stereotypical identifications?
2. Write an uncomfortable seduction scene between two characters encountering each other for the first time, in which one character is more proactive. Show how the characters' assumptions or expectations about gender and sexuality might emerge in their speech and actions.
3. A passive-aggressive person toys with someone they wish to disorient or undercut by contradictory messages of agreeableness and hostility, either as a pointed act of manipulation or mere power play. Write a dialogue scene that shows someone demonstrating marked passive-aggressive behavior toward another. How does the other person respond to it?
4. Write a scene of young adult characters exhibiting "offensive" or "taboo" public behavior. Portray the reactions of various onlookers.
5. Drama, to have life of its own, requires some form of conflict. Write a dialogue scene for two characters of different ethnicities or races, who meet for

the first time and who, under the pressure of some social force, fall into an uncomfortable encounter. How might tensions arise? What behaviors might emerge? What sort of conclusion could the scene have? Give attention to both the physicality and language of the characters.

The options above have proven effective with students who have had little or no direct experience with urban life or race interaction. Too often, sheltered students are quick to dismiss outspoken or brazen characters as "not nice" or "selfish" or "threatening" before they have accounted for the characters' backstories or the major signifying elements in the text they are reading. (I meet with the same difficulty in teaching Spike Lee's film *Do the Right Thing.*) These exercises seek to preclude any such prejudgment by putting students in the mindset of, or in imagined proximity to, culturally different people who, as drama demands, display a heightened form of assertive behavior. The dramatist's obligation to think through highly emotional interpersonal conflicts prepares them to observe Clay and Lula in the play to come.

When I assign these exercises, I let the students choose the option that attracts them the most. Two examples from a recent set of composed scenes illustrate the possible results. One student took on the issue of racial tension in her depiction of "taboo public behavior" (exercise 4). Set in a city school parking lot, the scene consists of two older boys, one white (John) and one black (Sam), each vying for the attention of a pretty female African American classmate (Sara) before a crowd of onlookers of both races. Although the boys had been friends, the developing prospect of an interracial couple infuriates Sam. When she chooses John, the two boys resort to racist taunts and end up in a brawl. The student writer demonstrated a remarkable ear for adolescent hate speech in the dialogue and revealed her understanding of how violence can occur when racial ideology directly informs a relationship.

Another student, combining elements from exercises 1 and 2, devised a train-platform encounter between a man (Adam) and a woman (Melissa) whose conversation begins as a comic flirtation but ends bitterly as an all-out volley of sexist remarks drawn from gender stereotyping (but without the factor of race). The overall scene was, finally, a sharply detailed and closely observed study in familiar sexual politics. Both examples reflected thoughtful engagement with difficult, troubling subject matter that, unbeknownst to the student authors, would figure boldly in the more electrifying action in *Dutchman*. Since assigning the "pre-" exercises, I no longer discern negative reaction to the play from even my most self-protective students.

Post-Reading Assignments: Five Sample Writing Exercises

1. Choose a section of the play and write the scene from the perspective of two of the unidentified subway riders on stage with Clay and Lula. Compose a whispered conversation that reveals their personal prejudices based on race and gender. What do they think they are witnessing? Whom do they blame

for what is happening? What might explain their desire to get involved or not? Remember to individuate the two passengers by age, gender, class, and state of mind (e.g., fatigue, inebriation, prejudices, nerve, cowardice).

2. *Dutchman* examines, among other things, the dilemma of middle-class black Americans pressured to assimilate into the white mainstream. Lula is the allegorical embodiment of all that attracts, intimidates, and maddens young men like Clay. Create a character of any sex, race, age, status, or appearance who, in a prolonged encounter, could have the same impact on you: i.e., make you feel inferior or absurd by virtue of your dreams and aspirations. Points of attack might include where you live, what you drive, what kinds of passions you indulge, or how you choose to present yourself publicly.
3. Reconceive a scene in *Dutchman* by reversing either the racial identities or gender roles of Clay and Lula. What different tensions might emerge in their encounter? Who might be the aggressor and for what reasons? How would the other respond to the aggression? Depict how these tensions would manifest themselves and how the encounter might end.
4. Clay grew up in postwar, segregated America. At twenty, he has already stored up a lifetime of suppressed anger and outrage, which finds voice in his tirade against Lula. What in your life has come closest to these feelings? How has any segment of society presumed to know and judge you and then tried to define you to suit its own self-interest? Dramatize your own deepest outrage over social injustice or a personal affront in a monologue that indicts a world that decides your worth. Show, as best you can, how society leads you on, only to punish you for either conforming or not conforming to its expectations.
5. Near the end of the play, after the passengers throw Clay's body off the train, Lula "takes out a notebook and makes a quick scribbling note" and then "[d]rops it in her bag" (37). What did she write? Copy out the last several pages of Lula's notebook, as you imagine them to be.

I assign the "post-" exercises if I observe any confusion about the play or if I sense that students feel alienated from its ideas or action. The aim here is to have the students work from the textual specifics of *Dutchman* to create a personalized expression of their own dissatisfaction with American values, economic opportunity, or social expectations. To do so, they must be open to the play's perspective on the history of American race relations and be willing to interact with (and assume responsibility for) the play's characters and dramatic arc. I describe here a few examples of my students' work to illustrate their efforts to gain a deeper appreciation of the play.

Students are free to adapt the first exercise above as they see fit, since it requires them to imagine the inner lives of unnamed characters who already figure physically in *Dutchman*. In one recent response to this prompt, a student developed a scene for the "old Negro conductor" who appears at the very end of the play. He is training a new transit employee (white, callow, naive) in the next car when the characters take note of Clay and Lula through the rear-door windows. When the trainee asks about transit policy for dealing with the couple's increasingly outrageous behavior, the conductor says to let things be, for experience has taught him that such degradation is the norm, that Lula and her kind live by their own rules, and that any indignant protests by men like Clay will only meet with public indifference. (Although the conductor witnesses the murder, the trainee, with his back turned, does not, and the conductor feels it is pointless to inform him of it.) The student-writer explained her scene as a means of understanding why the old conductor figure had been rendered as an antiquated racial stereotype of deference and compliance (dancing and tipping his hat to Lula), while holding inside the psychological pain of racial injustice. Her text also captured the generational differences in social attitudes as well as white ignorance of the realities of racial politics.

Exercise 3 provisionally reworks Baraka's conception of the characters so that students might further investigate the complexity of racial and sexual politics as they can play out in even casual interaction. One student reversed *Dutchman*'s pretext to have Clay, now a brash, sexily dressed young white male, hitting on Lula, presented as a demure, professionally outfitted young black businesswoman, on a subway train. Clay makes presumptions about her sexual availability and blurts out racist clichés about what he guesses her family to be like (poor, lazy, drug-addicted); Lula is both repelled and fascinated by him and gives as good as she gets, exposing him as an opportunistic player who seeks only to realize his interracial fantasies. The purpose of such rewriting, of course, is not to divert students from Baraka's allegorical character clash but rather to bring it into sharper focus by means of a comparison scenario. Thus, in the example above, the student felt she could not envision a fatal ending for her characters, and that Clay would merely laugh off a lengthy indictment speech from Lula. The student herself concluded that Baraka's particular choices in delineating character and action are essential to creating *Dutchman*'s explosiveness and articulating its ideas.

The last examples to consider are responses to exercise 4, which, as the most frequently chosen option, has proven a popular outlet for students' intense identification with Clay's rage. The assignment asks students to generate a highly personal tirade that taps into their resentments and social anxieties. Some students develop the tirade in a fully imagined scene; others write bluntly autobiographical monologues with little or no dramatic context, and assign themselves, rather than character surrogates, to deliver them. One sample scene opens with an arrogant journalism instructor lecturing on cases in which obituary writers are justified in disclosing embarrassing personal information about a deceased public figure, such as (the instructor adds) one's homosexuality. Appalled by this attitude, a female student indignantly challenges the instructor's professionalism for labeling any sexual orientation as embarrassing. Her fierce retort, by turns sarcastic and earnest, eventually becomes a public acknowledgment of her homosexuality and of her willingness to shout down anyone who would diminish her because of it.

In a standout autobiographical monologue, a student rails at length against the increasingly obvious disparity between the American promises of reward and success through hard work and the American reality of a stalled economy, lifelong student debt, and a rigged system of opportunity and compensation. With bitter eloquence, he denounces the rhetoric of twenty-first-century America, which feeds its young people lies about their command of the future. The monologue gives clear evidence, in both content and expression, of catching the fire in Clay's long rebuke to Lula in the last fourth of *Dutchman*. In subsequent class discussion of these and other monologues, students remarked on the surprising affinity they had with twenty-year-old Clay and his inner fury, despite the clear circumstantial differences between Clay's life and their own. Inviting them to compose their own heartfelt harangues appeared to increase their identification with Clay and heighten their recognition of Lula's tactics, so that they could assess the action of Baraka's play with greater attentiveness and empathy.

As more than mere directed-therapy strategies for voicing discontent, the "pre-" and "post-" exercises have allowed my students to find common ground with Clay and Lula by understanding how they themselves negotiate America's anxiety-inducing expectations concerning identity and social conduct. Even with scant personal testimony to the African American experience of race prejudice and its socioeconomic barriers, the students who fill my classes find themselves (to a certain degree) in Clay's story. They recognize the seething frustration in Clay's existence as, somehow, a counterpart to their own, and they become more open to hearing the truth of Clay's journey. The scene work they create, whether in anticipation of or in reaction to reading the play, is an act of engagement that not only gives Baraka's work the fair hearing it deserves but also brings students to a higher understanding of his achievement as a theater artist.

NOTES

[1] Individual students may have varying experiences with such exercises, as Bernstein et al. note: "for older participants and those with histories of high betrayal trauma, the PlayWrite workshop might rouse painful experiences to the surface in a way that may be difficult in the short term" (461). This is a possibility to consider and prepare for when implementing personal writing in the classroom.

[2] The instructors remind teachers to "be prepared to address instances of stereotyping 'the other' or tendencies to write about issues from a distance and not make connections between issues and one's own role/life/country" when guiding students through this creative process (Buckley-Marudas and Block 107).

Dutchman in the Round

Jim Cocola

Amiri Baraka's *Dutchman* presents a particularly linear dramatic occasion. Set in a subway car, the play hurtles toward a violent denouement, only to turn back on itself with a culminating plot twist that proves chillingly fatalistic in its circularity. Although *Dutchman* startles from first to last, it can also elude students a half century removed from its conceits and cultural references. One way to involve students more closely with Baraka's *Dutchman* is to teach the play "in the round," turning the classroom into a theatrical space where instructor and students are interpellated on a pedagogical stage. Such a method clarifies the performativity of Clay's and Lula's characters, while also underlining the performativity of the instructor and student roles. Confronting the racialization of Baraka's characters in the round, students in turn confront the racialization that marks them, their classmates, and their instructor in everyday life.

To teach *Dutchman* in the round is to encounter a confrontational text in a setting that fosters dialogue, bringing everyone in the room onto the scene, especially if instructors deliver lectures or moderate class discussions using the same configuration. Restaging excerpts from *Dutchman* allows for considered reflection, while examining the impact of different dramaturgical choices in the round can motivate students to think more carefully about the ways that class, gender, sexuality, and race intersect in the play. Debates about seemingly minor production details can prove revelatory, whether these concern dress and decorum, incidental props, or approaches to staging involving blocking and lighting.

In the round, students attend to not only the text of *Dutchman* itself but also one another. Indeed, this is the logic by which the play itself begins: with a man, later identified as Clay, "holding a magazine but looking vacantly just above its wilting pages," save for those occasions when he "looks blankly toward the window on his right." How often our own students drift in similar ways! Yet, as the subway stops, "the man looks idly up, until he sees a woman's face staring at him through the window; when it realizes that the man has noticed the face, it begins very premeditatedly to smile" (3–4).

The play is thus set in motion by a moment of recognition—however depersonalized, however fraught, however rote. As Mary F. Brewer observes of Clay and Lula's first meeting, "their encounter has the appearance of routine" and "their meeting symbolizes a long-standing social ritual between Blacks and Whites in the United States" (96). Yet, as Matthew Luter notes, Clay and Lula intersect precisely because "their eye contact constitutes an implicit agreement" to "break the accepted codes of etiquette together" (34). These are the very choices students face: the classroom as space of ritual and routine or as space of transgression and transformation. Crucially, this communal choice is also particular to each student, for those resembling Clay face different consequences for embracing ritual and routine—or transgression and transformation—than do those resembling Lula.

In the larger span of semester and syllabus, the sense of *Dutchman* can be further rounded through comparative analysis. By juxtaposing Baraka's play with others like it—or, perhaps better, with others unlike it—students might glean a clearer sense of what is at stake (and what goes unarticulated or underarticulated) in Baraka's own work. Taken in comparison to the mid-century canon, *Dutchman* tends to read as an exceptional text. In comparison with a wider selection of multiethnic and postcolonial texts, it may assume a more representative quality.

One's first inclination might be to teach *Dutchman* in the wider context of Baraka's career or as a signal moment in the African American literary tradition. Examining *Dutchman* alongside other Baraka plays, such as *The Slave* (1964) and *What Was the Relationship of the Lone Ranger to the Means of Production?* (1978), provides students with synchronic and diachronic senses of his career as a dramatist, thereby illustrating his transition from bohemian virtuoso in 1950s Greenwich Village to black cultural nationalist in 1960s Harlem to revolutionary Marxist and Third World liberationist during his later career in Newark. But teaching him in isolation as an exemplary figure risks recapitulating the very logics of autonomous aestheticism and bourgeois individualism that Baraka himself repudiated in the wake of *Dutchman*.

Meanwhile, to teach Baraka alongside contemporary African American plays like Suzan-Lori Parks's *The Death of the Last Black Man in the Whole Entire World* (1990) or August Wilson's *Two Trains Running* (1992) offers an instructive lesson in literary history. And yet, to teach *Dutchman* in the context of the African American literary tradition alone risks recapitulating the logic of a provincial black cultural nationalism. Another approach would be to teach *Dutchman* through a pan-Africanist lens, for when we read this play in the company of plays by the Nigerian Nobel laureate Wole Soyinka—for example, *Kongi's Harvest* (1965) or *Death and the King's Horseman* (1975)—our attention returns to the transnational legacies embedded in Baraka's titular invocation of the Dutchman. Such comparisons also bring Lula and Clay into further relief by juxtaposing these two characteristically American characters with African analogues that proceed by distinct codes in distinct cultures. If Clay's life and death in *Dutchman* express the vulnerabilities of the African diaspora in terms of an American tragedy, Olunde's life and death in *Death and the King's Horseman* evince the pathos of an African tragedy sparked by the encroachments of British colonization.

Several other plays that also treat questions of assimilation, pluralism, prejudice, and racialization can provide comparative, multiethnic, and transnational points of departure for considering Baraka's *Dutchman*. To take just a few instances from the dramatic canon, instructors might draw on Dion Boucicault's *The Octoroon* (1859), Israel Zangwill's *The Melting Pot* (1908), William Saroyan's

An Armenian Trilogy (1986), Anna Deavere Smith's *Twilight: Los Angeles 1992* (1994), or Young Jean Lee's *Songs of the Dragon Flying to Heaven* (2009). When paired with Arthur Miller's *A View from the Bridge* (1955), Baraka's *Dutchman* reveals itself more clearly as a one-act play in two scenes. In addition to the relation between these two scenes, students might also think about the structure of Miller's play, which first premiered on Broadway as a one-act play, coupled with a second one-act play, *A Memory of Two Mondays* (1955), only to be revised and expanded into a single two-act play. A one-act play in two scenes, two one-act plays, a single two-act play: How do these slight differences in formal structure shape their respective dramatic arcs?

Among ethnic American plays that can be productive pairings with Baraka's *Dutchman*, Luis Valdez's *Zoot Suit* (1979) merits special mention. Linking these works in the same syllabus might provide students with broader and deeper contexts for both works and their respective traditions in modern American theater history. Like *Dutchman*, *Zoot Suit* stands as a central document from a prominent theater troupe committed to and emerging from a subset of multiethnic American culture in the wake of the civil rights movement. Just as Baraka's Black Arts Repertory Theatre/School, founded in 1965 in Harlem, functioned as a key node in the African American literary tradition, so too Valdez's El Teatro Campesino, also founded in 1965, in Delano, California, functioned as a key node in Chicano literature, providing a cultural platform for the United Farm Workers of America.

Considering *Dutchman* with *Zoot Suit* prompts a reconsideration of the respective subject positions of Baraka and Valdez, their respective theater companies, and their most famous protagonists, Clay Williams and Henry Reyna. Do students find one of these protagonists more sympathetic than the other? more alienating? more threatening? Are they more indifferent toward one case than another? What can they learn from the fact that many will regard the *Dutchman* dynamic between Lula and Clay as a multiracial relationship, even while labeling the *Zoot Suit* romance between Henry and Alice as cross-cultural or multiethnic?

A comparison of *Dutchman* and *Zoot Suit* brings several important contrasts into relief: black power versus Chicanismo; dramatic dialogues and monologues versus dramatic ensembles and polyphonies; the public spaces of New York versus the public spaces of Los Angeles. Since *Zoot Suit* depends on a variety of settings and speakers, staging it in the round works in consonance with Valdez's dramatic vision, whereas staging *Dutchman* in the round contrasts with Baraka's stark binaries of character and singularity of setting. While the courtroom, domestic, and neighborhood scenes of *Zoot Suit* unfold quite plausibly in the round, the subway car of *Dutchman* would seem to defy such staging by its unceasing rail-bound linearity.

And yet, to proceed in the round is to bring the claustrophobia of *Dutchman* into the midst of the classroom with even greater force. After setting minimal parameters, a small group of students can choose the relevant excerpt, cast the relevant players, and produce any relevant props. Instructors might highlight dramaturgical choices that any company should consider in staging the play. Preformed or self-selected groups can make these decisions days or even weeks ahead of time, perhaps punctuated by several brief assignments devoted to process writing. Alternatively, the assignment could be given at random, on the spot. A scattershot group of students might develop a more spontaneous implementation of a scene, incorporating found materials into an improvised read through of Baraka's script. In any event, consideration of various alternatives for performance can lead to reflexive discussions about the play itself, further enriching collective classroom engagement with Baraka's text.

In such a scenario, every choice of staging becomes a potentially significant gesture. Should Lula and Clay be cast according to type? Beyond questions of racial identification, does it matter if a first-year student plays the older Lula, and a third-year student plays the younger Clay? Should Lula be a natural redhead? If not, should she color her hair? If so, should she include "a gray hair for each year and type I've come through" (13)? Need she be longhaired, or tall, or slender, or beautiful, as the script suggests? How many of these attributes are indispensable in performance? Which are the most expendable?

Props also matter. At the end of the play, when Clay's successor enters the subway, "*with a couple of books under his arm*" (37), which books should he be carrying? Such choices speak volumes. And when Lula suggests that "eating apples together is always the first step" (11), should the apple in question be red or green? How much license should dramaturgs take? Perhaps Clay should eat an orange while Lula eats an apple—or maybe he should eat a watermelon, per one of LeRoi Jones's favored college capers at Howard University, where he would sometimes "sit out on the campus eating half a watermelon and scandalize . . . the patron saints of middle-class Negroes way off in Negro heb'n" (*Autobiography* [Lawrence Hill] 125).

In the round, on the campus, these dramaturgical choices resonate not only at the level of the performed excerpt but also at the scene of teaching and learning, permeating even the cut of one's cloth. As an instructor, should one introduce oneself into the drama by wearing Lula's sandals or Clay's three-button suit? Consciousness of such decisions engages a class in a kind of sartorial pedagogy, where matters of dress and deportment can assume an implicitly didactic relation to the text. Such lessons bear on students and teachers alike. Whether dressed casually, formally, or somewhere in between, the clothed body consciously aware of other clothed bodies will inevitably read Lula's rebuke of Clay's fashion sense in a distinct manner. "Boy," she admonishes him, "those narrow-shoulder clothes come from a tradition you ought to feel oppressed by. A three-button suit. What right do you have to be wearing a three-button suit and striped tie? Your grandfather was a slave, he didn't go to Harvard" (Baraka, *Dutchman* 18). How do instructors wearing three-button suits and striped ties address this passage? How should instructors who wouldn't be caught dead wearing three-button suits or striped ties speak to that same passage? And how can instructors who deliberately don three-button suits and striped ties for the express purpose of teaching *Dutchman* best call attention to this passage?

Whether completed before or after these classroom performances, short writing assignments can allow students to reflect on their embodied and spatialized encounters with the play. In my drama courses, I ask students to prepare brief dramaturgical essays that explain, justify, and theorize how they staged and performed excerpts from plays under consideration, attending to specific details from the texts as they advance their arguments.

In response, many students have offered profoundly destabilizing readings of *Dutchman*. Some students focus on depictions of gender and sexuality in Baraka's work, noting the striking asymmetry in his principal characters' introductory treatments. We meet Lula as a "thirty-year-old white woman" (3) only to reencounter her, a couple of pages later, dressed "*in bright, skimpy summer clothes and sandals . . . wearing sunglasses, which she pushes up on her forehead from time to time.*" Baraka elaborates on this image by describing her as "*a tall, slender, beautiful woman with long red hair hanging straight down her back, wearing only loud lipstick in somebody's good taste*" (5). Meanwhile, Clay is merely described as "a twenty-year-old Negro" (3).

To exploit this asymmetry of characterization, one student suggests an alternative staging, recasting Lula as a man named Louis and recasting Clay as a woman named Cleo, while otherwise retaining the differences in other aspects of their identities. Transforming these roles calls attention to the traumatic contours of class, gender, and race in American history and literature, hearkening back to foundational traumas in the Garden of Eden and on the Southern plantation. This proposed restaging rearticulates the play's focus on racism, confronting prejudices deeply rooted in a religious and social unconscious that Baraka himself drew on and reinscribed. For if a prevailing stereotype in American society projects guilt upon the black male body by default, a defining moment from the creation narrative in the Book of Genesis projects guilt on the female body as a matter of course.

Another student suggests a staging underscoring Lula's ambivalence. In this variation, a single actor portraying Clay interacts with a pair of actors portraying Lula, with one Lula behaving erratically and confrontationally and the other Lula behaving evenly and civilly. As the two Lulas would be clothed identically, the audience would find themselves confronted with the question of which Lula committed the murder, left to speculate whether that act came as the rash insurgency of an outspoken eccentric or as the more typical reaction of an establishment conformist. One can imagine a similar bifurcation in the casting of Clay. In either case, such dramaturgical innovations inevitably evoke W. E. B. Du Bois's notion of "double consciousness," originally formulated in the pages of *The Souls of Black Folk* (1903; *Souls of Black Folk: Essays* 3), but applied more broadly in the twentieth century and thereafter to a multiplicity of dispossessed populations.

To stage *Dutchman* in the round is to bring the force of double consciousness home to students and perhaps even to impart a hint of the Du Boisian "sense of always looking at one's self through the eyes of others, of measuring one's soul by the tape of a world that looks on in amused contempt and pity" (*Souls of Black Folk: Essays* 3). To watch a performance in the round is not merely to watch but also to perform: to be watched by a set of watchers whom you watch as they watch you watching them. In such a scene of watching, critical thinking about the play takes on wholly different valences. When analyzing *Dutchman*, should one be more preoccupied with the tools of critical race theory, or the tools of feminist theory, or the tools of Marxist theory? Asking individual students to respond to this question in isolation may yield relatively definitive answers, but asking everyone in the room to respond has different stakes when all these students are looking to everyone else for answers even as they produce their own.

Posing questions to students in the round also leads them to pose unstated questions of their own: who looks at this, in what way, how do they look, how do I look at them, and how do they look at me? In classrooms where historically underrepresented students remain underrepresented, or even wholly absent, the sublimated dynamic of attraction and repulsion between Lula and Clay will take on different tones than it will in more diverse classroom settings. In either case, one need not hail the underrepresented student in order to underscore the dynamic at work; by seating students in the round, the stage is set for the bodies made invisible to become more apparent to those who might not otherwise have thought of them as such. These small epiphanies happen, and they happen without anyone's needing to explicitly note the configuration that makes these new forms of awareness possible.

Will students so situated agree with Fred Moten that Lula ultimately represents "the embodiment of predatory white femininity" (271) or concur with George Piggford that *Dutchman* finally turns on "exposing the horror of race relations in America" (82)? Such postulates can be clarified when students encounter the play in ways that foreground human embodiment and relation and thereby underscore what Samy Azouz, following Kimberly Benston, identifies as Baraka's methexis: "the collective keeping and continuation of the action" (26). When *Dutchman* is performed in the round, the play's methexis can carry beyond classrooms and off the stage, into campus centers and dormitory hallways.

Dutchman is a play that involves readers in a constellation of issues related to class, gender, and racial identity. One of the greatest challenges in teaching the play comes with its insistence on extending beyond the typical "happy family multiculturalism" (C. Nelson 52) that reproduces a universally flattened and historically evacuated sense of diversity. By teaching *Dutchman* in the round, instructors may find further routes to engagement with a confrontational, provocative text, in a spirit of openness to dialogue and difference. Talking through these differences without necessarily resolving them proves to be among the most important opportunities that a classroom encounter with *Dutchman* provides. In my courses, students who are transformed by the play are given the floor to praise it, students who find few redeeming qualities are given the floor to dismiss or even condemn it, and students who find strengths and weaknesses are given the floor to offer qualified endorsements along with particular criticisms.

One of the greatest rewards in teaching the play comes in watching this contestation, especially as it pertains to the play's conclusion, which students have been trained not to comprehend, much less to accept. After years of exposure to mass-mediated narratives that criminalize African American subjects per the discriminatory logics of the United States prison-industrial complex, *Dutchman* presents students with an unfamiliar denouement. For in Baraka's drama, it is the "thirty-year-old white woman" who stands as the perpetrator and the predator, while the black male object of her desire, victimized on numerous levels, returns to the scene of the crime as a perpetual martyr in an unending cycle of white-on-black violence.

As Robert Stam and Louise Spence observe, the "cultural and ideological assumptions" that structure knee-jerk associations between blackness and blameworthiness run deep (20) —so deep, in fact, that prominent professional critics failed to comprehend the significance of Baraka's *Dutchman* when it was condensed, transformed, and incorporated as a minor subplot in Jean-Luc Godard's *Masculin Féminin* (1966) (figs. 1 and 2). As a case in point, Stam and Spence flag a review of *Masculin Féminin* by the auteur theorist and film critic Andrew Sarris and express their dismay at Sarris's mistaken inference that the scene concludes as "a Negro nationalist . . . draws out a gun with phallic fury in the metro" (qtd. in Stam and Spence 19). Writing as a Greek American, poised uneasily with respect to the dynamic of racialization that Baraka examines, Sarris nevertheless "ignores the visual and written evidence that it is a woman who

Figure 1. Jean-Luc Godard, director. *Masculin Féminin*. 1966. (26:45).

wields the gun" and "projects his own racial and sexual expectations on to the film" (Stam and Spence 19). For while Godard layers a certain amount of sartorial ambiguity into the scene, dressing "la femme dans le metro" and "l'homme dans le metro" in similar trench coats (fig. 1), a careful examination of the relevant close-up (fig. 2) confirms that the woman, played by Chantal Darget, brandishes the weapon at the conclusion of this *Dutchman*-inspired vignette.

In the classroom, screening this brief scene from an important French new wave filmmaker and relating it to Sarris's suggestive misreading can clarify an important crux of Baraka's drama for students attempting to gain a more thorough grasp of this landmark play. Such a move stands as one of several intertextual juxtapositions that might further elucidate the underlying prejudices shaping the dramatic arc of *Dutchman*—prejudices marking the play's own time and place in the New York of the 1960s as well as many other historical locations (e.g., Boucicault's Louisiana of the 1850s, Soyinka's Oyo State of the 1940s, Valdez's Los Angeles of the 1940s, and Smith's Los Angeles of the 1990s).

Drawing on comparative, multiethnic, and transnational canons and discussing such material in the round can provide students more direct experiences of performativity, not only as it operates in dramatic texts but also as it manifests in the world that the students inhabit. How do they perform their own senses of self and other in relation to ideas of class, gender, and race? How do the audiences of their stagings authorize, receive, and transform such performances, and how do such negotiations vary from one subject position to the next? Asking students to consider such questions can propel them toward keener understandings of the stakes involved in Baraka's play, giving them a better grasp of the hand that wrote the hand that holds the dagger in *Dutchman*.

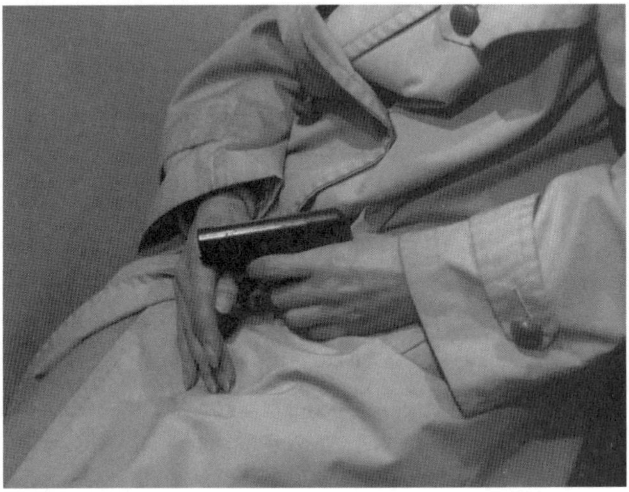

Figure 2. Jean-Luc Godard, director. *Masculin Féminin*. 1966. (28:18).

Teaching *Dutchman* from an International Perspective

Katarzyna Jakubiak

In a 2010 interview for *Black Camera*, the performance artist and filmmaker Jefferson Pinder describes *Dutchman* as "rich" because "it's grounded in something that is very real [Baraka's personal experience] and people can take and run with it in different directions" (qtd. in Martin and Wall 81). Pinder's view parallels the experience that most of my students have with *Dutchman*. While they are initially drawn to the play's biographical context—its author's dramatic transformation from Jones to Baraka—they are intrigued when guided beyond this dimension, and they appreciate *Dutchman*'s potential for surprise. And I ultimately lead my classes to an international perspective that may indeed be surprising. It seems to contradict the ideals of Baraka's "revolutionary theater," which informed the work of the Black Arts Repertory Theatre/School and which called for art that responded specifically to "the needs and aspirations of Black America" (Neal, "Black Arts Movement" [Gates and McKay] 2039). However, some contemporary critics have observed that *Dutchman*'s complexity transcends the polarized categories of this cultural nationalist ideology,[1] opening the play to multiple audiences. The pleasure of teaching *Dutchman* from an international perspective lies exactly in helping students imagine audiences outside United States theater culture and discover the multiple interpretative directions that the new contexts highlight.

Dutchman's ability to increase students' motivation for literary analysis is the main reason I chose to teach it in the Literary Research and Analysis course required of all undergraduate English majors at Millersville University. Our classes on *Dutchman* take place late in the semester, after students are familiar with major schools of literary and cultural criticism. Immediately preceding *Dutchman*, they study the Bedford/St. Martin's edition of William Shakespeare's *The Tempest*, which positions the play as "a case study in critical controversy" (Graff and Phelan). The final article in this volume, Gerald Graff and James Phelan's instructional essay "Writing about Critical Controversy and *The Tempest*," identifies three methods of engaging with critical arguments about literary texts: disagreeing; agreeing (saying "yes and . . ."); and partially agreeing, partially disagreeing (saying "yes, but . . ."). Our study of *Dutchman* uses Graff and Phelan's methods; in a series of assignments over the course of two weeks, students identify some critical controversies surrounding the play and, eventually, write an essay in response to selected interpretations. Before students begin their own research, I assign a sample of existing scholarship on *Dutchman*, three articles representing different periods and critical approaches: Willene Taylor's "The Fall of Man Theme in Imamu Amiri Baraka's *Dutchman*" (1973); Andrzej Ceynowa's "The Dramatic Structure of *Dutchman*" (1983); and Matthew Rebhorn's

"Flaying Dutchman: Masochism, Minstrelsy, and the Gender Politics of Amiri Baraka's *Dutchman*" (2003).[2]

Treating these three interpretations as a "critical controversy" around the play, we list the critical positions in the debate. The list typically looks something like the following:

> *Dutchman* is about victimization of black men by white America, symbolically represented by Lula.
>
> The play should not be read in a symbolic way. *Dutchman* is about a specific relationship between "one white girl and one Negro boy" (Baraka, *Home* [Akashic] 187).
>
> Lula and Clay do not fall easily into the oppressor/victim dichotomy. Both are guilty; Clay's guilt derives from his decision to assimilate and thus betray "his people" (Ceynowa) or from his choice to embrace the "macho" identity, which renders abject both women and homosexuals (Rebhorn).
>
> The interpretation of *Dutchman* should not be limited to racial matters. The play could be read as a criticism of unjust power hierarchies in general (Ceynowa) or as a universal allegory of human fallibility (W. Taylor).

It is the last item on the list, the universalist reading of *Dutchman*, that directs students' attention toward the play's international reception. One of the two assigned critics who support this interpretation is Ceynowa, a Polish scholar and a Fulbright fellow at the City University of New York in 1981. Unlike Taylor, who simply attaches secondary importance to blackness in the play, Ceynowa radically deflates color, declaring it "immaterial" and "symbolic" (18). He supports this controversial claim with a reference to his own cultural milieu:

> If the interest in *Dutchman* were limited to racial matters only, especially Black-white relations, the play could be expected to have little appeal to audiences for whom such problems are nonexistent. In 1967, however, the play was successfully presented by an all-white cast in Warsaw, Poland at [T]eatr Kameralny. If I may speculate about what held the audiences in this racially-uniform society, I would say that, free from being preconditioned to see a racial problem, the Polish theatregoers saw *Dutchman* as a play about honesty towards oneself and the wages of betraying one's people in the hour of confrontation with suppressive, alien power. (18)[3]

Of course, before students can reasonably respond to Ceynowa's claims, I must explain that his phrase "suppressive, alien power" implies the Soviet Union, which between 1945 and 1989 exerted various degrees of political control over Polish governments. I also confirm that in the 1960s, in the aftermath of the Nazi Holocaust, which had almost entirely wiped out the country's significant Jewish minority, Polish society was indeed overwhelmingly homogenous. Only two percent of Poland's nearly thirty million people were members of ethnic minorities (Roszkowski 253).[4] Then I ask students whether such new contexts of *Dutchman*'s production, and the resulting ability of an all-white Polish audience to identify with Clay as an oppressed person, can indeed make the character's blackness "immaterial." A common reaction is resistance, often supported by claims that the play's references to African American culture (e.g., the blues, Bessie Smith, and Charlie Parker) would defy translation. I counter this assumption with a brief explanation about the role of the blues and jazz as forces of resistance in the Eastern Bloc during the Cold War.[5] Another popular question among students is whether a Polish audience would have fully understood the moral dilemma of Clay's assimilation into white American culture. In response, I explain that to many Poles, adoption of the Communist value system posed similar ethical problems. Many aspiring Polish writers accepted the system against their convictions because they were offered significant privileges in exchange for works that glorified Communism.[6]

These considerations convince students of Polish audiences' transracial identification with Clay, and I stimulate further discussion about the meaning of race in Polish contexts by sharing copies of the Warsaw production's archival records, which I examine in my current research on representations of African American culture in Polish theater. Not surprisingly, the most disturbing items are photographs of Clay in blackface (fig. 1). To help students situate these images in a Polish context, I pair the photographs with excerpts from an interview I conducted with Maciej Englert, the actor who played Clay. In his reminiscences, Englert is reluctant to endow blackface with the same baggage of racial stereotyping that it carries in the United States. Instead, he defines it as "a sign of difference." Echoing Ceynowa, Englert describes the goals of the Polish production in the

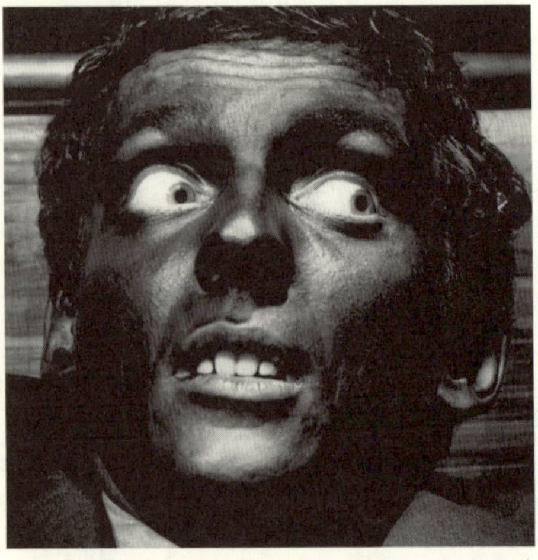

Figure 1. Maciej Englert as Clay at Teatr Współczesny, Warsaw, 1969. Photograph courtesy of the Archives of Teatr Współczesny.

following way: "[I]t was not really about reconstructing some other world, but about matching this world . . . with what we had in Poland. Nobody played an American. . . . We assumed that these were people; only one was white and the other black, which just meant that they were different" (Englert).[7]

When I asked Englert why, in the absence of an American referent, the producers decided to use blackface, he said, "Otherwise, at that time, people wouldn't have known what was going on. And if he spoke with a Jewish accent, or wore a red tie and a badge of the communist youth, the censorship wouldn't have approved it. *Or if, God forbid, she wore that badge*!" (my emphasis). When I read these excerpts to students, I highlight Englert's automatic association of otherness with "a Jewish accent," a remark indicating that, even in a "racially-uniform" society, racial problems are hardly ever nonexistent. Drawing on this remark, as well as Englert's suggestion that it is Lula, not Clay, who could be perceived as the other, I have students examine the treatment of Jewishness in *Dutchman*, an important theme, especially in the light of later controversies surrounding Baraka's alleged anti-Semitism. At various points in the text, Lula and Clay alternately call each other "Jewish," using the term as a mock insult. Scoffing at Clay's excessive "seriousness" and immaturity, Lula compares him to "Jewish poets from Yonkers," who, in her conception, are obsessed with mother figures (28). Later, deriding his assimilationist aspirations, Lula accuses Clay of having "crawled through the wire . . . to [her] side," and her subsequent question, "Don't they have wire around plantations?," interfuses slavery with the Jewish Holocaust (29). Clay's rebuttal, on the other hand, mocks what he takes to be Jewish people's preoccupation with their own victimhood: "You must be Jewish. All you think about is wire" (29). Students usually know enough about World War II and the Holocaust to realize that these passages would have resonated with new intensity when performed in a country that twenty-four years before had been a site of Nazi concentration camps.

A Polish context brings new meaning also to the play's final reference to Jewishness, Lula's seemingly nonsensical exclamations during her bout of wildness: "Red trains cough Jewish underwear for keeps! Expanding smells of silence" (31). Trains carrying naked, dehumanized people to their deaths are an iconic image of the Holocaust. Thus, when read with World War II as a background, Lula's statements link the subway train of *Dutchman* with the trains of the Holocaust, helping students realize that the play's apparently surreal climax—a public murder approved by silent witnesses—may be more realistic than they thought. Emphasizing the Holocaust references, I draw students' attention to the play's indictment of Western institutionalized and rationalized genocide. When the class rereads Clay's final prophecy of future murders committed with "rational explanations" by "ex-coons" who have finally learned to be like "Western men" (36), students' thoughts sometimes turn to nineteenth-century racial sciences like craniology, which provided support for Nazi racial politics. If students do not make this connection on their own, I remind them that the same theories were used to justify racial hierarchies in the American South.

The discussion of *Dutchman*'s possible evocations of the Holocaust makes students conclude that an international production of the play cannot eliminate the importance of race, even if black-white relations recede from the foreground. However, some students continue to wonder about viewing Lula as the other in the Polish context. We usually notice that this perception explains why Ceynowa rejects all interpretations that position her as a victimizer or a representation of "white America" (16). If we regard Lula as a member of another alienated group, we are more likely to accept Ceynowa's claim that she represents a judicial body presiding over the trial and execution of a traitor (17).

The full historical context of the Warsaw production makes Lula's position even more complex. *Dutchman* was brought to Poland just a year after the country's most severe postwar political crisis, often called "March 1968." Provoked by the 1967 Arab-Israeli war, the crisis developed out of a rising nationalist and anti-Semitic faction in the ruling Communist Party. The faction, popularly called "the partisans," exploited anti-Israeli sentiment to mount an attack on their political enemies. Among these enemies were Polish college students, who, following their international peers, had organized nationwide protests against state limitations on civil liberties. Influenced by the partisans, the government propaganda manipulated the public opinion to identify the student protesters and their sympathizers (including many leading Polish intellectuals) with Zionism. Because this anti-Semitic propaganda fed on a mythic alliance between Jews and Communist elites, it led to a paradox: although the protesters had criticized the Communist system, the public came to view their alleged Zionism as a sign of their secret affiliation with Communism. Their well-intentioned call for political reform was dismissed as a mere provocation (Osęka). At length, the consequences of this political conflict were grievous: because of their Jewish background, about eight hundred people in managerial positions lost their jobs, and fifteen thousand people emigrated from Poland permanently (Eisler 347).

The evocation of a mythic Jewish-Communist alliance may have created Lula's otherness for the Polish audience. Before Clay's banter identifies her as possibly Jewish, Lula mentions that her mother was a Communist (19);[8] later, she signals her Communist sentiments again when she belittles Clay as a "middle-class black bastard" (31), a name that might echo the Polish government's antibourgeois rhetoric. Consequently, in the context of late 1960s Poland, it was possible to view both Clay and Lula as victims of racial myths. For some playgoers, the characters' violent confrontation in scene 2 may have recalled March 1968's blurred distinctions between the oppressor and the oppressed.

However, the main goal of my class is not to probe into the complex historical context of the Polish production but to inspire students' general appreciation for context and audience as crucial factors in the meaning-making of any literary text, especially a dramatic one. The example of *Dutchman*'s Polish production fleshes out concepts that the class studies during a unit on poststructuralism: the idea of meaning as a fluid structure constantly remade by the ever-shifting contexts of reception.[9] Consequently, when students take their stands in the critical controversy surrounding *Dutchman*, they often refer to context as the defining factor of Lula's and Clay's roles. For example, one student, in his retort to Ceynowa's claim that the characters become racial antagonists only in scene 2, states: "[T]he racial undertones already existed [before] because the [American] audience/reader had already subconsciously put them into the context of the play." Another student, Shane Acker, supports his view of Clay as a victim by linking the play's title with the context of European colonization of Africa and the Dutch participation in it.[10] Shane proposes to treat one legacy of Dutch colonialism, South African apartheid, as "a model" of oppression to be "placed within the context of how America dealt with and used Africans during the time of slavery and after." For Shane, such a contextualization legitimizes reading the title *Dutchman* as an implication of Clay's social inferiority and victimhood.

Together with an appreciation for context, the international perspective on *Dutchman* introduces my students to transnational approaches to literary studies, a relatively new methodology, which adds to their knowledge of research and analysis in the field of English. Offering the class an opportunity to learn about the challenges of transnational research in theater, I explain that there is no single resource that would allow them to identify all past and present international productions of *Dutchman* (or any other play).[11] Students must accept that to conduct such research, they will use a combination of methods, which may not yield comprehensive results. One method is researching the author's manuscript collections. Various collections of Baraka's papers include records of *Dutchman*'s international presence. The collection at Columbia University has at least two: a program for a 1968 Brazilian production directed by Fernando Peixoto at Teatro Oficina (under the tile *Poder Negro*, or "Black Power") and a text of the South African adaptation cowritten by Baraka and the South African playwright Duma Ndlovu. Also, the collection at Syracuse University holds a copy of a program from Cherry Lane Theater's guest performance of the play at the prestigious Literary Colloquium Berlin in 1964.

However, research in manuscript collections, while fascinating, may be appropriate for only advanced students, considering the costs and the time commitments that are often involved.[12] For undergraduates, a more convenient method of researching international productions of *Dutchman* would be to do an author or title Google search, setting regional and language limits. (Students can restrict the search to the languages or the areas of the world that interest them.) This method can lead students to discover international theater resources, for many countries' national theater and art institutions have online platforms that provide access to records of domestic theater productions.[13] A thorough engagement in research on international productions of *Dutchman* is, once again, beyond the scope of my class, but some exercises in the methods discussed above can be useful for any class that incorporates a transnational approach to the play.

Obviously, the Polish perspective is only one among many that can inspire lively class discussions. Baraka and Ndlovu's South African version of *Dutchman*, set "on a train in Johannesburg" and full of specific local detail, offers another compelling perspective ("An Adaptation" 1).[14] The adaptation had one performance at the Schomburg Center for Research in Black Culture in Harlem in the 1980s but was never produced in South Africa (Ndlovu). Other South African sources, however, indicate that the original *Dutchman* has been staged in South Africa. In 2008 Market Theatre in Johannesburg presented a production of *Dutchman*, directed by Lindiwe Matshikiza, at Flare Festival, a celebration of emerging female directors ("Flare Festival"). In 2011 a dramatic reading of the play, directed by Lara Bye, was staged at the Gordon Institute for Performing and Creative Arts at the University of Cape Town during an event called The Names We Give, a weekend of "performances, jazz, film and public interventions" ("Names"). Many images from the Johannesburg production are available on the Web site 75, which is devoted to South African photography (nhlanhla).

Because of *Dutchman*'s evocation of Dutch colonial history, students may also be curious to examine the play's presence in the Dutch language, into which it was translated by the prominent writer Cees Nooteboom. The online catalogue of Theatre Instituut Nederland (TIN) records four productions that took place in Holland between 1966 and 1996. Unfortunately, access to most of TIN's archival materials is reserved exclusively for its members. Only the poster from the first Dutch production, staged by Stichting Incidenteel Theater Experiment in 1966, is available on TIN's sister Web site *Theaterencyclopedie*.

The film version (1966), directed by the British filmmaker Anthony Harvey and shot mainly in a British studio, offers another international perspective on *Dutchman*.[15] Students may be interested in discussing whether the British context could have influenced the play's screen interpretation, as expressed through the editing and framing choices, soundtrack, camera angles, and so on.[16] Another example of British reception, the 1967 United Kingdom production at the Hampstead Theatre Club, if juxtaposed with the Polish production, may give students some insight into the play's transnational circulation. *Dutchman* appeared at the Hampstead Theatre on a double bill with *Neighbours* (1964), a one-act play by the British writer James Saunders. The 1969 Polish production, discussed earlier, was also a double bill with Saunders's play, which suggests that the Polish producers may have drawn inspirations from their British colleagues.

It may be an interesting exercise in contextualization for students to reread *Dutchman* together with *Neighbours*. On one level, the British play pairs well with *Dutchman* because of parallel protagonists, a white woman and a black man, whose encounter reenacts sexual racial myths. However, on another level, *Neighbours* perpetuates stereotypes, which, when performed alongside *Dutchman*, may distort Baraka's political message.[17] Discovering the plays' common international production history, students could debate how race and gender dynamics in one play may have colored the audience's perception of such dynamics in the other.

Ultimately, an examination of what *Dutchman* has lost and gained through international productions makes students realize that the meaning of this work does not belong to its author. Baraka suggested as much, in his autobiography, when he confessed that after the play's rapid success, he had to "read [it] again, just to understand it" (*Autobiography* [Lawrence Hill] 277). *The Autobiography* also reinforces the critical argument that *Dutchman* is more than a manifesto of black nationalism; Baraka's personal story presents the play as a fruit of great confusion in his life.[18] Ironically, the ambiguity that was a source of anguish for Baraka has been *Dutchman*'s major point of attraction. It has helped fulfill its author's ambition of reaching more people and has sustained the play's dynamic international afterlife. Most important for teachers of literature, the play's ambiguity continues to intrigue and motivate students, making them eager to contribute their interpretations to the *Dutchman* debates.

NOTES

[1] See, for example, Nita Kumar's "The Logic of Retribution," which argues that, although some of Baraka's contemporaneous essays articulate an essentialist theory of black identity, *Dutchman* "contend[s] with the oppressive structures [i.e., black/white, Europe/Africa, etc.] of the binary, racial logic" that prevails in the United States (279).

[2] The file assigned to students also includes Baraka's essay "LeRoi Jones Talking" (1964), which features Baraka's often-quoted statement that "*Dutchman* is about the difficulty of becoming a man in America" (Baraka, *Home* [Akashic] 188).

[3] Ceynowa cites the wrong date in this passage; the Warsaw production of *Dutchman* took place in 1969. The production was done by Teatr Współczesny, which had been Łódź Teatr Kameralny (the name Ceynowa refers to) until 1949.

[4] These were chiefly Jews, Ukrainians, Belarusians, Germans, and Lithuanians. There were only about two thousand Africans, predominantly students on government-sponsored scholarships (Ząbek 40).

[5] See Penny von Eschen's *Satchmo Blows Up the World* for a discussion of this phenomenon.

[6] The most famous depiction of this situation can be found in Czesław Miłosz's *The Captive Mind* (1953).

[7] All quotations from the interview with Englert are in my translation.

[8] Baraka, in a 1991 interview and in his 1984 autobiography, mentions an Old Left Jewish bohemian friend who was a "model" for Lula (*Conversations* 255; *Autobiography* [Lawrence Hill] 208–09).

[9] Our study of poststructuralism is based on Peter Barry's *Beginning Theory*.

[10] Shane develops his argument from Robert Cardullo's "Names and Titles in Amiri Baraka's *Dutchman*," which proposes that in the context of the play the word *Dutchman* connotes the Dutch participation in the slave trade.

[11] While licensing companies hold this information, they do not routinely share it with the public. Samuel French, the licensing company for *Dutchman*, denied my request for a list of international productions. However, records of all domestic productions of *Dutchman* (and all other plays since 1945) can be found in *Theatre World* (Willis).

[12] While some archival materials can be ordered online (for a fee), some can be accessed only in person.

[13] These platforms include, for example, E-teatr.pl (the vortal of the Polish Theatre Institute), the online archive of the Akademie der Künste in Berlin, the Virtual Study (ViS) of the Theatre Institute of the Czech Republic, and the Web site of the Theatre Instituut Nederland (Netherlands). The databases of the last two platforms can be searched in English.

[14] In this version, American place names have been replaced by South African ones, and the main character has a South African name, Clay Bumba. There are also changes in vocabulary. For example, Lula calls Clay "black kaffir" instead of "nigger."

[15] A paraphrase of *Dutchman*'s violent confrontation between Clay and Lula in scene 2 was also included in Jean-Luc Godard's film *Masculin Féminin* (1966), another international source that can be shared with students. Werner Sollors briefly discusses Godard's choices for the scene and their links to surrealism (127).

[16] In my course, if time allows, we watch clips from Harvey's film and treat them as yet another interpretation in the critical controversy surrounding the play. Students sometimes note that the ominous tone of the soundtrack gives the story an air of a thriller rather than that of an allegory of race relations.

[17] Saunders criticizes white British liberalism represented by the female protagonist's desperate and absurd attempts to prove that she is not racist. While the satire on liberalism is well executed, Rastus, the play's West Indian protagonist, enacts the stereotype of black sexuality in reverse. He forces his neighbor to have sex with him, not through violence but through emotional blackmail, and, at the moment of consummation, he is symbolically castrated because he proves "incapable" (46).

[18] Drawing on an account of Baraka's personal history, Sollors reads *Dutchman* as a drama of "the divided self" (125). He argues that Clay and Lula can be interpreted as "two opposing forces" of Baraka's artistic consciousness, forces that "are again divided in themselves" (128). Lotta Löfgren makes a similar argument in "Clay and Clara."

Dutchman Heaped in Modern Cinema

William Thomas McBride

My introduction to formal analysis came from my film professor, Alan Spiegel, who taught me how to identify, describe, and interpret what he called stylized moments, significant expressions of meaning in the language of film. When I teach film, my students read closely the use of camera (framing, spatial relationships, point of view), editing, lighting, and set and costume design. My approach to teaching film, fiction, and drama also has been shaped by cultural studies. As it evolved, cultural studies has found that writings in philosophy, psychoanalysis, politics and social theory, anthropology, feminism, and cinema can be most valuable for understanding and reading texts—that is, for interpreting culture and the ideology embedded in it. I demonstrate how to perform the work of cultural studies through describing and interpreting stylized structural and linguistic authorial choices.

In both my asynchronous online film and synchronous face-to-face drama classes, I teach works chronologically by date of appearance. By the time we reach the 1960s, students have already analyzed several classics that precede the theatrical and film versions of *Dutchman*. They are now equipped to find those formal ingredients as well as elements of myth, psychosexuality, philosophy, race, and ethnicity that make up this work. Students in my film course read the play, screen the film, and then post their responses in a discussion forum where classmates and I continue the conversation. Because Anthony Harvey's film version runs under an hour, it is ideal for a seventy-five-minute version of the face-to-face class, in which the film can be shown in its entirety with time remaining for reactions and discussion. In the class meeting prior to the screening, students present interpretations of passages they have chosen to elucidate. Students then post their reflections on the play, film, and discussion in a similar online forum.

Heaped in Modern Myth: A Flying Dutchwoman

Students need to unpack the title of the work they seek to interpret. *Dutchman* is, on one level, a highly allegorical retelling of the Flying Dutchman myth that expresses the emerging radical black consciousness of Amiri Baraka. The author confirms that the title refers to the "ghost story" of the Flying Dutchman (*Autobiography* [Lawrence Hill] 187). The legend depicts a Faustian bargain between the Devil and the ship's captain, who exchanges his soul for passage around the forbidding Cape of Good Hope. "*Heaped in modern myth*," as Baraka writes in his stage directions (3), the play adds a layer of historicity by conjuring up a poignant reminder that Dutch textile merchants and their ships were major players in the transatlantic slave trade, making all the more sinister the play's title and Lula's murderous identity. The play overdetermines (or heaps) that identity by cross-gender casting, making the damned Dutch ship's captain a thirty-year-old "tall, slender, beautiful" white woman with "long red hair hanging straight down her back" whose allegorical sea vessel is a New York City subway train (5). Baraka cleverly expresses his radical black consciousness through both Lula as the militant prosecutor of "middle-class, fake white" men (34) and Clay as the emerging but soon retreating black avenger of white racism. Lula's gender is further problematized when, in the stage direction, Baraka refers to the "woman" as "it" (3). (I remind students, though, that stage and film audiences do not read these directions; they are intended for practitioners and interpreters alone.)

Another mythic layer, courtesy of the Book of Genesis, is heaped on the play by naming the ever-malleable black man "Clay." In Sumerian, Greek, Hebraic, and other ancient creation myths the first human is made of earth or clay, and the ancient Hebrew word for "Adam" is also the word for "clay." Baraka's heaping of modern myth allows me to introduce to students the notion of "overdetermination" and trace its history to Hegel, Freud, the New Critics, and Althusser. Lula is symbolically overdetermined as the sculpting Yahweh, evidenced when she imagines the evening that she and Clay will spend together:

> LULA. I mean, we'll look in all the shop windows, and make fun of the queers. Maybe we'll meet a Jewish Buddhist and flatten his conceits over some very pretentious coffee.
> CLAY. In honor of whose God?
> LULA. Mine.
> CLAY. Who is . . .?
> LULA. Me. . . . (23–24)

Lula is also both the seductive Eve and the Devil—she is therefore both the damned and she who damns. Throughout the play, Lula molds Clay, first as her sexual prey, who literally eats out of her hand, and then as the murderous, abusive black man she has been conjuring from the beginning. She says early on, "You're a murderer, Clay" (21).

Lula and Clay Framed

When Harvey's audience first encounters Lula posing for Clay's gaze, we see her internally framed through Clay's window. This shot invites a voyeuristic contemplation of her beauty and depicts Clay as the gazer eyeing the bait. Often created by a film set's doorways and windows, an internal frame visually brackets characters and props like a picture frame to invite aesthetic and hermeneutic contemplation. The wardrobe designer Brenda Gardner takes as a cue Baraka's dressing of Lula in "skimpy summer clothes" by costuming the femme fatale in typical black and white noir fashion with stripes, which generically represent prison garb, prison cell bars, and certainly a mysterious, inscrutable mixture of good (white) and evil (black). Stylized metaphors are usually this direct.

It is important for my students to know the history of the fatal temptress to whom the male hero is attracted but whom he must resist and defeat. The misogynistic characterization in Western culture goes back at least as far as Eve in the Hebrew Bible and the Sirens and Circe in Homer's *Odyssey*. Later in the play, a raging Clay pushes Lula back down into her seat, calling her "Tallulah Bankhead!" (34), the classic Hollywood temptress and the inspiration for Disney's Cruella De Vil in *101 Dalmatians* (Cubria). In keeping with noir's stock-in-trade femme fatale, Harvey's black-and-white cinematography creates a noir ambience and a visual correlative of the script's meditation on race in America. Lula's red hair, unreadable when filmed in black and white, is changed to blonde, which better italicizes the polar opposition to Clay's skin and hair color. Black and white is the most antirealist medium—Mike Nichols used it that same year in *Who's Afraid of Virginia Woolf?*—and further distances the audience from comfortable consumption of a true-to-life narrative. It points out that we are watching a film (of a play) that thereby invites attention to and creative analysis of style and detail.

The internal framing at the beginning of the film continues with a medium close-up of Clay outlined by poles to his left and right (fig. 1). The cinematographer Gerry Turpin's effect of also composing this shot in soft focus renders Clay already isolated and trapped. Soft or shallow focus photography is achieved with a specific lens that concentrates the depth of field so objects targeted by the camera appear in sharp, clear focus, while everything else in the shot remains out of focus. Soft-focus photography isolates certain images for inspection, granting a heightened interest in those objects in sharp focus. A meaningful distance or isolation can be indicated among two or more characters or objects in the same frame when only one is in focus at any time.

I encourage my students to develop an eye for meaningful spatial relationships, often executed as blocking on the theatrical stage. I want my students to

Figure 1. Still from *Dutchman*, directed by Anthony Harvey, 1966. Internal framing and soft focus photography render Clay isolated and trapped.

Figure 2. Still from *Dutchman*, directed by Anthony Harvey, 1966. Lula and Clay separated by a subway pole.

Figure 3. Still from *Dutchman*, directed by Anthony Harvey, 1966. Lula and Clay enclosed by the same pole.

see how power and intimacy are expressed through the placement of actors and objects, which cinema does by directing our gaze to such stylized placements. When we first see Clay and Lula together, the pole that separates them visually objectifies the social distance between them (fig. 2). Later in the first scene, and in the second scene, the same pole encloses them together and brackets them off from the rest of the train, forming an encompassing internal frame that expresses Lula's intimacy and Clay's capture (fig. 3).

Bet You Can't Eat Just One

Just as the work's title, character names and costumes, internal framing, camera focus, and spatial relationships are potentially significant, so is a play or film's set design. Set designers or decorators are in charge of all items visible in the set—e.g., furniture, wall hangings, etc.—that stylistically contribute meaningful elements. It is unclear precisely who is responsible for the two significant, stylized

Figure 4. Still from *Dutchman*, directed by Anthony Harvey, 1966. Production designers extend the play's modern myth by connecting two enslavers with the famous print ad for Dutch Masters Cigars (after Rembrandt's *The Staalmeesters*).

background print advertisements inside the subway car. Is it the set decorator Ian Whittaker, art directors Jim Morahan and Herbert Smith, first-time British director Anthony Harvey, or some combination of collaborators? A long shot down the length of the car as Lula enters it reveals the famous advertisement for Dutch Masters cigars, an ad that employs a reproduction of Rembrandt's 1662 *The Staalmeesters* (fig. 4). The connection between the aristocratic Dutch cloth merchants and the transatlantic slave trade is highlighted as the large ad perches right above the head of the vampiric slave mistress, Lula.

America's original sin of slavery is further illustrated with the placement of a second stylized backdrop: the famous "Bet You Can't Eat Just One" Lay's potato chip ad campaign from the 1960s, which features the famous Cowardly Lion, Bert Lahr, as the tempting devil. The ad is subtly placed, first visible behind Lula when she leans forward in the seat that she shares with Clay, and then when she leans back, at which point the white devil's horns seemingly grow out of her head as her seduction unfolds (figs. 5 and 6). Near the end of the film, the ad is clearly visible on both sides of the subway car as Lula recruits the crowd and as Clay rages, slapping Lula (fig 7). Temptation has permeated the train, and Clay too has accepted Lula's devilish bargain to act out.

My Christ. My Christ.

Baraka's play introduces students to a work with more than one protagonist, for the play is arguably as much about Lula as it is about Clay, and Harvey establishes this by cinematically splitting point of view. After Clay's death, Lula continues her eternal murderous quest of young, intellectually minded, middle-class black men who aspire to assimilation within hegemonic white culture. The play is named after Lula; she is the eternally damned Dutchman fated to search endlessly aboard her modern ship. Point of view (POV) shots are taken from

Figure 5. Still from *Dutchman*, directed by Anthony Harvey, 1966. Bert Lahr in devil horns to advertise Lay's potato chips.

Figure 6. Still from *Dutchman*, directed by Anthony Harvey, 1966. The devil horns align with Lula's head as her seduction of Clay unfolds.

Figure 7. Still from *Dutchman*, directed by Anthony Harvey, 1966. The ad becomes clearly legible on both sides of the subway car as Lula recruits the crowd.

a character's subjective perspective as if seen through that character's eyes. A director grants a privilege to any character afforded such a shot, since the audience is let in on that character's view of the world. Most POV shots suggest that the subject is the center or protagonist of the film. Harvey, however, splits point of view several times between Lula and Clay. Near the film's end, for example, as Lula stands on a seat and dances like "the lady who smoked up her grass skirt" (31), the audience is shown first Lula's point of view with the camera tilted down on her victim, Clay, and then in the next instant, Clay's point of view as he eyes the superior white devil pole-dancing above him. The split point of view helps develop Baraka's indication that both Clay and Lula are victims with whom we can identify: Clay suffers under the murderous femme fatale's seduction and racism, and Lula suffers from her inability to extricate herself from the devil's bargain (figs. 8 and 9).

Figure 8. Still from *Dutchman*, directed by Anthony Harvey, 1966. Lula's point of view.

Figure 9. Still from *Dutchman*, directed by Anthony Harvey, 1966. Clay's point of view.

Much like the bifurcated point of view so often employed by Hitchcock—as in *Vertigo* (1958), when the real Judy Barton drops her Madeleine mask during several revealing moments—Baraka's play and Harvey's film give us revealing moments when Lula drops her sweet-young-thing pose. For example, as a result of her bargain with the Devil, she emerges as an only slightly aging undead: "My hair is turning gray. A gray hair for each year and type I come through" (13). She is also the exhausted eternal wanderer as she flops down in her seat: "LULA: . . . *as if she is very weary.* Oooof! Too much weight" (6). Harvey uses an intense close-up of Lula in profile to signal Baraka's most obvious dropping of her mask: when she cries out to herself in an aside, "My Christ. My Christ" (20). The text clearly signals her identity as the damned Faustian character hopelessly pleading for mercy from her would-be savior as she echoes the wretched appeal by Marlowe's Doctor Faustus.

Thank You for Your Support

Lula's strategy to bring out Clay's hidden avenger of racism includes enlisting the slowly building crowd as surrogates for the American population at large. The assimilated Clay in scene 1 more easily shrugs off Lula's insults when he is not on public display. It is public humiliation on which Lula now relies. As spokesperson for Baraka's emerging black radical agenda, a figure who violently denounces and punishes those bookish young African Americans who are "middle-class, fake white" men (34), Lula exposes for the onlookers the seething righteous violence beneath Clay's mild-mannered surface. Lula is reassured she has found the right, soulless black sellout when Clay names his God: "A corporate Godhead" (24).

In his 1965 manifesto "The Revolutionary Theatre," Baraka calls for a "theatre of victims"—a theater of blacks like Clay and the "Young Negro" next in line for execution—that will help "their brothers in the audience . . . to understand that they are the brothers of victims" (Baraka, *Home* [Akashic] 238). These victims, in turn, will become "new heroes, and their enemies most of you who are reading this" (241). By acknowledging in the final line of his essay an intellectual, hip, and likely white readership, Baraka acknowledges two audiences: victimized black men being spurred to action and educated white audiences being threatened. The script lists in the characters section "RIDERS OF COACH, white and black" (3) but never refers to them again. Yet several of the subway riders of whom the film adaptation affords close-ups are black. By populating the train with African American, white, and Asian riders (figs. 10 and 11), Harvey is able to indict all for their complicity in Lula's violence, to heighten Clay's embarrassment and outrage at Lula's "Uncle Tom" salvo (32), and to provide Clay with a sympathetic black audience for his long vindication of murder as an alternative to metaphor. Lula's incendiary dance among the riders significantly foreshadows Clay's fate. I challenge students to detect and in-

Figure 10. Still from *Dutchman*, directed by Anthony Harvey, 1966. White and Asian American witnesses.

Figure 11. Still from *Dutchman*, directed by Anthony Harvey, 1966. Complicit yet sympathetic black riders heighten Clay's embarrassment.

terpret a performance's changes to the original script as evidence of a director's interpretation. Harvey casts young black men as two of those riders with whom Lula physically and violently interacts. She purposefully bumps one black male rider, backside to backside, and she seems to cut another black male rider across the forehead by recklessly swinging her bag. Why are these violent interactions between Lula and black male riders acted out for the camera? This action, only suggested in the script as her "*bumping into many of the standing people*" (30), rehearses Lula's marking out for violence Clay's black male doubles.

Flora Cameron Gambit

By openly riling Clay up and capping her assault with the stinging epithet "Uncle Tom," Lula manipulates the black man into publicly slapping a white woman. This culturally forbidden violence wins her allies among the other riders. Lula's insurance policy is the passengers' willingness to do her bidding.

It is underwritten by the fear behind a long-standing racial stereotype of, as Lula calls Clay, the "escaped nigger" (29). This white paranoia is best illustrated in D. W. Griffith's *Birth of a Nation* (1915). The newly emancipated, amorous renegade slave Gus (Walter Long in blackface) pursues Flora (Mae Marsh), the delicate daughter of a Ku Klux Klan sympathizer, into a forest, and despite Gus's assurance that he will not hurt her, she runs to the top of a rocky cliff and jumps to her death rather than face what she believes is certain miscegenistic rape. The Klansmen discover Gus, arraign him, and lynch him. His corpse is then deposited on the steps of the lieutenant governor's house. Similarly, Lula is able to stab Clay in view of several motionless and uninvolved witnesses, both black and white, who seem to submit to her authority.

The play represents Lula's murder of Clay as a kind of inverted rape. As Lindsey Campbell writes, "The scene has become that of predator and prey in which the white female possesses phallic power and the black male is reduced to the feminized position of object within this sexual economy." The Vampire Lady inserts her fangs (phallic knife) as the choker close-ups capture her drinking in her victim's stunned look (fig. 12). This clever reversal echoes the Hebrew Bible's depiction of Jael hammering her tent peg into General Sisera's temples (Judg. 5.24–28). Sacrificial Clay can only sputter forth muffled cries, "*his mouth working stupidly*" (37). As the lights dim in the train, Lula's delighted grunts and Clay's ever more violent cries easily double as the diegetic soundtrack of vigorous, indeed lethal, lovemaking.

To enhance the sexualized element of this murderous, knifelike rape for the passengers and, by extension, his audience, Harvey has Lula pull Clay down to the subway floor on top of her (in the script he merely "*slumps across her knees*" [37]) in order to simulate the sexual positioning for which Clay had hoped. I encourage students to ponder the ambiguous or unspecified identity and mindset of the riders who serve as surrogates for the play's and film's audience. Are they

Figure 12. Still from *Dutchman*, directed by Anthony Harvey, 1966. Vampire Lady sticks in her fangs and drinks the muffled cries of her prey.

representatives of a culturally conservative America who fear miscegenation? Are they part of Lula's crew, accomplices in her murderous quest for "middle-class, fake white" men? Or is their identity an overdetermined heaping of both possibilities?

Cinematic Deaths

In Baraka's script, a racially undifferentiated group of passengers heeds Lula's call to "[g]et this man off of me" (37), but, in the film, only the white riders respond. The African American riders sit passively still. Harvey intercedes here and indicts only the white passengers as manifestly complicit. Lula's next lines in the script—"Open the door and throw his body out" and "All of you get off at the next stop" (37)—are cut from the film, though this is presumably what the nameless riders do in the film as well. I urge students to imagine the actual staging of the dramatic work they study, and I remind them that plays are meant to be experienced primarily on stage, not on the page. In stage productions, Clay's dead body is likely flung across and through the fourth wall, in front of the first row or orchestra pit, although Baraka does not designate this action. In the theater, the fourth wall is that invisible line between actors and audience. Everything that happens behind that imaginary line is virtually real for the duration of the performance. It is a social convention we all accept: as explained by Samuel Taylor Coleridge's formula, "the willing suspension of disbelief" (341). In traditional proscenium arch theatrical productions, that line is never crossed in order to maintain the illusion that what happens behind it, on stage, is real. Clay's inert body deposited there is not unlike the body of Gus deposited on the steps of the lieutenant governor's house in *Birth of a Nation*. The tossing of Clay's body across this illusory but all-important line grants meaning to that body as it invades the audience's space.

Cinematic deaths are necessarily and notoriously handled differently than stage deaths. By shooting Clay's face out of focus in faux documentary style as he is carried past the camera, Harvey nods to the inexpressibility of death and cinema's inability to render it palpable when compared to the stage experience of the dead body lying in the front row until "curtain" (fig. 13). Another shot immediately follows this stylized gesture: a deep-focus canted angle shot of the clean subway platform and the sparkling light of the oncoming high-speed F train (fig. 14). A canted frame is achieved by tilting the camera on its axis, producing a framed shot at an oblique angle. A canted frame usually depicts a world gone awry. These two moments are the film's only out-of-focus and canted-angle shots, one depicting cinema's ultimate inability to represent physical death and the other signifying how askew the racist world is according to Amiri Baraka. The F train is not a random choice by Harvey and perhaps serves as a double entendre nod to the sexualized nature of Lula's ghostly death ship and her inverted rape of Clay.

Figure 13. Still from *Dutchman*, directed by Anthony Harvey, 1966. Out-of-focus shot shows cinema's inability to render death.

Figure 14. Still from *Dutchman*, directed by Anthony Harvey, 1966. The canted frame represents a racist world askew.

By working from the inside out, accurately describing the formal elements of *Dutchman*, my students and I strive to do justice to the work and guard against merely importing our own ideological sensibilities—although mine are certainly established, to an extent, simply by my including the play and film in the curriculum. I have been arguing that teachers and students can identify, describe, and interpret stylized moments by attending to formal filmic detail such as camera angles and lenses, framing, POV, set design, and costume. To that analysis we can also bring our historical knowledge by identifying and interpreting myth (e.g., the Bible and Faust), economic and social orders (e.g., commerce and slavery), and film itself (e.g., *Birth of a Nation*, *Who's Afraid of Virginia Woolf?*, and *Vertigo*). The hybrid historical and formal approach detailed here can be an effective way to understand this and any other film that engages in cinematically stylized choices.

Dutchman in the Drama Class

Meenakshi Ponnuswami

Because students are often shocked and silenced by *Dutchman*'s social and political implications, I find it useful to approach the play by providing a rich, textured introduction to its historical background.[1] This essay describes three interrelated approaches that contextualize *Dutchman* through the history of theater and performance. The first locates the play at home, examining its relation to the black liberation struggles of the 1960s as well as to the theater of the period. The second approach places *Dutchman* in the context of the postwar European theaters of the absurd and their American counterparts. The third situates the play in the history of the staging of the black body. By relating the contemporary historical and political contexts of *Dutchman* to performance traditions and theories worldwide, these three approaches, when pursued in tandem, provide students with a more nuanced understanding of the personal and political shifts that unsettle the play: Baraka's representation of searing contemporary debates concerning assimilation and authenticity; his interrogation of the languages of modernism and the absurd; and his exploration of the long, complex histories of black inscription and performance that young African Americans, especially artists, must confront and engage.

Dutchman *at Home*

Even students who have encountered other examples of violence in drama can be cowed by the racially and sexually charged confrontation in *Dutchman*. Analysis of the play's immediate context can help first-time readers work through the disorientation and hostility many experience. After studying the play, my classes examine documents and audiovisual materials related to the civil rights, black arts, and black power movements. Documentaries such as *Eyes on the Prize* and video clips about events such as the assassination of Medgar Evers and the Birmingham church bombing convey a vivid sense of the volatility of 1963. It is important for students to comprehend both the emergence of black nationalism and its appeal for young artists and intellectuals, so our readings emphasize Baraka's relation to both the beats and the nascent black arts movement. William J. Harris provides a useful description of Baraka's early years in the Village and his engagement with the beats, his subsequent disengagement, his move to Harlem, and the personal, political, and aesthetic commitments that attended this shift (Introduction). To highlight the emerging political and aesthetic priorities of the black arts movement, I ask my students to read Baraka's manifesto "The Revolutionary Theatre" (1965) and Larry Neal's "The Black Arts Movement" (1968); references to Antonin Artaud's work in "The Revolutionary Theatre" additionally introduce students to the avant-garde's reckoning with identity and power. Harold Cruse's *The Crisis of the Negro Intellectual* (1967) is also useful, for the book includes an important recollection of the Black Arts Repertory Theatre/School, which Cruse cofounded with Baraka in 1965. Such background materials prepare students to understand the assimilation, cultural authenticity, and cultural responsibility expressed in Clay's speech.

Students also benefit from reading the work of the period's white liberal writers (e.g., Norman Mailer's "The White Negro" [1957], Norman Podhoretz's "The Know-Nothing Bohemians" [1958], and Podhoretz's "My Negro Problem—and Ours" [1963]).[2] These essays, which can surprise and offend students, help clarify the many shifts in Lula's stance, from her crassly racist rants to her apparent adoption of the language of black nationalism.[3] As Carol Bunch Davis argues, "Lula's interaction with Clay reveals that while white liberals experience guilt and remorse for racism in America, ultimately, there is no moment of conscience about the distribution of power—even in the struggle over the ways that African Americans seek to define themselves" (65).

Understood historically, *Dutchman*'s first scene positions viewers at a moment when the struggles against segregation seem to have ushered in a new era of openness and equality. The young, apparently naive Clay's experience gives students a reassuringly tidy if schematic account of *Dutchman* as an allegory of American history in the aftermath of desegregation. Suggesting that Rosa Parks and her segregated bus are a thing of the past, the "subway heaped in modern myth" (3) blasts its way into a dark future while white society, in the form of the many-faced Lula, invites Clay into an experiment to see whether the past can be left behind. As she commandingly promises, or threatens, at the end of the opening scene, "We'll pretend the people cannot see you. That is, the citizens. And that you are free of your history. And I am free of my history. We'll pretend that we are both anonymous beauties smashing along through the city's entrails" (21). Lula seems to promise Clay a utopian future in which they will be free to enjoy a new kind of anonymity and invisibility, perhaps even a radical reconstruction of American democracy. Some of my students suggest that Lula is subtly invoking Martin Luther King's "I Have a Dream" speech, delivered only months before *Dutchman* opened; they also conceptualize her statement in postracial terms, imagining an identity that transcends history, politics, and biology.

The dream, of course, rapidly devolves into nightmare as Lula's "pretend[ing]" becomes a trap for Clay, an invitation only to act in a script of her devising. Analysis of *Dutchman*'s metatheatrics clarifies the power dynamics between Lula and Clay. Lula's autocracy is apparent from the outset as she scripts their encounter, ignoring Clay's protest. She is not, she insists, an actress herself, or, as Clay muses, "[a]ll scribed" (27); rather, as a director or indeed auteur, she encodes and delimits his character, motivation, and social background. It is important to emphasize that Lula is not a three-dimensional character but Baraka's representation of the contradictory, confusing faces of white society as experienced by a young black intellectual. In an interview conducted during the 2007 Cherry Lane Theatre production of *Dutchman*, Baraka stated, "I saw her as a metaphor for America," a figure who "represented temptation and seduction, but also death, if not of the flesh then of the spirit" (qtd. in McGee A7). But she can also be identified as a free-floating signifier, sliding without endpoint or origin from one pose or performance to the next. At the same time, she resists change in Clay, accusing him of becoming unknowable: "But you mix it up. Look out the window, all the time. Turning pages. Change change change. Till, shit, I don't know you" (28). Students tend to accept Lula's claims to "know" Clay, but a closer reading of the opening scene can also suggest that Clay's responses are coded and ambiguous and that his subtle negotiation of her cues does not necessarily betray acceptance or acquiescence. This unknowability can be seen as Clay's counterpoint to Lula's efforts to reinscribe him; it paves the way for his ultimate retaliation, where he reclaims identity and denies Lula access to it, by declaring that black art consists of "curses . . . in code" (36).

Baraka's underexamined relationship to Edward Albee becomes especially significant in this context. When he wrote *Dutchman*, Baraka had been involved, as he explains, in a "drama/playwright's workshop initiated by Edward Albee and his producers" at New York's Cherry Lane Theatre, where *Dutchman* eventually premiered (*Autobiography* [Lawrence Hill] 275–76). Albee's *The Zoo Story* is many students' first encounter with the period's Greenwich Village avant-garde, and it prepares them for *Dutchman*'s modernist elements as well as its gritty urban setting and broader social milieu. When students read *Dutchman* immediately after the original version of *The Zoo Story*, they are struck by the structural similarities: Albee's play depicts the bizarre and ultimately violent encounter between Jerry, a talkative and intrusive resident of a seedy Upper West Side tenement, and Peter, a dull, conformist publishing executive who is minding his own business on a Central Park bench when Jerry accosts him, demanding his attention and involvement. Students see both plays as examples of the period's ongoing cultural ferment and radicalism, but they also astutely identify how Baraka answers or reframes *The Zoo Story*. In both plays, a "hipster" targets a "square," evoking the rhetoric of spiritual awakening to provoke and intrigue. While in each case the conformist seems to be attracted by the hipster's vivacity and passion, he is ultimately unable to shed the "neurosis" of his bourgeois circumstances and mask—as Clay finally declares, he wants to be left "[s]afe with my words, and no deaths, and clean, hard thoughts" (35). Both plays mock the square's naïveté and timidity, but each hipster is a deeply ambivalent figure whose self-styling as an agent of radical transformation is dangerously narcissistic.

Lula adapts Jerry's role as a bohemian and folk artist. She repudiates bourgeois culture and attacks Clay's physical and spiritual emasculation as Jerry does Peter's; she rouses him in similar terms, mocking his middle-class aspirations and "three-buttoned suit" (18) and his being "so full of white man's words" (31). But whereas Albee gestures toward the potential for transformative healing in the bohemian storyteller's assault, Baraka questions whether white America will ever relinquish the privilege and the power to tell the story. For Albee, the bohemian's solipsism is self-destructive, but in Baraka's telling, the bohemian destroys the black artist, who could murder hegemonic white culture but whose passivity and conformity have rendered him impotent.

The Modernist Dutchman

In a drama class, this textual pairing makes clear that Baraka manipulates the languages of modernism and the absurd, inherited from the beats and Albee as much as Samuel Beckett and the postwar French absurdists.[4] *Dutchman* opened at the Cherry Lane Theatre on a triple bill with Beckett's *Play* (1964; first performed in 1963) and Fernando Arrabal's *The Two Executioners* (1958), plays that position Baraka at the heart of the American alternative theaters' experimentation with modernism and the theater of the absurd in the 1960s.[5] The term *theater of the absurd* was coined by Martin Esslin in his influential 1961 book about the work of the Parisian avant-garde (Beckett, Eugène Ionesco, Jean Genet, and others). Although the relationship of the so-called absurd to modernist and postmodernist drama has never been explicit, the term has stuck, becoming a useful descriptor of certain linguistic and stylistic techniques as well as thematic or philosophical attitudes.

Werner Sollors argues that *Dutchman* is "provocative and unsettling" because its "'realistic' elements are outweighed by absurdist drama techniques" (118). More precisely, Baraka's modernism maps a path through Artaud's theater of cruelty to political theater and revolutionary change. Artaud's theories help students interpret the shock tactics in *Dutchman* as well as the poetics of the black arts movement, which are rooted in Artaud's conviction that theater must rouse audiences from complacency and "stagnation," from "the boredom, inertia, and stupidity of everything." As Artaud argues in *The Theater and Its Double* (1938):

> A violent and concentrated action is a metaphor of lyricism: it evokes supernatural images, a bloodline of images, a bloody gush of images in the poet's mind as well as the spectator's. . . . Therefore, I propose a theatre in which violent physical images pound and hypnotize the sensibility of the spectator, who is caught in the theater as if in a whirlwind of higher forces. (258–59 [ed. Sontag])

In class, Artaud's work initiates debate about whether *Dutchman* simply shocks, whether it awakens its audience, and whether it inspires social or political change.[6]

However, *Dutchman* also seems to imply that modernism is white art containing a revolutionary attitude and language that the young black artist must negotiate but not internalize. As Sollors puts it, "[L]iterature is held responsible for alienating the writer from his Black identity" (146). Both *Dutchman* and Adrienne Kennedy's *Funnyhouse of a Negro* (1964) warn that white arts can interpellate young black intellectuals: the possibility of being a Baudelaire (19) lures Clay in, leaving him vulnerable to Lula's racism and her cutting reminder that he can assume no identity outside her script. Through Lula's unstable, racist language, at times parodic of Dada and beat imagery, Baraka challenges the politics of the modernism he embraced in other writings and in *Dutchman* itself. When Lula rattles off incomprehensible metaphors such as "Red trains cough Jewish underwear for keeps," the play implies that modernism (arguably in the hands of beatniks) has become a meaningless jumble of random images rather than a force for revolutionary change. Moreover, Lula reveals a fundamental racism in urging Clay "to break out" and embrace an unassimilated inner self that is uncivilized and primitive (31). In juxtaposing Lula's modernist aesthetics and her racial attitudes, the play argues that racism remains integral to beat culture despite its iconoclasm and counterculturalism. However, Clay remains intellectually and spiritually independent and untamed at the end of the play; his modernist aspirations have not (yet) divested him of an authentic black self.

Dutchman *and Race in Performance*

Discussions of modernist elements in *Dutchman* thus pave the way for a broader analysis of the history and politics of the black body in performance. Few students today have the "cultural literacy" to know Bessie Smith or Charlie Parker; they cannot visualize "four-eyed ofays popping their fingers" or readily understand why Clay ridicules discussions of "the tortured genius of Charlie Parker," let alone grasp how Clay reclaims Smith's meaning and message in saying, "Before love, suffering, desire, anything you can explain, she's saying, and very plainly, 'Kiss my black ass'" (34–35). Students can miss Clay's indictment of the white appropriation and colonization of black culture unless they are acquainted with the broader history of the display, representation, and impersonation of the black body. To complete the three-part historical contextualization of *Dutchman*, my students examine racist caricatures, more complex ethnic portrayals, and ethnic counterstereotyping by contemporary playwrights and performers.

In varying degrees, depending on the class, students study an array of background texts, including literary works that represent race and ethnicity. We often start with Shakespeare's *Othello* (1603–04) to explore early modern concepts of race and to consider how *Dutchman* inverts the racist logic of Shakespeare's play. Students then trace the persistence and evolution of the Shakespearean images into the nineteenth century by examining Victorian-era show business: British music halls, which included minstrel shows; travelling displays of Africans shipped from the continent (most notoriously, Saartje Bartman, the Hottentot Venus); and the display of Africans, Asians, and Native Americans in world's fairs, freak shows, and carnivals in the United States.[7] Joseph Conrad's *Heart of Darkness* (1899) supplements this material well, as does Artaud's *Theater and Its Double*; both exemplify the modernist (and high-cultural) tendency to write the black body as possessed of an intrinsic savagery that white civilization must subdue or control.

European representations of blackness usefully frame the politics and poetics of the minstrel era in the United States, from Jim Crow shows to the work of Bert Williams. Marlon Riggs's powerful documentary *Ethnic Notions* (1986) describes how minstrelsy shaped images of African Americans, and the film reveals the social functions of these images at key moments in American history: images of servile, happy slaves helped justify slavery, while the Civil War and its aftermath produced vicious images of brutish, lusting men. Such images persisted well into the twentieth century, in films like *Birth of a Nation* (1915) and *Gone with the Wind* (1939), mid-century animated cartoons, and postwar television. After watching *Ethnic Notions*, students view performances by Bessie Smith and Charlie Parker, considering the difficulties confronting African American performers in segregated theaters and the music industry.[8]

It is important to introduce students to the ways African American playwrights have challenged the racist legacies of slavery, colonialism, and minstrelsy. *Dutchman* can be taught alongside plays such as Lorraine Hansberry's *A Raisin in the Sun* (1959), James Baldwin's *Blues for Mister Charlie* (1964), Kennedy's *Funnyhouse*, Ntozake Shange's *For Colored Girls Who Have Considered Suicide* (1975) and *Spell #7* (1979), August Wilson's *The Piano Lesson* (1987) and *Fences* (1983), and Suzan-Lori Parks's *The America Play* (1994).[9] Class sessions comparing *Dutchman*, *Funnyhouse*, and *Spell #7* are especially useful for teaching the history of blackness on the American stage. While *Dutchman* and *Funnyhouse* both appear to treat the cultural promises of desegregation as lies,

Funnyhouse warns that the contradictions caused by assimilation will destroy the integrity of the black self. *Dutchman*, by contrast, asserts that the true black self is finally untouchable. This question is raised also in Shange's postmodernist *Spell #7*, where the looming minstrel mask is a disquieting reminder that black subjectivities are shaped by the racist past and carry the burden of identities and masks imposed over centuries. But while the actors in the play are haunted by the shadow of the mask, the play invites them to create new narratives and performances of black selfhood.

Finally, Spike Lee's *Bamboozled* (2000) works well as a supplement. Clips from the film give students a visual experience of blackface minstrelsy and demonstrate that the performances demanded vivacity and artistic skill. Cleverly deconstructing the entertainment industry's exploitation of black performance arts, Lee's film invites viewers to contrast fake, masked performance, which is colonized by and operated under white power, with a variety of authentic, black-owned performances. Some of these are gently mocked, as for example in the audition scene (where Lee incidentally showcases a rich array of comic talents). But a poignant note is struck later by the most real performer of them all, Junebug, played by real-life comedian Paul Mooney. Junebug's unquestionable authenticity (playing for black audiences in black venues, or what Clay calls "dark places, with big hats") helps students see the kind of performance that, according to Clay, belongs to "the pure heart," beyond "lies" and "device" (34).

This triply historicized approach to teaching *Dutchman* yields a much more complex understanding of Lula's efforts to confer an identity on and to mold Clay, and this approach correspondingly makes possible a more nuanced appreciation of Clay's final statement. Students sometimes even sense how to read the play's puzzling denouement, where the elderly conductor shuffles through the car. The nature of his gait (seen by some as subservient and by others as confident) is often subject to debate, because students question whether his presence is likely to deter Lula, or at least caution her new victim. After our history sessions, they are able to see that he is a descendant of the minstrel stage's Uncle Tom but also of the Pullman porter: embodying a long history of secret resistance and survival, he has "overcome 'em with yeses" (16), like the narrator's grandfather in Ralph Ellison's *Invisible Man*. As such, his appearance warns young African Americans of the dangers not only of passivity and assimilation but also of unmasking and self-revelation. Although he is not an artist, his gesture of respect, tipping his hat, is as surely a curse in code.

NOTES

This essay was written in memory of my inspirational teacher and beloved friend, James Hurt, who taught modern literature at the University of Illinois at Urbana-Champaign.

[1]Since 1991, I have taught *Dutchman* at least twice annually at Bucknell University, a small, private, liberal arts university in central Pennsylvania. Both the college and the

surrounding community are predominantly white; typically, classes of any size include only one or two nonwhite students.

[2]Podhoretz is now best known as a neoconservative thinker, but he describes himself as "a white liberal" in "My Negro Problem—and Ours" (100).

[3]Sollors's chapter on Baraka's beat years provides a brief overview of Mailer's essay and of Baraka's first publication, which was his response to Podhoretz's "The Know-Nothing Bohemians" (24–30).

[4]Comparing *Dutchman* to Eugène Ionesco's *The Lesson*, Sollors argues that "*Dutchman* is more 'European absurdist'" than Albee's *Zoo Story* because its characters are "social masks rather than 'individuals'" (122). See also William J. Harris's "Amiri Baraka's Adventures with the Out and the Gone." Harris argues that "it is not surprising [Baraka] ended up an avant-garde artist" given his formative exposure to 1940s and 1950s popular culture, such as the film *Pandora and the Flying Dutchman* (1951), which was one of *Dutchman*'s inspirations (484). Harris proposes that such influences prepared Baraka for the avant-garde and shaped his aesthetic, which "demanded the extreme, the outrageous, both in art and life" (483).

[5]Interestingly, revivals of Jean Genet's *The Maids*, Ionesco's *The Lesson*, and Beckett's *Play* won Obie Awards in 1964, alongside *Dutchman* and Adrienne Kennedy's *Funnyhouse of a Negro* (1964). For a full discussion of Baraka's relationship to modernism, see chapters 1, 2, and 6 of Sollors.

[6]Students are intrigued by Howard Taubman's review of one of the play's first performances. Taubman wrote, "If this is the way the Negroes really feel about the white world around them, there's more rancor buried in the breasts of colored conformists than anyone can imagine. If this is the way even one Negro feels, there is ample cause for guilt as well as alarm, and for a hastening of change."

[7]Bernth Lindfors's essay collection *Africans on Stage* (1999) offers several excellent examples of what the title calls "ethnological show business."

[8]Baraka's *Blues People* (1963) and *Black Music* (1967) are useful sources.

[9]Earlier twentieth-century plays, including Georgia Douglas Johnson's *Blue-Eyed Black Boy* (1930) and Langston Hughes's *Mulatto* (1935), are also useful to consider.

Baraka's Aesthetic Radicalism: *Dutchman*'s Modernist Roots

Daniel Morris

I teach *Dutchman* in a survey of American literature, and I place it in the final third of a reading list that stretches back a century before Baraka wrote the play. My training in modernism, with special emphasis on poetics, also informs my approach. My students read Baraka as a playwright, but he is arguably best known as a poet who merged avant-garde aesthetics with black nationalist ideology. Baraka was featured in *The New American Poetry: 1945–1960* (Allen; 1960), an anthology containing works in the tradition of experimental modernists such as Ezra Pound, William Carlos Williams, and Louis Zukofsky. The collection included politically radical and formally innovative writers identified with beat, Black Mountain, San Francisco renaissance, and New York school poetics. It is also worth recalling that the young Baraka edited work by the Black Mountain poet Charles Olson, whose "projective verse" was characterized by the use of form as an extension of content and by spontaneity and improvisation (Sollors 33).

Certainly, we should locate *Dutchman* within the context of civil rights and black liberation politics in order to understand Baraka's ambivalent treatment of Clay Williams. A young urban black man, Clay masks anger at a racist society through an assimilationist posture. He suggests that art—even the traditional African American artistic expression in the blues and jazz—sublimates a desire for vengeance. Baraka invokes and critiques disparate models of black male identity in the 1960s. Clay's initial persona is a bourgeois with bohemian flair—Lula notes that he is "trying to grow a beard" and that he reads "Chinese poetry" (8). At the end of scene 2, Clay becomes a militant who can no longer contain his rage: "And I sit here, in this buttoned-up suit, to keep myself from cutting all your throats" (34). Through Clay, Baraka mocks conformist tendencies among middle-class blacks, and Clay embodies Baraka's belief that the arts, including drama, should serve social protest. As Houston Baker remarks, Baraka's conception of "Black as a country—a separate and progressive nation with values antithetical to those of white America—stands in marked contrast to the ideas set forth by Baldwin, Wright, Ellison, and others of the fifties" (*Journey* 106). Ellison, for instance, believed that African Americans are profoundly American and are crucial to defining American identity. Baraka, by contrast, moved toward a black separatist ideology. In a slightly later work, a manifesto entitled "The Revolutionary Theatre" (1965), he said drama "should force change": "[white] Americans will hate the Revolutionary Theatre because it will be out to destroy them and whatever they believe is real" ([National Humanities Center] 3). Unquestionably, Baraka intended to shock audiences and readers through Lula's murder of Clay—and through the suggestion that another black male awaits her knife blade after the curtain closes.

Yet there are other important contexts, in addition to the civil rights and black liberation movements, in which the play should be read. *Dutchman* was "designed to shock" through "its basic idea, its language and its murderous rage," as a *New York Times* reviewer states on the back cover of the 1964 Morrow edition (L. Jones), and, in this regard, the play belongs to a continuum of twentieth-century transatlantic culture that Werner Sollors calls an "international camp of aesthetic protest and antibourgeois Bohemianism" (18). Lula's sexual advances toward Clay on a subway are themselves a manifestation of modernism's intent to scandalize. So is her Dadaist performance of screaming, dancing, throwing items out of her purse, and chanting suggestively lyrical nonsense phrases: "Red trains cough Jewish underwear for keeps! Expanding smells of silence. Gravy snot whistling like sea birds" (31). When Clay was in college, he fancied himself a "Baudelaire"—and Lula mockingly calls him a "Black Baudelaire" (19)—but, as Sollors notes, Baraka may be a "Black Breton" (127). In his "Second Manifesto of Surrealism" (1930), André Breton advocates an art "not afraid to make for itself a tenet of total revolt, complete insubordination, of sabotage according to rule" (125). Stylistically, Baraka follows Breton in crafting deliberate anti-art. *Dutchman* is an answer to the "well-made play" epitomized in black theater of this period by such works as Lorraine Hansberry's *A Raisin in the Sun* (1959). Lula's demeaning chatter (e.g., "Screw yourself, Uncle Tom. Thomas Woolly-head" [32]), Clay's physical intimidation and verbal aggression (e.g., "I could murder you now. Such a tiny ugly throat" [33]), and, of course, Lula's murder of Clay recall Antonin Artaud's theater of cruelty, to which Baraka's "The Revolutionary Theatre" is explicitly indebted. As Matthew Rebhorn writes, "Baraka engaged in innovative theatrical techniques—techniques built on earlier twentieth-century experimental dramaturgy. . . . Artaud wrote that what modern society really needed was 'a theater that wakes us up: nerves and heart'" (799).

When my class reaches *Dutchman*, students have already discussed American modernisms, including Gertrude Stein's Dadaism, the mythic strains of T. S. Eliot's *The Waste Land* (1922), and the images of bourgeois alienation in Eliot's "The Love Song of J. Alfred Prufrock" (1915). We've even discussed the racial context of modernism: Harlem Renaissance writers' lyric expression of their "individual dark skinned selves" (Hughes, "Negro Artist" [Belasco and Johnson] 561). When interpreting *Dutchman* as "radical," therefore, I want students to consider the adjective's Latin etymological meaning. We think of "radical" as meaning "root" rather than exclusively viewing radicalism as drastic change.

Among *Dutchman*'s many and various roots are some of the radical modernist aesthetics of the early twentieth century. As is typical of much modernism (e.g., *The Waste Land*), *Dutchman* is a compositional pastiche, depicting Baraka's creativity through his appropriation of other texts. The materials that Baraka appropriates are derived from early-twentieth-century experimental arts movements, albeit recast to represent issues of race, interracial desire, violence, and masculinity in urban America in the 1960s. As Sollors puts it, Baraka "appropriates modern poetry to his own uses" (37), and Baraka himself recalled his early "Eliot period," albeit as a "shell" from which he needed to emerge (qtd. in Sollors 38). "Eliot is certainly present in Baraka's works," Sollors further argues, "even if Eliot's 'objective,' 'academic' art is what Baraka struggles away from" (38). In what follows, I discuss the focus of my course unit on Baraka's *Dutchman*, the play's appropriation of not only an Eliotic mythopoesis but also Eliot's work itself. Through this appropriation, I explain to my students, Baraka represents the peril of the black subject's seeking recognition on the other side of the color line.

In "*Ulysses*, Order, and Myth" (1923), Eliot praised James Joyce's experimental novel for its "mythical method" (178). Creating "a continuous parallel between contemporaneity and antiquity" provided Joyce with "a way of controlling, of ordering, of giving a shape and a significance to the immense panorama of futility and anarchy which is contemporary history" (177). Baraka, too, undergirded his radical art with myth. The play's setting is "the subway heaped in modern myth" (*Dutchman* 3). From the earliest scholarship on the play, critics have noted affinities between *Dutchman* and the archetypal imagination of modernists who framed their period with templates from long ago.

Tom Reck, writing in 1970, implicitly connected *Dutchman* to the modernist "mythical method":

> *Dutchman* is, in fact, worked around the most archetypal of all myths: the seduction of the male by the beautiful but deadly female, with particular inference to the myth of Adam and Eve in the Garden of Eden. The name of the Negro male, Clay, seems to suggest an Adam and Everyman; and the white temptress, Lula, is not only a direct descendent of Lilith, Circe, and Delilah, but particularly of Eve. (67)

In 1979, George Levesque took a similar approach to the play and made explicit Reck's linkage of *Dutchman* to transatlantic modernism. Baraka follows August Strindberg, for example, in building conflict by drawing male and female figures as "representative" types rather than as the particularized characters that one expects from realist drama (Levesque 34).

Baraka renders Clay and Lula as types, even as stereotypes, to suggest how their conflict illustrates general concerns. At the start of scene 1, Lula is described in stage directions as "*the face*," implying that, for Clay, Lula represents the oppressive gaze of white America. When Lula tells Clay, "I lie a lot. It helps me control the world" (9), we read her remarks as Baraka's assessment of America as an empire whose dominion is predicated on deceit. As Victor Leo Walker has argued, those more general cultural concerns recall a tradition of African American authors—W. E. B. Du Bois, Paul Laurence Dunbar, and Ralph Ellison—who challenged stereotypes such as Uncle Tom and Jim Crow and who asserted their identities despite a felt need to "wear the mask," to conform to white expectations for behavior and appearance. Following Alain Locke, Walker writes, "[W]hite America has historically controlled African American public images . . . using symbolic types such as 'Uncle Tom' to represent assimilationist roles that have been forced upon them" (237). Walker argues that, at the end of *Dutchman*, Baraka invokes and then destroys the Uncle Tom archetype.

The play's title is itself an expression of Baraka's archetypal imagination:

> [The] Flying Dutchman, a ghost ship in several maritime legends, was a sign of bad luck, particularly for sailors. In most versions, the ship appeared off the Cape of Good Hope, the southern tip of Africa. The legend was inspired by the story of a Dutch sea captain named Vanderdecken who boasted that he could complete the journey around the cape during a fierce storm. He swore that he would do so or keep trying forever. As punishment for his rashness, he was condemned to sail around the cape until the end of time. ("Flying Dutchman")

The Flying Dutchman achieved lasting fame through Richard Wagner's opera of the same name (1843). In this variant, the captain returns to land once every seven years, and if he can find a faithful wife during one of these respites, the curse will be lifted. Baraka appropriates this legend to dramatize a racially inflected romantic conflict. Rebhorn writes that the play projects "the relationship between the doomed sailor and his lover onto Clay and his 'loving' and erotic murderess Lula" (796).[1]

In reading *Dutchman* as an expression of a modernist mythopoetic imagination, we link the play to Eliot's work, which we encountered earlier in the semester. Furthermore, we discover that Eliot's work is some of the "modern myth" in which Baraka's subway is "heaped." In some remarkable ways, *Dutchman*'s tone, setting, characterization, and plotting allude to "Prufrock." Here Eliot depicts a purgatory environment prior to the paradiso that he glimpses at the end of *The Waste Land*. *Dutchman*'s plot involves two strangers who cast eyes on each other, flirt, and argue as they consider the prospect of going to a party together. Scene 2 begins with Clay and Lula imagining how they will behave at the party, how others will regard them, and what will happen after they leave. The implied narrative in "Prufrock" is strikingly similar to this action: a neurotic, bourgeois man strives, and fails, to reach a party with another. "Let us go then, you and I," Prufrock pleads, envisioning a room in which "the women come and go/Talking of Michelangelo" (672). Baraka alludes to "Prufrock" when Lula and Clay discuss the party's aftermath. Lula's prediction—"After the dancing and games, after the long drinks and walks, the real fun begins" (24)—recalls the following lines from "Prufrock":

> And would it have been worth it, after all,
> After the cups, the marmalade, the tea,

> Among the porcelain, among some talk of you and me,
> Would it have been worth while. . . . (675)

Lula, who, as George Knox writes, "'comes on' as a kind of Prufrockian 'lady' carried to an erotic extreme," is taunting Clay with her comment (245–46). Her innuendo of sex after the party is twisted later in scene 2 when Lula uses her knife as a deadly phallus. In Eliot, Prufrock's skepticism, ennui, self-consciousness, and inability to live in the present tense render him unable to meet those women talking about Michelangelo. Clay, too, is eager to know and be known by another—to project himself across the color line—though *Dutchman* ultimately suggests the hopelessness of this desire.

Baraka again references Prufrock's struggles to convert chatter into physical intimacy when Lula tells Clay, "You don't know what I mean" (28). Throughout Eliot's poem, Prufrock feels misconstrued by women even as his female interlocutors feel he misunderstands them. Any affirmation he makes is likely to be rejected with the words "That is not what I meant at all./That is not it, at all" (675). Like Prufrock, Clay is a split self. His desires for sex and an integration of appearance and reality, character and body, cannot be satisfied. Lula reads Clay not as a unique individual but as "a well-known type" (12)—so much so that Clay feels that she controls his image. Similarly, Prufrock avoids the party because he feels others will judge his age, body, masculinity, and overall appearance:

> (They will say: "How his hair is growing thin!")
> My morning coat, my collar mounting firmly to the chin,
> My necktie rich and modest, but asserted by a simple pin—
> (They will say: "But how his arms and legs are thin!") (673)

The unruly dialogue between Lula and Clay, set in a subterranean urban setting, resembles Prufrock's linguistic labyrinth, which Eliot figures as sinister streets that the speaker travels without reaching his destination. When Lula drifts from her conversation with Clay to muse about a life "[h]ugged against tenements, day or night" (13), readers may recall Prufrock's wanderings through "certain half-deserted streets" that "follow like a tedious argument/Of insidious intent" (672). Lula's "argument" turns out to be similarly treacherous, and Clay's struggle for recognition just as hopeless as Prufrock's. Clay waits far too long to abandon his fantasy of truly crossing the color line.

In focusing on the connections between "Prufrock" and *Dutchman*, my class looks closely at one of the play's engagements with early-twentieth-century modernist aesthetics. Other instructors may choose to place *Dutchman* and Baraka's other works in conversation with post–World War II modernisms (or even with early postmodernisms). As William J. Harris has argued, Baraka's "jazz aesthetic" draws significantly on Olson's lessons about open-form poetry. Harris writes, "From the Projectivists, and from Olson in particular, Baraka absorbed his sense of the poem as open form, his sense of line, his sense of the poem as a recorder of process, and his conception of the poem as definition and exploration" (35). In fact, as the *Poetry Foundation* Web site notes, Baraka is most often associated with experimental poetry that developed after World War II:

> The white avant-garde—primarily [Allen] Ginsberg, [Frank] O'Hara, and leader of the Black Mountain poets Charles Olson—and Baraka believed in poetry as a process of discovery rather than an exercise in fulfilling traditional expectations. Baraka, like the Projectivist poets, believed that a poem's form should follow the shape determined by the poet's own breath and intensity of feeling. ("Amiri Baraka")

Furthermore, it is certainly the case Baraka came to Dada, surrealism, and the theater of cruelty through his involvement in the new American poetry and other post–World War II avant-garde movements.

Yet Eliotic mythopoesis is one of *Dutchman*'s roots, and I have found that exploring *Dutchman*'s appropriation of this tradition opens up the play for my classes. Many students come to my survey course already interested in archetypal texts and prepared for the kinds of analysis that these texts require. Also, by the time we study the play, my students have learned a lot about the history of modernism, and they have begun tracing literary genealogies. To be sure, there is much more to be said about *Dutchman*'s many roots, but our work with the play's mythopoetics is one worthwhile exploration along these lines.

NOTE

[1] In 1991 Baraka said in an interview that the idea of representing the subway as a modern ghost ship was suggested in part by advertisements for Albert Lewin's 1951 film *Pandora and the Flying Dutchman* (*Conversations* 255), a revision of Wagner's opera (1843).

Breaking from the Beats: Teaching *Dutchman* as a Critique of Bohemianism

Kurt Hemmer

The final unit of the beat generation course that I teach at a community college in the northwest suburbs of Chicago focuses on Amiri Baraka's *Dutchman*. My students have tended to be predominantly traditionally aged, middle class, and white and have had little or no contact with beat literature and just as little contact with African American literature; my approach therefore tactfully introduces them to material that they may initially greet with some resistance. The class begins with examinations of novels by Jack Kerouac (*On the Road* [1957] or *The Dharma Bums* [1958]) and William S. Burroughs (*Junky* [published as *Junkie* in 1953], *Queer* [completed in 1953 and published in 1985], or *Naked Lunch* [published as *The Naked Lunch* in 1959]). In the middle of the semester, we immerse ourselves in beat, San Francisco renaissance, and Black Mountain poetry. I teach a major poem by Allen Ginsberg ("Howl" [1956] or "Kaddish" [1961]), alongside a variety of poems covering a number of beat-related topics (sexuality, drug use, jazz, racism, sexism, antimilitarism, environmentalism) by an eclectic group of poets associated in various ways with the beat movement: Gregory Corso, Gary Snyder, Michael McClure, Lawrence Ferlinghetti, Charles Olson, Robert Creeley, Ed Dorn, Janine Pommy Vega, Anne Waldman, Joanne Kyger, Diane di Prima, Ted Joans, Bob Kaufman, and Baraka. By the end of the semester, I usually have several students who have become beat devotees. But, in an effort to complicate students' understanding of the beats and to contextualize the racial complexities of the time period, especially in relation to bohemianism, I end the semester with a close examination of *Dutchman*, which allows us to reflect on the romantic primitivism, the idealization of the uncivilized, found in Kerouac's novels and the racial otherness found in Ginsberg's poetry.[1] It also allows the students to see a critique of bohemianism that encourages them to grapple with a more nuanced view of the white beat writers and examine them in a more critical, rather than glamorized, light. More often than not, this is one of the most highly charged and engaging units of the semester. To enhance the type of reading I would like us to do, I supplement *Dutchman* with excerpts from Baraka's *The Autobiography of LeRoi Jones* (1984), Hettie Jones's memoir *How I Became Hettie Jones* (1990), Norman Podhoretz's "The Know-Nothing Bohemians" (1958), Baraka's response to Podhoretz's review (1958), and Baraka's essay "Cuba Libre" (1960). The primary focus of this final unit is to reveal and examine Baraka's critique of bohemianism, which led to his break from the beats.

"Cuba Libre," an account of Baraka's visit to revolutionary Cuba with a group of African American intellectuals, expresses his growing embarrassment with being associated with the bohemianism of the beats, whom he views, for the first time, as lacking true political commitment:

> Later in the evening, the two middle-class ladies from Philadelphia turned up, drawn I suppose by all the noise that must have been coming out of our room. The one pretty middle-class lady talked for awhile [*sic*] about not being at the Riviera, and what people in Philadelphia had said when she told them she was going to Cuba. I was pretty surprised, in one sense, at the relation of those comments, because the comments themselves, which I suppose must have come from people pretty much like herself, *i.e.*, middle-class, middle-brow young Negroes living in Philadelphia, were almost exactly the same as the comments that had been tossed my way from the various beats, bohemians and intellectuals in Greenwich Village, New York City (of course, given that proper knowing cynicism that is fashionable among my contemporaries). It made me shudder. I mean to find how homogenous most thinking in the U.S. has become, even among the real and/or *soi disant* intellectual. (20)

Later in the essay, Baraka turns a self-critical eye on himself: "The rebels among us have become merely people like myself who grow beards and will not participate in politics. Drugs, juvenile delinquency, complete isolation from the vapid mores of the country, a few current ways out" (61). Baraka is clearly not satisfied with mere bohemian disaffiliation, and students' recognition of this fact encourages them to reexamine aspects of the novels by Kerouac and the poems by Ginsberg to see if this disaffiliation is an attitude that we had not noticed entirely before. The class now wonders to what degree Baraka thinks of Kerouac and Ginsberg as two of "the rebels among us" whom he criticizes. "Cuba Libre" offers an explanation of the dramatic ideological shift that Baraka was beginning to make, a transformation that can be seen as a subtext of *Dutchman*.

From the late 1950s until the mid-1960s, Baraka generally identified with the beat movement or, more generally, with the bohemian avant-garde. I enjoy telling my students about Baraka's transformation into a beat. In 1957, inspired by "Howl," he mailed a piece of toilet paper to Ginsberg at the "Beat Hotel" in Paris. Baraka wanted to know if Ginsberg was "for real" (*Autobiography* [Freundlich] 150). This Dadaist gesture instigated a forty-year relationship. The exchange was also one of the critical moments in Baraka's transformation from a "middle-class intellectual" into a bohemian. Baraka became an important editor of the seminal beat journals *Yūgen* (1958–62, with his wife, Hettie Jones) and *The Floating Bear* (1961–63, with Diane di Prima), both of which published several authors we study in our class. Baraka would also publish some of the major beat authors through Totem Press and (with Eli Wilentz and Ted Wilentz) Corinth Books. In 1961, Baraka and di Prima were arrested for using the mail to distribute obscene materials when an issue of *The Floating Bear*, containing a piece by Burroughs, was intercepted at a New Jersey prison. Baraka's eloquent two-day defense helped the editors beat the charges.

It was Baraka, moreover, who vindicated Kerouac and Ginsberg after Podhoretz's vitriolic essay "The Know-Nothing Bohemians" appeared in the *Partisan Review*. Podhoretz had linked the beat sensibility to a variety of social ills:

> I also believe that juvenile crime can be explained partly in terms of the same resentment against normal feeling and the attempt to cope with the world through intelligence that lies behind Kerouac and Ginsberg. Even the relatively mild ethos of Kerouac's books can spill over easily into brutality, for there is a suppressed cry in those books: Kill the intellectuals who can talk coherently, kill the people who can sit still for five minutes at a time, kill those incomprehensible characters who are capable of getting seriously involved with a woman, a job, a cause. (318)

Baraka deftly defended his fellow beats and bohemians in a letter published in the magazine's next issue: "As with Dada, Beat represents a line of departure rather than a concrete doctrine. And even if this departure never produces another poem as influential or controversial as Allen Ginsberg's 'Howl,' there is no doubt in my mind that it will produce better ones. The same is true of Kerouac's *On the Road*. It breaks new ground, and plants new seeds . . ." ("Beat Generation" 473). By building this bulwark against Podhoretz's assault, Baraka established in no uncertain terms his alliance with the beats and bohemianism.

Yet, by 1964, the year *Dutchman* won the prestigious Obie Award from the *Village Voice* for best off-Broadway play, Baraka was in the midst of another transformation, which had begun with his visit to Castro's Cuba, and which would culminate in his embracing black nationalism, leaving his white Jewish wife, and moving from Greenwich Village to Harlem.[2] During a time that William J. Harris calls Baraka's "transitional period" (Baraka, *LeRoi Jones/Amiri Baraka Reader* 19), Baraka produced his most famous play, *Dutchman*, which made him a literary celebrity. Nilgün Anadolu-Okur argues that

> real credit is due to *Dutchman*, more than any other play, for heightening black consciousness and promoting the Black Arts movement. Baraka's unique contribution was the advocacy of an end of the centuries-old dream of integration. . . . The direction among black playwrights from then on, and a justified one, was to follow separate paths from the American mainstream in art, aesthetics, and drama. . . . (*Contemporary* 12)

Dutchman can be read as a crucial moment in Baraka's break from the beats. What caused this radical break becomes the focus for the end of our class.

If Baraka's beat friends paid close attention to the language of *Dutchman*, they would have discovered the play's frustration with white bohemia. Hettie Jones recalls how she became conflated with Lula, who embodies white supremacy in the play: "the glances of strangers were sideways rather than confrontational. Who was that at the playwright's side—Lula the murderer, his white wife, or the former Hettie Cohen? And then, as I'd dreaded, one day they all became one" (218). Baraka's break from the beat world would become final when, spurred by the assassination of Malcolm X on 21 February 1965, he left the Village and his wife for life and work in Harlem, eventually marrying an African American woman, Sylvia Robinson (later Amina Baraka). At the time of his break from the beats, Baraka was in the midst of cofounding the Black Arts Repertory Theatre/School, an immensely important (though short-lived) black arts institution. Based in Harlem, and later in Newark, New Jersey, Baraka became a major figure in the black arts and black power movements. When we regard *Dutchman* retrospectively, the play can look very much like a prelude to this radicalization or like an early phase of this process.

After reading *Dutchman* and screening Anthony Harvey's film adaptation (1966), and before beginning a formal analysis of the play's complexities, our class looks at how it relates to the works we have previously read. We look, for example, at the othering of blackness in Ginsberg's "Howl," with its bohemian "best minds" "dragging themselves through the negro streets at dawn looking for an angry fix" (9). Ginsberg's bohemian world is separate in a meaningful way from the black streets that "the best minds" tour. The class wrestles with just how these worlds are different. We also return to *On the Road* and reexamine the romantic primitivism of Sal Paradise's "wishing [he] were a Negro, feeling that the best the white world had offered was not enough ecstasy for [him], not enough life, joy, kicks, darkness, music, not enough night" (179–80). The exchange between Clay and Lula reminds students of beat images of the white bohemian encounter with blackness.

Clay can be read as an allegorical "young naive black intellectual" (*Autobiography* [Freundlich] 187), as Baraka describes him, and more specifically as a stand-in for Baraka himself—or that part of himself that he sought to transform. And students tend to read the character along these lines. At times, Clay strikes students as a self-critical caricature of Baraka. At other times, Clay becomes the mouthpiece for Baraka's partially veiled attack against the beats and white bohemia.

When Lula, the allegorical temptress and tormentor, first engages with Clay, she says, "You look like you've been reading Chinese poetry and drinking lukewarm sugarless tea" (*Dutchman* 8). Our class immediately thinks of the tea-drinking Gary Snyder, who translated Han Shan's Chinese poetry as "Cold Mountain Poems" (1958). Kerouac's *The Dharma Bums* is dedicated to Han Shan, a legendary ninth-century Chinese poet, and the novel's protagonist, Japhy Ryder (inspired by Snyder), along with all "the Dharma Bums" (who are mainly white beat poets), is portrayed as a modern-day incarnation of Han Shan. Ray Smith, the narrator, says, "Finally [Japhy] learned Chinese and Japanese and became an Oriental scholar and discovered the greatest Dharma Bums of them all, the Zen Lunatics of China and Japan" (6). Lula implicitly identifies

Clay as an aspiring "dharma bum," a hipster dabbling with the new fad of Easternism (partially inspired by writers like Snyder, Kerouac, and Ginsberg), which is preventing Clay from embracing his authentic blackness. Students readily see problems with Lula's presumptuous tone and her ungrounded sense of authority. But to what degree does she see something in Clay that he does not like about himself? Clay's embrace of white bohemianism, he begins to realize, has simultaneously been a repression of his innate blackness.

In the second scene of the play, Lula also equates Clay's bohemianism with homosexuality, Jewishness, and Buddhism—all associated with the beat poet Ginsberg. Proposing a night out on the town, Lula says to Clay, "I mean we'll look in all the shopwindows, and make fun of the queers. Maybe we'll meet a Jewish Buddhist and flatten his conceits over some very pretentious coffee" (23). My students here find a Ginsbergian figure under attack, defined as an obstacle to Clay's self-realization. Lula again refers to such a figure when she says, "I bet you're too serious to be psychoanalyzed. Like all those Jewish poets from Yonkers, who never leave their mothers looking for other mothers, or others' mothers, on whose baggy tits they lay their fumbling heads. Their poems are always funny, and all about sex" (28). After reading "Kaddish"—a eulogy for the poet's mother that is, at times, funny and about sex—our class cannot help but think that Baraka had Ginsberg in mind when he put these words into Lula's mouth. Lula, like Ginsberg, also claims to have had a Communist mother (19). By thus alluding to Ginsberg, Baraka is setting up the Ginsberg-type as Clay's metaphorical shackle.

Shortly after *Dutchman*'s appearance, Baraka would vehemently repudiate the bohemian world peopled by "Jewish Buddhist[s]" and "those Jewish poets from Yonkers." William J. Harris writes:

> [Baraka's] exorcism of white consciousness and values included a ten-year period of professed hatred of whites, and most especially Jews. . . .
>
> This time marked a period of thorough disassociation from liberals, bohemians, and whites in general, due, he has written, to his perception of their inability and their refusal to take the political action he saw as essential. (Introduction xxiv–xxv)

Jerry Gafio Watts believes that we cannot fully understand Baraka unless we confront his sometimes unseemly stances. Speaking in particular about Baraka's black nationalist period, Watts contends that "[t]he viciousness of [Baraka's] sexism, the obscenity of his anti-Semitism, and the ridiculousness of his pipe dream to usher black Americans into African feudalism demand a day in the public court" (477). *Dutchman* itself suggests that the black intellectual's association with a bohemian figure like the gay and Jewish Ginsberg frustrates his search for a black aesthetic. One moment in which the play draws a connection between Clay's bohemianism and his alienation from blackness occurs when Lula spouts some Ginsberg-like poetry after calling Clay a "middle-class black bastard" (31) and "just a dirty white man" (31).

When Clay, outraged by this provocation, admits that he *is* a "middle-class fake white man," he reveals a deeper, authentic side that had previously been buried, and his attack seems directed at hipster bohemians, like Ginsberg, Kerouac, and other beats, as much as at Lula: "Charlie Parker? Charlie Parker. All the hip white boys scream for Bird. And Bird saying, 'Up your ass, feeble-minded ofay! Up your ass.' And they sit there talking about the tortured genius of Charlie Parker. Bird would've played not a note of music if he just walked up to East Sixty-seventh Street and killed the first ten white people he saw. Not a note!" (35). Baraka would have been aware of Kerouac's *Mexico City Blues* (1959), which includes three "choruses" in praise of Parker. The first one, the "239th Chorus," begins:

> Charley [*sic*] Parker Looked like Buddha
> Charley Parker, who recently died
> Laughing at a juggler on the TV
> after weeks of strain and sickness,
> was called the Perfect Musician.
> And his expression on his face
> Was as calm, beautiful, and profound
> As the image of the Buddha
> Represented in the East, the lidded eyes,
> The expression that says "All is Well"
> —This was what Charley Parker
> Said when he played, All is Well. (241)

Clearly Baraka wanted to say that even white jazz aficionados like Kerouac could not penetrate the true significance of Parker's music, for they had not experienced being black. Clay, speaking for Baraka, is also angered by white bohemians' fetishization of Bird and their appropriation of Bird as a musical talisman with which to enter black cultural arenas. At the time of *Dutchman*'s appearance, then, Baraka's journey from bohemia toward blacker regions was well underway. In his essay "American Sexual Reference: Black Male" (1966), Baraka would call integration "a beatified decadence" (226), an allusion to Kerouac's linkage of "Beat" and "beatific" ("Beatific" 571). Whether Kerouac knew it or not, Baraka was clearly breaking from "the King of the Beats."

I end my *Dutchman* unit by discussing with the class why Baraka felt he had to break from the beats. We return to the beats' early work to see if we can find signs of political engagement that Baraka may have overlooked and if we can discern the ways it is in dialogue with the racism of its era. We ponder political art's relation to organized political activism. We consider the trauma and heartache experienced by Hettie Jones, who had been rejected by her family after her marriage but was embraced by Baraka's family after the couple's divorce. Baraka's break from Hettie was certainly not easy for him, but he saw it as a necessary step in his development into a political activist. He was also troubled by his movement away from the beat and Black Mountain poets who had played such a crucial role in his development as an artist. He writes, "It was Olson, because of his intellectual example, and Ginsberg, because of his artistic model and graciousness as a teacher, whom I thought most about in terms of the road I was moving along. Where would they be in all this? Also, my friend Ed Dorn . . ." (*Autobiography* [Freundlich] 192). Hettie Jones recalls Baraka's saying that "Ed Dorn was the only white man who understood him" (212). But Dorn was not the only white bohemian poet to sympathize with Jones's struggle with racial identity. Ginsberg would write to his father in November 1965, "I see why LeRoi Jones gives up on the U.S. whites" (*Letters* 312).

Baraka's attitude toward whites could be brutally cold. Once, when a blonde female college student asked Malcolm X if there was anything she could do to help his cause, he replied, "Nothing" (*Autobiography* 330). When a white woman asked Baraka a similar question, he said, "You can help by dying. You are a cancer. You can help the world's people with your death" (*Autobiography* [Freundlich] 193). Baraka's volte-face and the homophobia that accompanied his black nationalism (exemplified in the essay "American Sexual Reference") were extremely distressing to Ginsberg.[3] Yet, in later years, Baraka would reject black nationalism and reconcile with many of the white beats, including Ginsberg, appearing with them on panels and at conferences, often praising them in documentaries. One of the last phone calls Ginsberg made before his death was to his friend Amiri Baraka. In his 2009 introduction to *Home: Social Essays* (1966), Baraka apologizes for the homophobia he had voiced in the past and acknowledges, in what is surely a nod to Ginsberg, "the homosexual giants we all have known, who have always been out front sexually and politically" (Introduction 16).

Though there is a great deal more to *Dutchman*, it is rewarding to recognize that Baraka saw his break from beat bohemianism as a momentous event in his cultural and political evolution. Understanding this break complicates and adds nuance to our reading of beat literature, the very notion of bohemianism, and what it means to be politically engaged. It brings to the forefront the racial tensions with which bohemians and others had to grapple in the 1950s and 1960s. These racial encounters help define who we are today and inform the struggles with which we are still challenged.

NOTES

[1] To read more about Kerouac's romantic primitivism, see Jon Panish's "Kerouac's *The Subterraneans*: A Study of 'Romantic Primitivism.'"

[2] Beginning in the early 1970s, Baraka would remake himself again, leaving behind the black nationalism with which he had become associated and adopting a Third World Marxist politics.

[3] To hear Ginsberg's take on Baraka's break from the beats, see Bourne, "Interview."

Dutchman as Black Avant-Garde Historical Drama

Matthew Calihman

I have taught Amiri Baraka's *Dutchman* in a variety of contexts: introductions to African American studies, surveys of African American literature, seminars on the black power and black arts movements, and other courses on United States culture in the 1960s and 1970s. When I teach the play in the African American literature survey, my unit on *Dutchman* comes more than a month after I first introduce modernism in general and the avant-garde in particular. During our work on the Harlem Renaissance, I define the avant-garde as the modernist impulse to destroy an unendurable but enduring past in order to make way for a livable future. The avant-garde, I explain, is antihistoricist; "futurism" is not only a name for a particular avant-garde movement but also a description of the avant-garde impulse itself.[1] But, when we reach *Dutchman*, we encounter something of a paradox: an avant-garde historical drama. Baraka's play, as I teach it, wages war against a present that has already declared victory over the ongoing past of black oppression.

The objectives of my *Dutchman* unit correspond with some important claims in black arts movement scholarship. I want students to see the history of the avant-garde as one of the contexts in which black arts must be placed. As Harry J. Elam, Jr., succinctly puts it, "[D]espite [their] vehement repudiations of Western aesthetics, black artists [of the 1960s and 1970s] were knowledgeable about, trained in, and influenced by avant-garde traditions" ("*TDR* Black Theatre Issue" 42). I also want students to see that, as Elam and others further argue, black artists engaged critically with these aesthetics and formed new avant-gardes of their own. Mike Sell aptly describes the black arts movement as "a radical aesthetic trend that was both 'inside' and 'outside' Euro-American aesthetic, philosophical, and critical traditions" (*Avant-Garde Performance* 277). And I want my students to see that the movement broke with these traditions by insisting that black aesthetic experiment must also be historiography. Kimberly W. Benston observes that black arts theater "diverges from its Euro-American counterpart in retaining commitment to remembrance and history even as it annuls inherited mechanisms of social reproduction" (29). My course unit on *Dutchman* explores the play's vanguard historicism.

In this three-hour unit, I rely on prepared minilectures, discussion prompts, and a handout that reproduces passages from the supplemental texts that I quote along the way. After introducing the black arts movement and Baraka's life and career, I ask students, "What are your initial impressions and questions about this play?" I begin with this most general question because students often come to this class session with a lot to say, and I do not want to begin by building a single channel through which all their responses must flow. Typically, some students are interested in *Dutchman*'s allusive and intertextual play with familiar master narratives of transgression; we observe that the play invokes Adam and Eve, Romeo and Juliet, and the Flying Dutchman legend. When I ask the group, "Which character has transgressed, and how so?," some students read the play as a tragedy of assimilation; we discuss Clay's "three-button suit and striped tie" (18), his identification as a bohemian citizen of the world, and Lula's calling him an Uncle Tom. Other students say that the black man's crime here is actually his struggle against Uncle Tom; we read race into Baraka's onetime assertion that "*Dutchman* is about the difficulty of becoming a man in America" ("LeRoi Jones Talking" 188).

I devote about an hour to this work, and then, referring to some of the foregoing discussion, I begin to sketch the literary history to which *Dutchman* belongs. I start by saying that, like other participants in the emerging black arts movement, Baraka began during the mid-1960s to theorize a black aesthetic. At this time, he often imagined black art as a black voice ceaselessly, ruthlessly refusing silence and insincerity, and he called this fierce, inexorable expressiveness "Black Dada." Baraka envisioned a black analogue to the European Dada of the late 1910s and early 1920s, which had proposed the destruction of bourgeois culture and championed a boldly antitraditionalist antiaesthetic of spontaneity, chance, and illogic. Like many young, bohemian experimental artists of his generation, Baraka was well versed in the history of the early-twentieth-century avant-garde, and, in his magazines, *Yūgen* and *The Floating Bear*, he published translations of the likes of Tristan Tzara and César Vallejo. I use a photocopied excerpt from Tzara's "Dada Manifesto 1918" to introduce students to Dada—"a protest with the fists of its whole being engaged in destructive action" (81).[2]

Then, to make the connection to Baraka, I turn to a passage that appears in his essay "LeRoi Jones Talking" (1964). In this passage, Baraka describes black Dada as a response to the struggle over desegregation in Birmingham in 1963 and, more generally, to the persistence of racial oppression:

> Something else I aspire to is the craziness of all honest men. (And as another aside: one way Negroes could force [America's] institutionalized dishonesty to crumble and its apologizers to break and run even faster than they are now would be to turn crazy, to bring out a little American dada, Ornette Coleman style, and chase these perverts into the ocean, where they belong. Say, if Negroes just stopped behaving, stopped being what Charles [i.e., white power] desires, and just flip, go raving in the streets, screaming in verse an honest history of America, walk off their jobs—as they should have done in Birmingham after those children were murdered—and watch the country grind to a halt, the owners cracking their knuckles as they got out their gold guns and got ready to blow out their own legendary brains. It is a good, and practical, idea. Why don't you try it, Negroes?) That is, a craziness that will make a man keep talking even after everyone else says he shouldn't. (183)[3]

We thus see that Baraka imagined black Dada, here epitomized by the avant-garde jazz of Ornette Coleman, as an aesthetic scourge on white supremacy and a nation too insincere to confront it. Although Coleman's music (I play a sample from his album *Free Jazz* [1961] in class) is instrumental, Baraka attributed to black Dada a distinctly vocal agency, "a craziness that will make a man keep talking even after everyone else says he shouldn't." This "screaming" or "raving" ("LeRoi Jones Talking" 183), Baraka thought, was the expressive basis of black liberation and a necessary aesthetic complement to revolutionary social violence (e.g., a black general strike).[4]

At this point, I ask my students, "Can you see these ideas in *Dutchman*?" During the first hour on the play, students typically point out that Lula abuses and manipulates Clay and that she attempts to define his identity. Now we focus on Clay's resistance. We recall that, near the play's climax, Lula tells Clay to "[g]et up and scream at these people" (31). I add that the version of the play published in Edward Parone's anthology *New Theatre in America* (1965) explicitly invokes Dada at this moment; immediately after enjoining Clay to "[g]et up and scream at these people," Lula summons the "dada man" within him (Parone 209). Lula seems to have this avant-garde subject in mind when she says, "You're a murderer, Clay, and you know it" (21). Clay later emerges as a "dada man" during his long, furious speech near the end of the play. In a grand performance of black aesthetic violence, he discloses the longing for murder that even black artists—Bessie Smith, Charlie Parker, and others—have kept secret. Lula had urged Clay to "scream meaningless shit in these hopeless faces" (31), but his black Dada turns out to be "an honest history of America" ("LeRoi Jones Talking" 183).

However, *Dutchman* does not conclude with this scream. Clay finally relents and chooses to engage Lula no longer: "Sorry, baby, I don't think we could make it" (37). And it is in this instant that Lula assumes the role of murderer and stabs Clay to death: "*As he is bending over her, the girl brings up a small knife and plunges it into* CLAY*'s chest. Twice. He slumps across her knees, his mouth working stupidly*" (37). In the analysis through which my students and I work, Clay's betrayal of his own black voice is his tragic transgression.

If time allows as we approach the end of our second hour on *Dutchman*, then I note that Eldridge Cleaver read *Dutchman* in much the same way that I have—as a call for a black revolutionary speech act. In the essay "Psychology: The Black Bible" (1969), Cleaver likened Clay's struggle to the sort of anticolonialist struggle described in Frantz Fanon's *The Wretched of the Earth* (1961; trans. 1963):

> Fanon teaches that the key factor is to focus all the hatreds and violence on their true target—the oppressor [i.e., not the oppressed]. From then on, says Fanon, be implacable. The same point is made by Leroi [*sic*] Jones in his play, *Dutchman*, when his character, Clay, screams to the white woman who had tormented him, "A little murder will make us all sane again." (Cleaver 19–20)

I stress here that, for Cleaver, among other black radical intellectuals of this period, Clay's murderous oration was akin to revolutionary political action.[5] I stress, too, that, in readings such as Cleaver's, Clay's tragedy is his final retreat from implacability.

But there is more for us to say during our final hour on *Dutchman* about Clay's advance and retreat, a sequence that is revealed as social ritual when another young black intellectual boards the train in the play's closing moments. This sequence suggests that *Dutchman*'s avant-garde violence is restrained by history itself, by the ongoing past of black racial subordination. As I note in class, when the play first opened in March 1964, the United States House of Representatives had already passed the bill that would become the Civil Rights Act, and the bill became law during the play's nearly yearlong run. But Clay and Lula do not get clear of Jim Crow, or even slavery. The difficulty of escaping the past is first signaled by Baraka's initial stage directions, which tell us that the play's subway is "*heaped in modern myth*" (3), freighted with the narratives that form modern American society even in its flux. Although Baraka's characters are hurtling along in a New York City subway train ten years after *Brown v. Board of Education*, they remain determined by the stories of Homer Plessy and the Scottsboro Boys, among other ur-narratives of race, citizenship, and national belonging. Students recognize the burdens imposed by these stories when I ask the class to do a close reading of the play's opening. There the white law indicts Clay's black male gaze, charging him with reckless eyeballing. "Weren't you staring at me through the window?" (6), Lula asks, even though it is she who initially lays eyes on the other (4). My students see here that, from the beginning, Baraka refuses to portray integration as an accomplished fact. They see that *Dutchman* recognizes the persistence of the past in the triumphal present.

To make these points in another way, I return with the class to the European avant-garde. But instead of returning to Dada, I talk now about futurism and its visions of modern velocity and technological transcendence. In the "Initial Manifesto of Futurism" (1909), which I excerpt for the class, F. T. Marinetti proclaimed that his movement stood on "the extreme promontory of the centuries" and that the futurists lived already "in the absolute, since we have already created speed, eternal and ever-present" (124). In another paean to modern technology and speed, he sang of "broad-chested locomotives prancing on the rails, like huge steel horses bridled with long tubes" (124). *Dutchman*'s first scene concludes with a send-up of such absolute antihistoricism. Proposing a make-believe romance, Lula says sarcastically to Clay, "And we'll pretend . . . that you are free of your own history. And I am free of my history. We'll pretend that we are both anonymous beauties smashing along through the city's entrails" (21). Whereas a futurist locomotive might have smashed its way out of the past, Baraka's subway ritually re-confronts the past in the present. And whereas futurist subjects might have sped their way beyond finite particularity, Baraka's subjects cannot become "anonymous"—raceless—"beauties."

Dutchman's recognition of the persistent past, I emphasize, is one of the play's black arts projects. So, too, I add, is the play's recognition of a distinctive and redemptive black vernacular culture. During the class sessions leading up to our *Dutchman* unit, my students learn that the mainstream civil rights movement of the late 1950s and early 1960s tended to downplay black cultural distinctiveness or to deny it altogether, and I make clear that, in Baraka's view and to his horror, the normative cultural ideology in mid-century America was assimilation. But *Dutchman* challenges this norm. The play enacts the black writer's anguished first effort to reclaim "Bessie Smith," "Charlie Parker," "belly rub" (34–35), and the ordinary blacks, the "blues people" (36), from whose lives black vernacular culture emerged. Clay's long, raving speech is not only a negative expression of aesthetic resistance but also an affirmative contribution to the vernacular tradition, for Baraka linked such Ornette Coleman–style Dada to the very beginnings of the blues: "These young [black avant-garde] musicians also rely to a great extent on a closeness of vocal reference that has always been characteristic of Negro music. Players like Coleman, Coltrane, and Rollins literally scream and rant in imitation of the human voice, sounding many times like the unfettered primitive [i.e., proto-blues] shouters" (*Blues People* 227). It is this tradition of "primitive shouters" that Clay betrays when he finally yields to Lula.

We also have some evidence, as I aim to show in class, that Baraka linked at least a few earlier black writers to the vernacular tradition. Though he had often argued during the early 1960s that the black literary past was a wasteland of middle-class conformity and mediocrity, he began to move away from this position at mid-decade. In the essay "Black Writing" (1964), Baraka cited as "proofs" of black cultural "nonconformity" books by James Baldwin, W. E. B. Du Bois, Chester Himes, Richard Wright, and the sociologist E. Franklin Frazier (164–65).

Baraka did not publish lengthy comments about Wright until the late 1970s, more than a decade after *Dutchman*'s premiere, but these comments reveal another origin of Clay's scream. In *The Autobiography of LeRoi Jones* (1984), Baraka recalled the first time he read Wright's *Black Boy* (1945), and he remembered the book as something like black Dada. Young Wright was slow in learning to censor himself among whites, or to tell them the requisite lies, and he never became reliably dissembling. He often violated Southern prohibitions on black speech, and it was the violence of his speech that impressed Baraka: "when I was thirteen I read *Black Boy*, . . . and I feared for R.W.'s life and wondered how he dared say such things and still walk around" ([Lawrence Hill] 62). In another reflection on his first encounter with *Black Boy*, Baraka recalled asking the same question ("Confessions" 19), and he quoted from Wright's almost encyclopedic list of the subjects blacks were not to broach with whites:

> Among the topics that southern white men did not like to discuss with Negroes were the following: American white women; the Ku Klux Klan;

> France, and how Negro soldiers fared while there; Frenchwomen; Jack Johnson; the entire northern part of the United States; the Civil War; Abraham Lincoln; U.S. Grant; General Sherman; Catholics; the Pope; Jews; the Republican party; slavery; social equality; Communism; Socialism; the 13th, 14th, and 15th Amendments to the Constitution; or any topic calling for positive knowledge or manly self-assertion on the part of the Negro. (Wright 231)

Reminding the class that my analysis of *Dutchman* has become speculative, I ask, "Isn't Wright's list a version of the 'honest history of America' that Baraka wanted blacks to scream in the streets?" Here, for Baraka, was the testimony that Southern blacks were forbidden to give but that young Wright could not help but give. A long, single-sentence list that threatens to continue indefinitely, this passage seems to express syntactically the sort of "craziness that will make a man keep talking even after everyone else says he shouldn't." Although Baraka wrote little about Wright's work in the years immediately preceding and following *Dutchman*, he later remembered having marveled, as a young reader, at Wright's unyielding social witness.

My class's exploration of *Dutchman*'s historicist aesthetic violence usually precedes a unit on Octavia Butler's *Kindred* (1979), a speculative neo-slave narrative. The novel's protagonist, a black woman named Dana, is literally thrust back and forth between her present in 1976 Los Angeles and her past in antebellum Maryland. Her bodily and subjective involvement in this past comes to represent the terrible difficulty of surmounting history. No fiat can get Dana clear of slavery, just as no confident decree can transform Clay and Lula into "anonymous beauties smashing along through the city's entrails."

NOTES

[1] Renato Poggioli's *The Theory of the Avant-Garde* (1962; trans. 1968) offers a foundational account of the avant-garde as a futurist impulse.

[2] This manifesto was one of many collected for English-speaking readers in Motherwell, *Dada Painters and Poets* (1951).

[3] A slightly different version of this statement appears in Baraka's "Philistinism and the Negro Writer" (1966).

[4] Among the other texts in which Baraka invokes black Dada is the poem "Black Dada Nihilismus" (1963), whose speaker unleashes black expressive violence on whites: "Black scream / and chant, scream, / and dull, un / earthly / hollering. . . ." (63–64). See, too, "The Revolutionary Theatre" (1965), Baraka's manifesto for a black arts theater. Although the revolutionary theater must ritually enact violence in the manner of Antonin Artaud's theater of cruelty, it must also "stagger through our universe correcting, insulting, preaching, spitting craziness—but a craziness taught to us in our most rational moments" (Baraka, *Home* [Morrow] 211). The short story "The Screamers" (1963) is about

a young black bourgeois intellectual who struggles to scream in this way. He is "too quiet to become a murderer" (74). But the black musicians named in the story's title are not so reticent.

[5] For a related discussion of Clay's scream and the many others in Baraka's oeuvre, see chapter 5 of Benston's *Performing Blackness* (189–227).

Culture and Violence in *Dutchman* and the Black Arts Movement

Deborah M. Mix

One challenge of teaching a play like Amiri Baraka's *Dutchman* is helping students understand the ways in which the play and the black arts movement more broadly envision the relation between violence and art. The descriptions and enactments of violence are rightly unsettling to many readers and require careful engagement in the classroom to ensure that students understand the impetus behind those visions without glossing over their challenges. Though Baraka advocated violent resistance to white racial violence, his career suggests that he also believed in art as a force for social change.

Near the end of the play, Clay suggests one perspective on the relation between art and violence when he asserts that black art—black music in particular—can function as a cultural pressure release for African Americans, converting rage into aesthetic expression:

> [Charlie Parker] would've played not a note of music if he just walked up to East Sixty-seventh Street and killed the first ten white people he saw. Not a note! . . . If Bessie Smith had killed some white people she wouldn't have needed that music. She could have talked very straight and plain about the world. No metaphors. No grunts. No wiggles in the dark of her soul. Just straight two and two are four. Money. Power. Luxury. Like that. All of them. Crazy niggers turning their backs on sanity. When all it needs is a simple act. Murder. Just murder! Would make us all sane. (35)

Clay goes on to insist that as African Americans increasingly regard "the great intellectual legacy of the white man" as their own, as cultural traditions like the blues disappear, and as African Americans become "stand-up Western men," they will be unable to resist the impulse to violence: "They'll murder you. . . . They'll cut your throats, and drag you out to the edge of your cities so the flesh can fall away from your bones, in sanitary isolation" (36). Clay seems to welcome direct expressions of violence, even if it comes as a result of deracination; whites, *Dutchman*'s plot suggests, are neither prevented from direct expressions of violence against African Americans nor punished for them, so why, Clay asks, should African Americans be? However, we must also remember that, along with the escalation in violence, there is an additional cost to such thinking: the impulse to create black art will be exhausted.

As we know, Clay is murdered and his body thrown from the subway car by Lula and her black and white conspirators; it is Clay's body that is slashed, his that is left in "sanitary isolation" somewhere in the tunnels beneath the city. The play concludes with Lula's cool appraisal of another young black man like Clay arriving in the same subway car, suggesting that the cycle of provocation, conflict, and violence is destined to continue. The question of what—if anything—can disrupt this cycle is at the center of Baraka's play and is where I focus when I teach it in my literature courses as part of a larger unit on black arts writing. I want to give my students the tools to understand both the context in which Baraka and his cohort were writing and the purposes they envisioned for their poetry and drama.

In order to provide contexts for students to think about the relation between art, politics, and violence, I incorporate three kinds of supplemental source material into the class sessions devoted to *Dutchman* and black arts writing: first, some of Baraka's poetry, most notably his ars poetica "Black Art"; second, other work by black arts writers, and recordings of these writers performing their poems; and third, popular rhythm and blues and soul music and scholarly discussions of that music. In this essay, I will explain how I use these elements to help students understand both why Baraka envisions art as a liberatory act and how he and other African American writers and musicians use art as an alternative to—but not a substitute for—social violence.

Baraka's political investments form an important context not only for reading *Dutchman* but also for thinking about his poetry. "Black Art" was published in 1966, two years after *Dutchman* was produced and published. Despite that publication gap, however, the poem offers a similar vision of black anger transformed into art. Its opening declaration that "Poems are bullshit unless they are/teeth or trees or lemons piled/on a step" (427 [lines 1–3])[1] often surprises students, who struggle to understand what "teeth or trees or lemons" have to do with one another or what they have to do with non-"bullshit" poems. I remind them of what the black cultural nationalist Ron Karenga identified as the three central imperatives of black art—"expose the enemy, praise the people and support the revolution" (33–34)—and I ask them to think about how the opening lines of "Black Art" might be read in the light of these directives. (Though Karenga's model of black cultural nationalism did not influence Baraka until 1967, I find Karenga's distillation of black art's principles to be a useful framework for thinking about Baraka's play and his social and aesthetic principles more generally.) We go on through the poem, considering how it aligns with Karenga's principles. Baraka envisions "live/words of the hip world live flesh &/coursing blood" (428 [lines 9–11]), suggesting generative power, as well as "Poems that shoot / guns" (428 [lines 20–21), reflecting the simmering violence of the time. The poem's final turn, however, toward a vision of poems that "[c]lean out the world for virtue and love" (428 [line 42]) and of a collective investment in the power of poetry, marks a potential endpoint to the poem's most violent visions of murder and mayhem, gesturing toward a future in which neither Clay nor Lula winds up dead on the subway. While aesthetic violence may be necessary to "[c]lean out the world," that violence is figured as creative and productive.

But even as the poem powerfully reflects the ideals of Karenga, Baraka, and others, it also illustrates the vexing challenges of teaching the black arts movement, challenges that are directly relevant to how students understand *Dutchman*. "Black Art" exhibits some of the misogyny and anti-Semitism that plagued the black cultural nationalist movement more broadly. Baraka writes of "dagger-poems in the slimy bellies/of the owner-jews" (428 [lines 14–15]), "[a]nother bad poem cracking/steel knuckles in a jewlady's mouth" (lines 39–40), and "the Liberal/Spokesman for the jews" vomiting and choking (lines 28–29). Anti-Semitism was, unfortunately, a persistent thread in much black nationalist rhetoric and writing, perhaps functioning to lash out at whites in general by vilifying a still-marginalized white subgroup. Anyone teaching black arts writing must confront this disturbing motif, locating it in not only the literary texts but also the larger historical contexts of the movement, and I ask my students to think about why an artist invested in empowering one group would leverage hatred toward another group to achieve those ends.

Misogyny runs through both *Dutchman* and "Black Art." In the poem, we see Baraka excoriating "girdlemamma mulatto bitches" as "Stinking/whores!" (428 [lines 16, 18–19]).[2] Similarly, he characterizes Lula as a "dumb bitch" and threatens to "rip [her] lousy breasts off," suggesting that Lula deserves a gendered retribution for her cruel and goading words (lines 32, 34). It is possible to interpret the play as suggesting that Clay has failed to achieve full manhood because he neither sleeps with nor murders Lula. Instructors must engage these issues directly with students, both to make visible the underlying assumptions about gender and sexuality in the play and to open up a conversation about the endemic sexism in any number of 1960s-era radical and countercultural movements.

But while Baraka and some of the other male poets of the black arts movement were strongly invested in remodeling black masculinity, sometimes at the expense of black and white womanhood, many other black arts writers attended to black women and to a nonmasculinist vision of black humanity. In order to illustrate this point, I introduce work by women poets involved with the movement, particularly Jayne Cortez ("I Am New York City"), Nikki Giovanni ("Nikki-Rosa," "Beautiful Black Men"), Audre Lorde ("Now," "Coal"), and Sonia Sanchez ("Homecoming," "When We Come," "blk/rhetoric"). These womanist and feminist black nationalist writers help deepen students' vision of the literary and political movement. In these poems, writers take seriously the idea that black art can "praise the people" and "support the revolution" without denigrating others in the process. Reading a few of these poets alongside Baraka helps students recognize that the violence in Baraka's work is not an essential element of black art. These poems suggest that it is possible to tell white audiences to "kiss my black unruly ass," as Clay hears Bessie Smith saying in her music (34), without coupling that dismissal with a kick in the teeth or a bullet to the brain.

Clay looks to popular music—specifically to jazz and blues—for examples of artists turning their rage into creativity. A central aim of the black arts movement was to ensure popular access to art. The movement thus privileged poetry and drama, creative media that were easier for ordinary black people to access.

Poetry was made available in inexpensive editions like those from Dudley Randall's Broadside Press, Naomi Long Madgett's Lotus Press, and Third World Press; individual poems were sometimes produced as poster-sized broadsheets and pasted up in black neighborhoods, the idea being that passersby could easily pause to read a poem, which might then help to shape their identity and engagement. Similarly, plays were often one-acts requiring minimal sets and scenery. Set directions for *Dutchman*, for example, specify that only subway seats and windows are required; the world outside the windows need only be suggested (3). This approach ensures that black arts drama, like its poetry, can be easily brought to the people, to those who might otherwise never enter a theater. In the same vein, writers in the movement emphasized vernacular language, creating what Larry Neal describes as "an art that speaks directly to the needs and aspirations of Black America" and that "consists of an African-American cultural tradition" (272, 274).[3] Given black arts' emphasis on bringing poetry and drama to the people, I find it useful to share examples of broadsheets and to play recorded versions of some of the poems in class.[4] This discussion also establishes a context in which students can think about Clay's invocations of Bessie Smith and Charlie Parker. In the play, Clay argues that while whites profess to love Smith's music, they "don't even understand that Bessie Smith is saying, 'Kiss my ass, kiss my black unruly ass.' Before love, suffering, desire, anything you can explain, she's saying, and very plainly, 'Kiss my black ass.' And if you don't know that, it's you that's doing the kissing" (34–35). He makes a similar argument about Charlie Parker, whose saxophone seems to say to the "hip white boys" who "scream for Bird," "Up your ass, feeble-minded ofay! Up your ass" (35). My students are largely unfamiliar with blues and jazz music and only passingly familiar with the mainstream soul music of the 1960s, so, to help them to understand what Clay means, I bring several music selections to class. We begin with Bessie Smith, many of whose songs Angela Y. Davis characterizes as social protest songs meant to "name and explore oppressive social conditions defining life in the black community" (102). Davis demonstrates, and I help my students recognize, that Smith's lyrics need not call out whites directly to be effective, if coded, critiques of white power in the ways Clay describes.

Discussion of what might have constituted common knowledge and shared experiences among Smith's African American audiences can help students recognize those coding strategies—strategies that Davis recognizes as rooted in "the music of slavery, in which protest was secretly expressed and understood only by those who held the key to the code" (111). For instance, Smith's "Washwoman's Blues" (1928) is certainly a heartfelt depiction of the life of a laundress, but in its references to a brand of soap powder that was packaged in a box featuring pickaninnies, and in Smith's acknowledgement that alternative employment opportunities for a black woman of the time would still require her servitude, the song also functions as a protest against racism (see A. Davis 98–100). I also play for the class a selection of Charlie Parker's music, usually "Ornithology" (1946), because it is a contrafact composition, weaving a new melody over an older one (in this case the standard "How High the Moon," from which I also play an excerpt). My students generally receive Smith's music better at first, probably because the lyrics make it more easily understandable, especially to those without backgrounds in music, but a discussion of how and why Parker remakes a familiar standard is quite constructive because it reveals to students ways of encoding critique and resistance.

Baraka's "The Changing Same (R&B and New Black Music)" (1967), which I sometimes assign to students, discusses contemporary black music (e.g., James Brown and Motown) as strategies of "dealing with the everyday, and how to get through it and to the other side (or maybe not) which for the most part still bees that world, but on top of it, power full, and beauty full" (128). Craig Werner's *A Change Is Gonna Come: Music, Race, and the Soul of America* (rev. ed. 2006) is another terrific resource on the cultural significance of African American artists like Aretha Franklin, Jimi Hendrix, and John Coltrane. In his autobiography, Baraka recalls the power of popular rhythm and blues music as a source of black identity and affirmation: "Martha and the Vandellas' 'Dancing in the Streets [*sic*]' was like our national anthem. Their 'Heat Wave' had signaled earlier, downtown, that the shit was on the rise. But 'Dancing in the Streets' which spoke to us of Harlem and the other places, then Watts and later Newark and Detroit, seemed to say it all out" (*Autobiography* [Lawrence Hill] 305). The songs to which Baraka refers were released in 1963 ("[Love Is Like a] Heat Wave") and 1964 ("Dancing"), and both were popular hits, appearing on the Billboard R and B and Hot 100 charts. Yet while these songs were clearly popular among white audiences, Baraka's remarks show how they were understood as containing a double message. While the white listening public may have heard them as party songs, as Martha Reeves herself insisted they were, many African Americans also heard them as speaking to growing unrest in African American urban communities and to the racially charged riots that swept across United States cities in the summers of 1964 (Harlem), 1965 (Watts), and 1967 (Newark).[5]

I play these songs in class, asking my students to listen carefully for lyrics that speak to a sense of disfranchisement and frustration or that suggest the singer is telling some listeners to "kiss my black unruly ass." Students often realize that they've heard the songs before—they're staples of oldies radio stations—but they also realize that they've rarely listened to the lyrics and that they've never connected the songs to political protest in the way that Baraka does. Students now hear a second narrative alongside the lament for lost love in "Heat Wave," identifying lines like "It's like a heat wave/Burning in my heart/Can't keep from crying/Tearing me apart" as suggesting experiences of frustration and anger. Similarly, students begin to hear "Dancing in the Street" as suggesting a more politicized solidarity among the people dancing in New York, Chicago, Detroit, New Orleans, and elsewhere.

Students can find hearing familiar songs in new ways eye-opening, and this experience resonates in productive ways with our discussions of Smith's and Parker's music. I point out that Baraka would not yet have heard "Dancing in the Street" while he was writing *Dutchman* (and he may not have heard "Heat Wave" at the time, either), but I also suggest that we might use Baraka's interpretations of those songs to understand what Clay hears in the music he invokes in the play. Through carefully listening to the music and thinking about its significance to the community, students can engage not only the contexts in which *Dutchman* was written and originally performed but also the play itself.

Clay's frustration and fury—his fantasy of murdering white people—and Lula's aggression and violence, then, become not literal representations of Baraka's vision of 1960s race relations but rather a manifestation of the subtexts that Smith and Parker wouldn't or couldn't make plain. Thus we end our discussion of *Dutchman* and black arts writing by returning to the question of art's role in social change. Is it enough, I ask my students, for art to function as a pressure release, keeping Clay or Baraka from "kill[ing] the first ten white people" he sees on the street? Do they believe that sublimating frustration and rage into art is an appropriate response to the brutality of racism? Do we believe that some people, like Lula, are allowed to commit violent acts without punishment—indeed with the support of those around her—while others, like Clay, are destined to be thrown away like so much garbage? These are, of course, difficult questions, but they are questions that resonated then and that continue to resonate now. In literature courses, it behooves us to foreground the responsibilities and potentialities of all art to participate in and even to provoke social change.

NOTES

[1] All quotations of "Black Art" are from the *Anthology of Contemporary American Poetry*, edited by Cary Nelson.

[2] Baraka's criticism of assimilationism is not directed at only women; in "Black Art," he also lambasts the "negroleader pinned to/a barstool in Sardi's," another "on the steps of the white house," and a third on his knees "negotiating coolly" and possibly fellating a presumably white sheriff (427–28 [lines 3–36]). In the play, stage directions note that there are both black and white passengers in the subway car, and the car's conductor is described as "*an old Negro*" (37).

[3] I cite the essay in Gayle, *Black Aesthetic* (272–90).

[4] Examples of broadsheets are available online and in books like Cary Nelson's *Anthology of Contemporary American Poetry*. Recordings of the poets reading their work are also easy to find online at sites like *PennSound* (writing.upenn.edu/pennsound) and *YouTube*, and in the supplementary CDs included with anthologies like the *Norton Anthology of African American Literature* and *Poetry Speaks*.

[5] Suzanne E. Smith's "*Dancing in the Street*" (esp. 169–71) is a great resource for understanding the song in a variety of contexts.

What's Love Got to Do with It? Everything! Teaching *Dutchman* and "The Revolutionary Theatre"

Koritha Mitchell

Because the black power and black arts movements have been vilified as divisive, teaching *Dutchman* requires overcoming students' assumptions that it is hateful. I therefore frame the play with Baraka's theater theory. I emphasize that Baraka's essay "The Revolutionary Theatre" (1965) is theory; it allows us to understand his vision of black theater's possibilities. Though published shortly after *Dutchman*, the essay represents, to a great extent, the conception of theater that informed the play. In the classroom, considering that vision helps guard against privileging our own perspectives while reading *Dutchman* and studying the black radical movements for which it became a foundational text.

Engaging Baraka's theory requires historical context, so before we read "The Revolutionary Theatre," I cover the many ways that our nation's policies have benefited white people, without regard to merit. I provide discussion-intensive minilectures based on George Lipsitz's The *Possessive Investment in Whiteness* and Ira Katznelson's *When Affirmative Action Was White*, and we explore the nation's most effective affirmative action programs, the ones that have not borne that label. Through consideration of these policies, students notice how our society has positioned itself against African Americans by awarding benefits to whites and withholding them from black citizens. Concrete examples help students see why the nation's most common practices depend on teaching everyone that African Americans do not deserve opportunities. The constant message that black people make poor decisions, are inferior, are lazy, and so on is crucial; it keeps citizens from questioning racial inequities. Once students consider the origin of inequities, they better understand the destruction Baraka seeks through revolutionary theater, the destruction of illusions that undergird the racist status quo—which oppresses black Americans financially, spiritually, and otherwise. Wanting to destroy illusions that perpetuate injustice is anything but hateful.

When assigning "The Revolutionary Theatre" (to be discussed for an entire class period before we engage *Dutchman)*, I ask students to read with these questions in mind: 1. In which ways does Baraka's logic depend on love for oppressed people? 2. In which ways does it depend on love for the American ideal of self-determination? 3. In which ways does it depend on love for that which is spiritual and human and cannot be labeled American?

Seeing love in this text is no easy task, so directing students to look for specific objects of love helps, and their search for these objects provides an invaluable framework for *Dutchman*. Together, we come to acknowledge the role of love in

Baraka's theory as well as the value his theory places on passion and the human spirit. Though these investments are woven throughout the piece, they are overshadowed by the essay's masculinist conception of power. "The Revolutionary Theatre" speaks aggressively, but the class's collective work reveals its preoccupation with love and spiritual affirmation. By analyzing Baraka's theater theory with an eye toward connections often obscured by the masculinist rhetoric of the black arts movement, we learn why black female energy manages to emerge briefly in *Dutchman*. Giving upper-level undergraduates this framework leads them to read more deeply.

An Antiblack Society?

United States citizens are educated to believe that racial inequality is an accident of history. Students typically assume, "Blacks may often end up on the bottom in terms of financial security and other measures of success, but not because opportunity is withheld." My boldest students will declare, "My grandparents didn't have much but they sacrificed and saved. Other people could've done the same thing." Because this is the belief with which most students enter my classroom, I present what Katznelson calls "affirmative action" for whites. Without this context, the intensity of the black arts movement can be too easily dismissed as unjustified, inspired by nothing more than black people's lack of gratitude and patriotism.

Showing students that white people have always benefited from affirmative action exposes the lie this country most often tells, that race is a factor only when people of color are involved. Black arts and black power intellectuals understood that real affirmative action has always been for white people. In the colonial period, the rules governing who could own land deemed whites worthy and disqualified Native Americans who had lived here for generations. Later, "almost all of [the] land [granted under the provisions of the Homestead Act of 1862] was allocated to whites through restrictions expressly designed to deny access to blacks." Therefore, black people are scarce among the more than forty-six million Americans who can trace the origins of their family wealth to that act of Congress. More recently, between 1932 and 1962, "98% of FHA loans . . . went to whites via the openly racist categories utilized in the agency's official manuals for appraisers." Thus, when white parents have a home (or equity) to pass down to their children, it is often from an investment that they would have been prevented from making had they been black. The tax code multiplies the benefit of past discrimination because assets primarily available to white people, such as inheritance income and capital gains, are taxed less, while earnings are taxed more, thereby "lessening the value of income gained through work" (Lipsitz 107). Though students may be resistant, this historical background helps them begin to see that white people have done well in no small part because of government aid.

Consideration of the G.I. Bill makes the point more forcefully because students associate military service with "earning" rights and privileges, but as Katznelson demonstrates, policies were implemented in ways that excluded people of color. Katznelson explains, "With the help of the GI Bill, millions bought homes, attended college, started business ventures, and found jobs commensurate with their skills" (113). However, while "the GI Bill helped to unleash a prosperity never before known" and created "a more middle-class society," it did so "almost exclusively for whites" (114). Though the bill was the first color-blind social legislation (118), the government allowed states to control the administration of every benefit, including education. With local preferences determining the distribution of federal funding, "the veteran status that Black soldiers had *earned* 'was placed at the discretion of parochial intolerance'" (128). Especially in the South, local agencies were resistant to the idea of black citizens benefiting from federal programs. Indeed, local authorities eagerly dashed African Americans' hopes that any status gained through military service and sacrifice would weaken segregation's hold (126). Students notice that the government's willingness to help whites and abandon nonwhites—as recently as their parents' generation—did much to determine the racial composition of the middle class.[1]

Where Is the Love?

Having acknowledged affirmative action for whites, students begin to see that white people hold most of the country's wealth and power, but not necessarily because they are the nation's best and brightest. Suddenly, students can consider the possibility that, likewise, people of color did not earn their reputations as poor decision makers and lazy parasites. In the United States, astonishingly unfair practices determine access to education, wealth, and health care and whether one will live constantly exposed to toxins (Lipsitz 109).

If students can consider how little merit determines white people's economic, social, and political position, they will be more prepared to engage the opening lines of Baraka's theater theory: "The Revolutionary Theatre should force change; it should be change" ("Revolutionary Theatre" 210).[2] Given the country's insistence on affirming whites at the expense of blacks, anything that does not automatically privilege whiteness would constitute change. If the default is to advantage white people and disadvantage others, then whiteness is an unspoken prerequisite for recognition as a United States citizen. Baraka is interested in what it would take to remove that prerequisite.

Love for the Oppressed

Love for oppressed people comes into view with Baraka's declaration that his ideal theater "must Accuse and Attack because it is a theatre of Victims" (211). Such a theater demonstrates love by seeing the people about whom it claims to care. An important part of the nation's violence against those not privileged with whiteness is that the country denies that they are victims at all. The United States limits the life chances of certain populations while declaring that they have equal opportunity. I remind students that, despite having been taught much American history, few (if any) of them had been exposed to readily available facts about the discriminatory distribution of FHA loans and G.I. Bill benefits.

Has not that omission aligned perfectly with our assumptions about who worked to build wealth and who did not? How many more examples of convenient amnesia might there be? Baraka wants to equip his audience to ask those questions. Schools discourage curiosity of this sort, so he wants theater to prompt it.

By recognizing that the United States has victimized and vilified African Americans, revolutionary theater advances ethics because it is ethical to acknowledge injustice. The only thing worse than wronging someone is to do so while denying that their circumstances result from your crimes against them. Yet this is exactly what American society does.

By acknowledging victimization and exploitation, Baraka's theater validates marginalized groups rather than denying their experience and labeling them "misguided" or "unpatriotic" for not accepting mainstream lies. By exposing that which the nation—especially its education system—insists on ignoring, this theater equips audiences to notice the unearned advantage of whiteness. Indeed, Baraka's theater constitutes an assertion of self-worth, a declaration that one deserves the rights that most white people take for granted.

Love for Self-Determination

Baraka's ideal theater moves beyond asserting the worth of those who are oppressed, however; his "theatre of Victims" is also a space for self-determination. Using self-worth as a foundation, Baraka hopes to empower his people to "change the drawing rooms into places where real things can be said about a real world, or into smoky rooms where the destruction of Washington can be plotted" ("Revolutionary Theatre" 212). Here, Baraka suggests the need to bring theatricality's transformative power to amateur and improvised performance spaces, not just professional venues. This is no surprise, given the premium the black arts movement placed on taking art to the streets. Baraka believed that, as with black arts work in other genres, the movement's theatrical efforts must affirm marginalized people outside venues validated by the arts establishment and controlled by mainstream market forces.[3]

"Why destroy Washington, D.C., though?," my students usually ask. Since the capital has been a site for denying the nation's wrongs against certain people and denying their contributions,[4] plotting its destruction demonstrates love for a very American project: self-determination. Rather than remain at the mercy of the powerful, who do not truly see you, you accept that you will have only the life that you are brave enough to create against the worst odds. Self-determination is considered an American principle, so if the United States simply used its own standards to judge black people who assert their worth and work to shape their own destiny, then it would admire them and not withhold opportunity. Instead, the nation chooses hypocrisy by adding the prerequisite of whiteness when deciding whom to respect and recognize as citizens. In other words, the nation punishes black people for seeing themselves as fully American, fully entitled to the same self-determination that is honored in white people.

Love for the Spiritual and the Human

Baraka's theory also insists on the need to transcend any standard based on social categorization, including nationality. More than a love for American self-determination, then, his theory is based on a love for the spiritual. Baraka's ideal theater calls for the destruction of that which denies spiritual supremacy. He declares, "The Revolutionary Theatre must hate [white men] for hating. For presuming with their technology to deny the supremacy of the Spirit" (211).

With what technology is the spirit denied? My students can answer that question because they have learned about the nation's tendency to embrace affirmative action only when it benefits whites.[5] Baraka seems to suggest that when the United States limits black Americans' life chances through social mechanisms it is denying "the supremacy of the Spirit." If African Americans are only what mainstream society says they are, then the nation can expect to treat them according to social hierarchy. However, if African Americans exist in a system of law that transcends social categories, then a justice much higher than that defined by the United States governs them. As Baraka's contemporary Audre Lorde reminds us, "powerlessness" is a "supplied state of being"—supplied by oppressors who want to see marginalized groups as "other," as fundamentally different from themselves ("Uses" 58). By declaring that "technology" is required "to deny the supremacy of the spirit," Baraka insists that differences among people are manufactured.[6] Therefore, as Lorde would later assert, "every oppression must corrupt or distort those various sources of power within the culture of the oppressed that can provide energy for change" ("Uses" 53).

Despite all that the country has taken from them, African Americans have spirit and imagination, and Baraka's theater will help them maximize these resources. Black Americans must understand themselves as spirits not limited by the nation's treatment of them, and they must prize imagination because it is "the projection of ourselves past our sense of ourselves as 'things.'" Baraka's ideal theater performs such a projection by inspiring a visceral reaction.[7] Baraka insists, "And what we show must cause the blood to rush, so that pre-revolutionary temperaments will be bathed in this blood, and it will cause their deepest souls to move, and they find themselves tensed and clenched, even ready to die, at what the soul has been taught" (Baraka, "Revolutionary Theatre" 213).

Because Baraka's revolutionary theater will put black people's spirits on display, he predicts, "Americans will hate the Revolutionary Theatre because it will be out to destroy them and whatever they believe is real. American cops will try to close the theaters where such nakedness of the human spirit is paraded" (214). Those invested in the American status quo do not want African Americans to be empowered by "a theatre of World Spirit. Where the spirit can be shown to be the most competent force in the world. Force. Spirit. Feeling" (212).

Insofar as Baraka's aesthetic privileges spirit and feeling, his ideas align with those later articulated by Audre Lorde, but Baraka's aggressive tone obscures the similarities. Baraka develops his theater theory by positioning himself against mainstream Americanism, what bell hooks calls white supremacist capitalist patriarchy. Nevertheless, because Baraka's theory seeks to assert the kind of power that dominant American culture will recognize, it often replicates that culture's masculinism. Baraka seems to sense the limitations of this strategy, but he cannot quite relinquish it. He admits, "The Revolutionary Theatre is shaped by the world . . ." (212). Providing "daring propaganda for the beauty of the Human Mind" requires that this theater be "a weapon to help in the slaughter of these dimwitted fat-bellied white guys who somehow believe that the rest of the world is here for them to slobber on" (212).

In short, Baraka's theory highlights the contradiction of wanting African American humanity and citizenship to be recognized in a society shaped by white men. He speaks in masculinist language to assert an uncompromising manhood, one that must suppress any emotion other than anger. It is an understandable trap; he reads his surroundings accurately. Baraka understands what the cultural historian Marlon Ross would later articulate: "in modern Western culture, feelings are assumed to be the province of . . . individuals, not social groups—and more tellingly of *vulnerable* individuals who cannot protect themselves, like properly feminine women and improperly effeminate men" (293). Even understanding why Baraka takes a masculinist approach and even seeing that he senses the limitations, my students and I admit that his stance may obscure his investment in spirit and feeling. We therefore consider Audre Lorde's famous caveat: "What does it mean when the tools of a racist patriarchy are used to examine the fruits of that same patriarchy? It means that only the most narrow parameters of change are possible and allowable. . . . *For the master's tools will never dismantle the master's house*" ("Master's Tools" 110–11, 112).

Spirit and Emotion in Dutchman

The tension between Baraka's masculinist discourse and his recognition of the power of spirit and emotion becomes palpable in *Dutchman,* and when it does, black womanhood makes its only appearance—almost in spite of Baraka's masculinist Afrocentrism. Lula describes Clay throughout the action, and when he does not accept her characterizations, she berates him. When Clay finally reaches his limit, he insists that murdering white people would be the truest sign of black sanity. During this tirade, he utters Bessie Smith's name, using her to understand his and his people's predicament.

Suddenly, Clay abandons all decorum and declares,

> [White folks] say, "I love Bessie Smith." And don't even understand that Bessie Smith is saying, "Kiss my ass, kiss my black unruly ass." Before love, suffering, desire, anything you can explain, she's saying, and very plainly, "Kiss my black ass." And if you don't know that, it's you that's doing the kissing. . . . And Bird [Charlie Parker] saying, "Up your ass, feeble-minded ofay! Up your ass." And they sit there talking about the tortured genius of Charlie Parker. Bird would've played not a note of music if he just walked up to East Sixty-seventh Street and killed the first ten white people he saw. Not a note! . . . If Bessie Smith had killed some white people she wouldn't have needed that music. She could have talked very straight and plain about the world. No metaphors. No grunts. . . . Just straight two and two are four. Money. Power. Luxury. Like that. All of them. Crazy niggers turning their backs on sanity. When all it needs is that simple act. Murder. Just murder! Would make us all sane. (34–35)

With these assertions, the play corroborates Angela Davis's assessment of the significance of blues women, their transformation of individual tragedies into touchstones for cultural consciousness. Indeed, even those unfamiliar with the particular hardships that inspired black women's expression nevertheless claimed to identify with the music. Davis explains, "If not for the blues, many individual tragedies affecting black working-class communities might never have been recast as social, collective adversities" (111). The blues are much more than complaint, then; they "articulate a consciousness that takes into account social conditions of class exploitation, racism, and male dominance as seen through the lenses of the complex emotional responses of black female subjects" (119).

Baraka seems unaware of this music's critique of male dominance, but he believes the art form crosses class lines; after all, the play underscores Clay's middle-class status (and presumed distance from most black people), but when he decodes the blues, he claims connection to working-class African Americans. Most important, Clay confirms Davis's observation that "the blues idiom requires absolute honesty" (107), and he insists that such honesty is unacceptable to those in power. Also, because Clay uses Bessie Smith's seemingly straightforward, lyric-based music to contextualize Charlie Parker's saxophone playing, Baraka echoes James Baldwin. In 1951, Baldwin argued, "It is only in music, which Americans are able to admire because a protective sentimentality limits their understanding of it, that the American Negro has been able to tell his story." The story, Baldwin added, has been told "in symbols and signs, in hieroglyphics" ("Many" 19). In other words, the blues are popular with white audiences only because the music articulates black reality using symbols and signs—"metaphors" and "grunts"—that white people do not actually comprehend.

When Clay analyzes his plight (and Charlie Parker's) through the lens of Bessie Smith, he claims a connection to working-class blacks, allows himself emotional affirmation, and decodes the blues. However, just as quickly, he retreats from the truth he speaks: "[*Suddenly weary*] Ahhh. Shit. But who needs it? I'd rather be a fool. Insane. Safe with my words, and no deaths" (35). By then, it is too late. Lula will soon murder him. Thus, black truth cannot be told plainly, lest those empowered to give or take life (and American opportunity) hear and understand. Clay is most in danger when he is most willing to translate the emotional truth that artists like Bessie Smith disguised with metaphors and grunts.

By reading "The Revolutionary Theatre" as theory and by looking for the love that drives it, my students and I uncover what Baraka never seems to appreciate directly: black female energy. We admit the damage that his masculinist preoccupations do to black women, but we do not use it to overlook what he does not feel safe acknowledging outright. Wanting desperately to be master, he uses the master's tools, but blues women's subversions nevertheless shine through, having worked on him too.

NOTES

[1] Also see Coates.

[2] Quotations from "Revolutionary Theatre" are taken from the Morrow edition of Baraka's *Home*.

[3] To help students understand the power of theatricality outside traditional theater spaces, I emphasize the role of performance in everyday life. Performance is any embodied practice that creates and conveys meaning, and it almost inevitably affirms our identities. A person who cooks will find that the repetition reinforces their self-conception. Their ease with "props" like pots and pans can bolster this part of their identity. Similarly, when a schoolteacher's behavior suggests that they see you more as a disciplinary problem than as a learner, the performance has an effect on both the student's and the teacher's identities. To be even more concrete, I highlight for students how the "setting" of the university and the arrangement of the classroom lends to my performance as an educator; how my clothing choices ("costumes") affect my performance whether it should or not; how their behaviors can lend to a performance as a voracious learner or not.

[4] Here, I urge students to think of the nation's capital as a setting for performances that create and convey meaning. They easily understand the procedures they see on C-SPAN as performances. And the resulting legislation underscores what the powerful deemed important to enact or not important enough to change. Students appreciate seeing the link between performance and material outcomes for people's lives, and they soon provide their own examples. For those who become more interested, I share ideas from Augusto Boal's *Theatre of the Oppressed*. Boal urged collapsing the barrier between actor and audience, and his techniques allow people to rehearse resistance to oppressive situations so that, when they encounter them in real life, they will have

already imagined empowered responses. Rather than the catharsis for audiences that Aristotle prized in tragedy, Boal valued creating circumstances in which "spect-actors" maximized "rehearsal." Boal's techniques help individuals see the world in ways that both expose oppressive forces and equip individuals to believe that they can alter their experiences of those forces—through their performances in daily life.

[5] Also see my "Supreme Court Agrees with Michigan Voters: Affirmative Action Must Remain for Whites Only."

[6] To underscore Baraka's investment in exposing the manufactured nature of social categories, I invoke Diana Taylor's theater theory, especially her concept of the "scenario." As Taylor explains, a scenario is a well-worn sketch or outline of action. Because it "resuscitates and reactivates old dramas," "the scenario makes visible, yet again, what is already there: the ghosts, the images, the stereotypes." Thus, a scenario "structures our understanding," and "because we've seen it all before," it can do so even if there are omissions (28). Because the United States has so relentlessly cast white people as contributors to society and everyone else as leeches, it does not take much to reinforce these ideas. I guide students in a conversation about how rarely negative stereotypes cling to white people. That's no accident; that too demonstrates the power of scenario.

[7] This emphasis on visceral reaction puts Baraka's theater theory in conversation with James Baldwin's interest in what I term "flesh-centered imaginative work." However, because Baraka is confident that white people will respond only with anger, his theory diverges from Baldwin's. See my "James Baldwin, Performance Theorist, Sings the *Blues for Mister Charlie*."

CULTURAL INTERPLAYS

"Free of Your Own History": Implicating Students in *Dutchman*

Andrew Sargent

> And we'll pretend . . . that you are free of your own history. And I am free of my history.
>
> —Baraka, *Dutchman*

My reading of *Dutchman* hinges on the idea that Amiri Baraka's play delivers a warning, to blacks and whites alike, that it may be impossible to escape America's tortured racial history. The crux of my argument is that the sexually charged conflict between Clay and Lula dramatizes how racial stereotypes and sexual myths fatally script interracial relations and, moreover, how those forces thwart black attempts to assert individual identities that might exist beyond white-constructed stereotypes. Read today, the play seems to imply that despite the promise of living in a "postracial" America, there may be no easy way to move past three centuries' worth of racial sins.

That such a reading runs counter to the worldview held by many of my students makes *Dutchman* a challenging, if also deeply rewarding, text to teach in the undergraduate classroom. Over the last several years of discussing Baraka's play with students of various ethnic, racial, and class backgrounds, I have been struck by how many seem to feel that they are (to paraphrase Lula in the above epigraph) "free" of the historical legacies of slavery, Jim Crow, and other forms of institutionalized racial oppression. They do not see their identities as overdetermined by forces beyond their immediate personal control but instead believe that their lives move forward largely by their own individual choices.

I suspect that this distancing from history goes hand in hand with a feeling of being safely outside the gravitational pull of *Dutchman* itself. Indeed, like many of the play's early reviewers, students often find *Dutchman*'s depiction of mid-twentieth-century racial tensions to be so melodramatic and artificial as to be almost ridiculous. They dismiss Anthony Harvey's 1966 film adaptation, which I often screen in my classes, as especially dated and contrived. A few years ago, in an introductory literature class, one student exclaimed that the film was "the stupidest movie [he'd] ever seen," in part deriding Harvey's arguably stagey filmmaking but also announcing his own sense of superiority to what he perceived to be the play's prehistoric and irrelevant concept of race relations.

Given such reactions, one of my central goals in teaching *Dutchman* is to implicate students in the racial history that Lula (at the end of scene 1) facetiously invites Clay to forget. What, if anything, does this admittedly strange text—with its stylized stage directions, violent denouement, and sexually provocative but mystifying dialogue—say about American race relations that might be valuable to students today?

I begin by asking my students to be open to the possibility that *Dutchman*, despite its strangeness, may only appear to be far removed from their own lived experience. I suggest that the play speaks to us if we make ourselves available to it—through class discussion, close reading, and creative interpretation. I am aided in this effort by competing reactions from a less dismissive set of students: those who are unsure of what *Dutchman* might mean but who try eagerly to interpret it. They are intrigued, even awed, by Baraka's abrasive lyricism, Lula's crazed antics, and the play's vision of race relations as a hostile battle of the sexes. Taking my cue from both these responses, I ask students to engage in two interconnected critical processes: first, to grapple with a literary text of mysterious power in a way that promises to build their confidence as readers and critics, and, second, to grapple with the dominant historical scripts of American race and sex relations in a way that makes us not free of those scripts but critically informed enough to understand and challenge their lingering influence.

Dutchman's power and brevity make it remarkably viable for any kind of course and teachable in a limited number of class meetings. I have assigned *Dutchman* in introductory literature courses, African American literature surveys, a senior seminar on the literature and culture of the civil rights and black power era, and others. In all these classes, I start by writing two questions on the board: "What underlying comments is Baraka's play making about race and sex in America, and how does his play make them?" and "Who or what are the play's primary targets of critique?" While initial student answers are provisional, I leave the questions on the board and promise that we will build deeper responses to them as we move through the text.

One practical way to spark a class discussion on *Dutchman* is simply to ask, "Who is Clay?" and "Who is Lula?" These questions provide students an accessible point of entry by giving them a chance to volunteer notable character traits and memorable lines of dialogue. This brainstorming exercise eases students into making more sophisticated critical evaluations of Lula and Clay and uncovering some of the larger thematic and ideological issues generated by these characters. Students flummoxed by Lula's sexual and racial manipulations of Clay, for example, often express how "unrelatable" (their word) she is as a character; her provocations seem so brazen, and her character so devoid of inner life or personal history, that she hardly even strikes them as human. But implicit in this reaction is the possibility that Lula is not meant to be human but rather to operate as any or all of the following: a grotesque caricature of white womanhood warped by the American rape complex; "a metaphor for America," as Baraka himself once put it (qtd. in McGee A7); the monstrous embodiment of American racism; or a duplicitous yet truth-telling catalyst for Clay's own political transformation.[1] I have also listened as a seemingly minor detail such as Lula's age—she is thirty years old and thus ancient by undergraduate standards—prompts students to feel sympathy for her, not only as a desperate "cougar" (again, their word), but also as a casualty, like Clay himself, of America's warped fantasies about race and sex.

It may seem self-evident that a close attention to the details of these characters must be matched by a careful investigation of the play's language. But Baraka the writer is, for better or worse, preceded by his reputation as a black arts movement ideologue. So it bears emphasizing that *Dutchman*'s language is highly—even flamboyantly—literary. There is not a single line in the play that isn't interesting in some way, and it is precisely this literary quality that beckons students to engage in imaginative close reading.[2] One of the most compelling lines we linger over is Baraka's enigmatic statement, in an early stage direction, that the subway is "heaped in modern myth" (3). I ask students how, if they were directing a production of *Dutchman*, they might represent this "myth" visually on stage. (We agree that it would be difficult to do so.) The line also prompts a discussion of just what myths Baraka might be referring to. As we consider how hard it would be for two individuals to achieve intimacy when pressed down by a "heap" of racial stereotypes (about, for example, black manhood, rape, and white womanhood), I observe that our own hesitancy even to verbalize these stereotypes suggests how we, too, are heaped in modern myth and burdened by anxiety about racial difference. The "modern myth" line also frequently sparks a spirited consideration of the significance of the subway setting. What are the distinguishing features of a subway? How is it different from, say, a car? What sorts of social relations does it structure? What mileage—dramatic, thematic, or otherwise—does Baraka gain from using the subway as the site of his play's action? In what way is the subway car's circular journey a metaphor for the circularity and repetition in American race relations?

To anchor these questions in the historical and cultural contexts of Baraka's play, I ask students to research and deliver in-class presentations on topics such as Scottsboro, Emmett Till, lynching, and other touchstones that bring to light the intricacies of the Southern rape complex. One recent student presentation in my Civil Rights/Black Power Era seminar focused on two well-known photographs of Emmett Till—the before shot of a smiling Till posing next to his mother, and the after shot of Till's mutilated corpse lying in an open casket. The student argued that the shocking contrast between these two images compels us to confront the social and cultural pathologies that led to Till's lynching, in much the same way that Clay's own shocking murder prompts us to acknowledge the price that African American men have historically paid for stepping out of their assigned places in a white-controlled racial and sexual order. Arming students with a knowledge of the history of race, rape, and lynching in America—by screening the PBS documentary *Scottsboro: An American Tragedy* (2000), for example, or directing them to consult James Allen's chilling book of lynching photographs, *Without Sanctuary* (2000)—enables them to consider how *Dutchman* compresses and reenacts this charged history in unexpected ways. Clay's embarrassed reaction to his sexual interest in Lula at the start of the play evidences the weight of this history on the black male psyche; Lula's eventual murder of Clay becomes a kind of lynching, in which a white woman wields the power to cause a black man's death while posing as an innocent victim of black male aggression and enlisting a mob to dispose of the black man's offending body.[3]

Students in my Civil Rights/Black Power Era seminar have also contextualized *Dutchman* by giving biographical presentations on Baraka, focusing on the author's personal and political transformation from beat poet to black nationalist in the mid-1960s. This background enables us to read *Dutchman* as a site of transition from the integrationist ethos of the civil rights movement to the more separatist discourse of the black power era. Students are always intrigued to discover that Clay's newfound militancy by the end of the play presages the author's own evolution from LeRoi Jones to Amiri Baraka and his divorce from his (white Jewish) first wife, Hettie Jones.

Still another means of contextualizing *Dutchman* is to teach it in dialogue with other key black texts that, like Baraka's play, depict encounters between black men and white women. In my own courses, this list has included Richard Wright's *Native Son* (1940) (or, when space is limited, "Big Boy Leaves Home" [1936]); Chester Himes's *If He Hollers Let Him Go* (1945); selections from *The Autobiography of Malcolm X* (1965) and Eldridge Cleaver's *Soul on Ice* (1968); and Alice Walker's "Advancing Luna—and Ida B. Wells" (1981). These texts, which replicate but also complicate the black man–white woman dynamic at the heart of *Dutchman*, affirm Baraka's shared belief with other black writers in the centrality of race, rape, and sex to understanding the historically precarious position of black men in America.

I have also assigned my students several touchstone texts of 1960s white liberalism that wrestle, in some cases evasively, with the same racial and sexual taboos that *Dutchman* audaciously confronts: Harper Lee's *To Kill a Mockingbird* (1960), John Howard Griffin's *Black Like Me* (1961), and the Hollywood romantic drama *Guess Who's Coming to Dinner* (1967). In my Civil Rights/Black

Power Era seminar, in fact, I assign *Guess Who's Coming to Dinner* on the same day as *Dutchman*, thus positioning these two texts as unlikely companion pieces with a shared focus on the romantic and sexual attraction between a middle-class black man and a white woman. Students unearth several intriguing parallels, particularly that *Dutchman* and *Guess Who's Coming* reveal how white fantasies about African American males act as straitjackets on black identity. Just as Clay must endure Lula's taunt that he is "a well-known type" (12), Sidney Poitier, the leading black film star of the 1960s, had to endure the limitations of conforming to Hollywood's narrow vision of nonthreatening black masculinity. Many of the students who earlier viewed *Dutchman* as artificial now observe that the slickly produced Poitier film feels like a hypercontrived depiction of interracial love, one that seemingly celebrates love's power to overcome racism but then emasculates its black lead and places all authority in the hands of a white male patriarch (Spencer Tracy) thrown into crisis by his daughter's desire to marry a black man. I suggest that *Dutchman*, in contrast, intentionally calls attention to its own artifice in order to reveal something else: namely, the inescapably performative nature of American race relations, in which blacks and whites carry out prescripted roles in stock situations shaped by hundreds of years of racial and sexual oppression. (To illustrate *Dutchman*'s self-conscious artificiality, I remind students of the stage direction in which Baraka states that the subway lights can be treated "as admitted props" [3] and of Clay's remark that his exchange with Lula is a "pageant" [37].) I add that while *Dutchman* critiques the overdetermining power of these racial scripts, *Guess Who's Coming to Dinner* timidly conforms to them.[4]

Our discussion of black masculinity in the cultural and political turmoil of the 1960s—and the ways in which Clay both adheres to and breaks from the Poitier screen persona—turns inevitably to Clay's explosive monologue at the end of the play. I usually set aside a large block of class time for a close reading of this long passage, as students often appear reticent to tackle the speech's raw language and racial essentialism, as well as Baraka's apparent contention that black art is a secret means of sublimating African Americans' desire to murder whites. I have seen white students unsettled by the play's suggestion that Clay's angry persona somehow represents true blackness, and I have seen African American students question the implication that blacks who fail to meet Baraka's rigid standards of racial authenticity are automatically race traitors.

A close reading of Clay's rhetoric can, and should, lead to a broader discussion of his speech's significance to the play as a whole: if Clay's venting of rage marks his turn toward the black nationalism that Baraka endorses (and that Lula has goaded Clay to adopt), then what is the value of Clay's metamorphosis when he is later murdered? In other words, does Baraka's killing of Clay cancel out the self-empowerment that Clay might derive from his speech? Or is the monologue's primary function to speak to an audience beyond the text?

These questions have elicited much thoughtful reflection. Some students argue that Clay's violent death renders him a cautionary tale about the dangers facing black men (like Martin Luther King, Jr., and Malcolm X) who speak truth to power. Others contend that Clay's speech lives on after his physical demise and thus encourages the audience to take up his mantle. Still others posit that Clay's problem is not so much that he speaks out but that he has waited so long to do so—and, even then, only after being driven to it by Lula. By letting Lula dictate his identity and history, Clay allows himself to be stripped of any real identity at all. In this line of thinking, students see Clay's murder as a comment on the barriers facing African American men who wish to achieve complex human identities that exist beyond racial stereotypes. While Baraka suggests that Clay's explosion might be an authentic expression of his own personal rage—a dispatch from Clay's "pumping black heart" (34)—the text also implies that Clay's anger is a result, or even a construct, of Lula's manipulations. Even as Clay no longer conforms to the "Uncle Tom" (32) label that Lula affixed to him, his spontaneous outburst gives Lula an opening to typecast him as a menacing black male threat to white womanhood. Thus by play's end, Clay has done little more than move laterally within a framework of predetermined racial types fashioned for him by Lula.

In recent semesters, I have had students compare Clay's dilemma to Barack Obama's own apparent effort to avoid being stereotyped as an angry black man in his public speeches and debates. We consider that Clay might, not unlike President Obama, believe sincerely in the possibility of living in a postracial America but finds that his interactions with Lula are almost completely shaped by race. *Dutchman* implies that we are foolish to think we live in a color-blind society; read in the context of the Obama era, the play challenges the notion that the election of America's first black president automatically resolves the country's longstanding racial problems.[5]

My students' ambivalence toward Clay allows us to see him as a victim not only of white racism but also of his willing accommodation to white normative judgments. Some students feel it unfair to label Clay a "sellout" simply because he wears a suit, and they suspect that Baraka is being too hard on his protagonist, essentially trapping Clay in a reductive version of black masculinity just as Lula does. Others point out that Clay should never have gotten involved with Lula in the first place, as his attraction to her only reinforces the dangerous myth that black men are inexorably drawn to white women. I ask students to consider that Clay's biggest mistake may be his willingness to let Lula force-feed him her false version of racial history; he lets Lula type him, or (as his name suggests) mold him, with false labels that elide his own complex struggles and the larger historical intricacies of black experience.

Our careful consideration of Clay's—and Lula's—culpability in Clay's demise leads us, inescapably, to consider our own accountability. Returning to the aforementioned list of Baraka's "targets of critique" (still on the board), we begin to understand that in *Dutchman*, no one gets away clean; everyone, perhaps especially the audience, becomes a target of Baraka's critique. One of the class's most interesting revelations comes when we see ourselves allegorized in

Baraka's subway passengers; as the audience watching the play, we, too, remain passive bystanders who do nothing to intervene in the racial and sexual "pageant" playing out before our eyes. This idea prompts students to consider the moral cost of remaining compliant spectators (as the subway riders are) to racial role-playing. The text implies that, like Clay and Lula, we, too, are not yet free from our country's controlling racial myths, even as exploring *Dutchman* has enabled us to see those myths with a more critical eye.

This sort of revelation can discomfit my students (as perhaps it should). White students in my classes have admitted to dim stirrings of racial guilt or shame after reading the play, while others deny accountability for America's oppressive racial history. Some African American students have rightly challenged the implication that persons of color must always be hamstrung by history, as Clay is, even as they remain disturbed by the acquiescence shown by the black subway passengers visible in the film version of *Dutchman*. Building on these reactions, I suggest that coming to an awareness of one's vexed relation to America's racial history need not be an occasion for feeling merely guilt, anger, or exhaustion. Rather, the realizations we reach in class can generate an empowering critical agency, one that derives from seeing ourselves represented—even implicated—in Baraka's text. In his 1965 essay "The White Man's Guilt," James Baldwin writes that even as "the great force of history comes from the fact that we . . . are unconsciously controlled by it in many ways," it is nonetheless our task to "assess the history which has placed one where one is" and to "attempt to achieve a level of personal maturity and freedom which robs history of its tyrannical power, and also changes history" (723). By offering us a vision of what can happen when we allow ourselves to become passive subway passengers—unconsciously controlled by the great force of history—*Dutchman* exhorts us to resist the scripts that structure Clay and Lula's encounter and that shape race relations even today. If we are all figuratively riding around in circles on a subway heaped in modern racial and sexual myths, then my hope, as a teacher, is that our own capacity for critiquing those myths—honed by discussion and analysis of Baraka's short, shattering play—might enable us to step off the train and begin the hard work of disrupting that pernicious cycle.[6]

NOTES

[1] Baraka's construction of Lula as a grotesque manifestation of whiteness also provides students and instructors an opportunity to read *Dutchman* through the lens of critical whiteness studies—and to consider more broadly the way African American writers have long engaged in what Stephanie Li calls "pointed stud[ies] of whiteness" (*Playing* 158). How do black writers represent whites and whiteness, and to what ends? Li's *Playing in the White* (2015) and Veronica Watson's *The Souls of White Folk* (2013) provide two recent scholarly examples of this approach.

[2] The outdated image of Baraka and other black arts movement writers as racial essentialists lacking artistic complexity has been amply refuted by recent scholarship on the

black arts movement, including Nilgün Anadolu-Okur's "Drama and Performance from Civil Rights to Black Arts" (2015), Amy Abugo Ongiri's *Spectacular Blackness* (2010), Lisa Gail Collins and Margo Natalie Crawford's *New Thoughts on the Black Arts Movement* (2006), and James Smethurst's *The Black Arts Movement* (2005). The movement's recuperated standing is also evident in the most recent edition of *The Norton Anthology of African American Literature* (Gates and Smith); volume 2 contains expanded and highly informative headnotes on both Baraka (660–65) and the black arts movement (533–61). In the critical framework established by these resources, *Dutchman*'s remarkable literary quality becomes a characteristic feature of black arts movement writing rather than an exception to it.

[3]The dynamics of race, rape, sex, and lynching in American culture have been amply theorized by contemporary critics and historians; among the most notable texts are Patricia Hill Collins's *Black Sexual Politics* (2004; 261–68) and Robyn Wiegman's *American Anatomies* (1995; 81–113). Teachers might also direct students to such classic analyses as Calvin Hernton's *Sex and Racism in America* (1965) and especially W. J. Cash's *The Mind of the South* (1941), which originated the term "rape complex" (115).

[4]In a sense, *Dutchman* both interrogates the politics of interracial performance and, in Clay, participates in the cultural construction of black masculinity during the civil rights and black power era. Indeed, both Clay and Poitier exemplify how African American men performed various kinds of racial masculinities—and in turn sought to achieve various forms of racial authenticity—during the shift from civil rights to black power in the mid- to late 1960s. Instructors looking for theoretical and historical contexts for interpreting these issues might consult Steve Estes's *I Am a Man! Race, Manhood, and the Civil Rights Movement* (2005) and E. Patrick Johnson's *Appropriating Blackness* (2003). Soyica Diggs Colbert's more recent study, *The African American Theatrical Body* (2011), suggests how the black stage itself might operate as an empowering site of both literal and figurative black performance.

[5]*Dutchman*'s sharp rebuke to the idea of a postracial America offers students a powerful lens for interpreting the racial dynamics of the Obama era. If the postracial is, as Stephanie Li has argued, "another iteration of the misguided aspiration for 'color blindness,' a way to ignore both the historical legacy of race and its abiding influence on all aspects of social life" (*Signifying* 3), then *Dutchman*'s skepticism that Americans could ever be "free of [their] history" might be a prescient critique of the premature postracial euphoria that, in some quarters, greeted Obama's election in 2008. The play might also be credited with anticipating the veiled racial hostility that frequently confronted Obama throughout his two terms in office. In addition to Li's *Signifying without Specifying* (2011), critiques of postracial discourse since Obama's election include Colson Whitehead's "The Year of Living Postracially" (2009) and Peniel Joseph's "Our National Postracial Hangover" (2009).

[6]The urgency of this work—and, it should be said, students' receptiveness to engaging in it—has undoubtedly been intensified by the emergence of Black Lives Matter as a national movement in 2014 and the increased public attention to the longstanding problem of police brutality against African Americans. The publication of Michelle Alexander's influential *The New Jim Crow* (2010) has also prompted students to reflect more deeply on issues of racial bias and injustice in contemporary America. In this changed—and charged—racial climate, *Dutchman*'s critical insights about imperiled black masculinity and the durability of oppressive racial scripts are likely to seem more relevant and compelling to students now than they would have only a few short years ago.

Reading *Dutchman*'s Setting

Richard Schur

Man, this subway is slow.

—Baraka, *Dutchman*

When I first started teaching African American literature survey courses, I relied primarily on chronology to organize them. I began with slave narratives and ended with the civil rights movement. My students tended to experience the course as a journey from slavery to freedom. Looking back on my early attempts to teach African American literature, I realize that covering such a wide range of eras, writers, and themes resulted in a fairly uncritical and overly simplistic account of African American literary history. The course became too much of a triumphalist narrative in which literature and society progress as racism recedes. More recently, I have been trying to cover fewer texts but to examine them more thoroughly to reveal the complexity and nuance of African American literature and culture. I have found that Amiri Baraka's *Dutchman* can illuminate several important aspects of African American literary history. In this essay, my goal is to show how teachers and students may read the play's subway car setting as a site of shifting attitudes and perspectives about integration and desegregation.

Dutchman can be assigned as either the first or last reading in a survey course to help introduce or summarize the class's main themes. The play's allegorical structure is deceptively simple, especially for students new to the study of African American literature. Moreover, the characters seem increasingly remote and strange to students. For me, the play's setting on a subway train is the key to Baraka's thinking about the tradition of black writing. Unfortunately, my students rarely take much notice of the setting or see the dialogue as anything other than an almost surreal conversation between a crazy white woman and a deluded African American man.

My first step in teaching in the play is to ask students to read the text out loud, which we can usually do in one class period. I usually have a few students interested in theater, and they enjoy getting into the roles.[1] As a class, we laugh at its humor and have a good time with it. While students want to talk about the symbol of the apple, Lula's strange interest in Clay, Clay's initial cluelessness, and his eventual murder, I try to defer those conversations and ask why Baraka set his play on a subway car. Usually there is not much of a response, although sometimes a student will make a connection to the Underground Railroad or segregation on public transportation. A great way to engage students in the text is to ask them to research the role of railroads in African American life and to think about the real similarities and symbolic affinities between railroads and urban subway systems. I ask students to read studies of the Underground Railroad, John Henry, *Plessy v. Ferguson*, African American laborers laying track in the South, Pullman porters, A. Philip Randolph, the Scottsboro Boys, the Great Migration, trains in black music (gospel, blues, and jazz), and subway graffiti in New York City.[2]

Such research deepens students' sense of African American history and helps them think in more concrete terms about how racial hierarchy worked during the late nineteenth century and much of the twentieth century. Railroads were linked with modernity, especially mass migration and the freedom involved in such movement. The research assignments show students that, for African Americans, railroads were identified with both new freedoms and new restrictions.[3] By no means did this new technology transform social relations completely; under the force of existing racist attitudes, the railroad generally respected the color line. This research is eye-opening for students, for they have not thought about the many ways that trains symbolize modernity for African Americans. Moreover, the research helps students clarify the differences between the interstate railroad and the urban subway system, which then helps them understand why the play takes place on a subway car.

Because I am interested in generating a collaborative account of the complex and contradictory history of trains in African American life, I ask students to report their findings orally. Once the presentations are completed, I have them develop a hypothesis or main idea about how trains have functioned in African American culture. Pretty quickly, students can see there is a significant gap between the hope for freedom embodied in railroads and the reality of working on or riding on a train.[4] Sometimes, it can take a while for students to see trains as a locus of social contradiction and struggle because many want to reduce them to either symbols of hope or examples of racial oppression.[5] I want my class to consider Baraka's insistence on the ambiguous and liminal nature of trains as potential vehicles for social change: vehicles that have left the station but not yet reached their destination. The subway is fitting for an exploration of the paradox of progress because, unlike the railroad, which allows riders to leave their town or state, the subway tends to travel in circles within a single city. Subway riders never escape their locations. And because the subway is associated with the urban North, *Dutchman*'s setting questions the grand social narrative wherein African American life in the northern city is a life beyond the reach of racism.

More than just focusing on the role of trains in African American life, my exploration of *Dutchman* asks students to reflect on the role of modern technology. Frequently, techno-optimists assert that new technologies—from the mass-production of consumer goods to the rise of the internet and cell phones—inevitably improve the quality of social life and make people freer and more equal. The class discussion about trains questions this narrative. The technology of the railroad promised an escape from racism and segregation. At the same time, migration created social conflict between those who liked the existing racial order and those who wished to escape it. In addition, existing racial attitudes frequently shaped how trains were incorporated into a segregated America. *Dutchman*'s subway car is a concrete symbol of the promise and failure of modernity to transform American social relations.

While many Americans saw the train's potential to change the American cultural and political landscape, the civil rights movement of the 1950s and 1960s created hope that racism could be dismantled through acts of civil disobedience, marches, and civil rights litigation. The next step in teaching the play is therefore to locate it within the history of the civil rights movement. My students, born now in the mid- to late 1990s, frequently want to read the play as a predecessor to Martin Luther King, Jr., the NAACP litigation strategy, and the mass demonstrations of the 1950s. Of course, this rewrites history, framing Baraka and the black arts movement as forerunners of the civil rights movement, rather than its critics. In other words, by reading *Dutchman* as a text that prepared blacks and whites to challenge Jim Crow, the students protect the civil rights movement from criticism. Focusing on trains as a contested site of modernity, I ask students how the play illustrates the limits of the civil rights movement's strategy for social change. At this point in the class conversation, I show how the play comments on integration as only a partial solution to the problem of white supremacy. In particular, students examine three moments in the play: (1) the description of the setting, (2) the symbol of the apple, and (3) the appearance of the conductor at the play's end.

Armed with their research and ready to reread the play as a commentary on 1960s race relations, we return to the play's opening lines: "*In the flying underbelly of the city. Steaming hot, and summer on top, outside. Underground. The subway heaped in modern myth*" (3). I have the students reflect on a key descriptor here: "Underground." This word, along with "flying," "subway," and "modern myth," I tell students, provides some important clues for understanding how Baraka constructs his modern allegory about race relations. A typical class will jump at the word "[u]nderground" and observe that it evokes the Underground Railroad. In response, I ask the students to think about how the Underground Railroad relates to a scene on a New York subway train in the mid-1960s. At first, students struggle with this question. Through some nudging, though, they see that Baraka is comparing Clay's effort to navigate the dangers of interracial sex to the flight from slavery. If I am teaching the play at the end of my African American literature course, I can draw comparisons between Clay and Frederick Douglass or between Clay and Harriet Jacobs, the authors of the two slave narratives that I teach most frequently. As one might expect, some students resist such comparisons because Clay is ostensibly free. Others, however, view the analogy as apt because Clay seems fairly guarded and suspicious early in his conversation with Lula. Lula claims to know his destination (a party thrown by his friend Warren). Clay, however, assumes that Lula must have some angle or interest in him. Clay distrusts Lula and fears that she is setting a trap. At this point, a student will usually question the comparison because Clay's freedom does not appear to be endangered and there are no slave catchers or owners in the story. Without much intervention on my part, students begin debating whether Lula functions as a slave catcher or owner. If we have read *Incidents in the Life of a Slave Girl* (1861), they will usually make the case that interracial sex and rape was a key part of slavery. Sometimes, I also draw a connection to train lyrics in blues songs, many of which deal with love gone bad. Other times, I will talk about how African American musicians, from the 1920s through the 1950s, used the sound of trains and train horns in their compositions to link musical innovation and racial freedom. Connecting *Dutchman* to this rich legacy of train allusions and meanings helps students see the play's setting as very intentional and indeed historically overdetermined.

At this point, I shift the discussion to *Dutchman's* allegorical reenactment of Genesis. When Lula appears onstage for the first time, "she is eating an apple, very daintily. Coming down the car toward Clay" (5). As the pair's conversation reveals almost immediately, Baraka wants audiences to understand Clay and Lula as a modern-day Adam and Eve. I ask students to identify the ways that Baraka recalls and reenacts the Adam and Eve story and explain how an urban subway train can be understood as a Garden of Eden.[6] Not surprisingly, the first task is much easier than the second, and students enjoy analyzing the play as a commentary on, or parody of, the biblical story. Students eagerly point out how the play's sexual tension echoes the original story. They have no problem identifying Lula as a modern-day Eve. I also note that the name Clay seems connected to the name Adam, which means "earth" in Hebrew. Some students question why Baraka relies on such a conventional view of women as temptresses. More than one of my classes has argued that the play reinforces stereotypical gender norms. Usually, one or two students will respond that some white women did play this role in Southern life (especially if we have read Sterling Brown's "Frankie and Johnny" [1932] earlier in the semester) and defend Baraka.

Eventually, we find ourselves discussing a key passage from the play:

> LULA. Come on, Clay. Let's rub bellies on the train. The nasty. The nasty. Do the gritty grind, like your ol' rag-head mammy. Grind till you lose your mind. Shake it, shake it, shake it, shake it! OOOOweee! Come on, Clay. Let's do the choo-choo train shuffle, the navel scratcher.
>
> CLAY. Hey, you coming on like the lady who smoked up her grass skirt. (31)

Here Lula becomes both Eve and the snake, tempting Clay to partake from the tree of knowledge. Typically, students point out that trains provide even some of the metaphors for sex. I then have students explore why sex gets framed in such terms and how the escapes that trains offered African Americans are imaginatively identified with both sexual release and sexual freedom. That the struggle for freedom was about more than civil rights produces epiphanies for contemporary students. Students can see that those who fought for equality and freedom were not simply high-minded idealists but real people.

I observe, however, that *Dutchman* diverges from the biblical story because Clay does not have sex with Lula. I stress that Clay's refusal to have sex is a renunciation of integration, or at least a simple-minded integration, as a solution to America's racism. Yet students always want to know why Clay must perish if he does not actually taste of the forbidden fruit. They ask why Clay is not free. This is another tough question, but it helps me shift the conversation back to the subway setting. I now ask students to patiently work through the failed comparison between the subway and the Garden of Eden. At first blush, the play seems to suggest that desegregation constitutes a new Garden of Eden or ideal social order. What Baraka shows, however, is that integration may not be quite the Eden it appears.

Rather, because subways are constructed underground, Baraka's putative Eden is more like a level of hell. This reading, of course, surprises and confuses many students. They have been taught that integration, especially as imagined by King, was the cure for America's ills. Moreover, the play suggests that it is whites who have nefarious motives for crossing racial lines—motives that may have little to do with social equality. Toward the play's end, Clay announces, "I guess I better collect my stuff and get off this train" (37). Of course, Lula will not let Clay exit, and she murders him. Her actions stun and surprise students, so much so that they want to frame her as crazy or some sort of lunatic. My job, however, is to make students grapple with her symbolic role. Because of the play's allegorical nature, it would be a mistake to ascribe her actions to a psychological illness. Lula represents the crazed longings and desires of white America. I use students' reactions to encourage them to look back through the course materials or read the semester's texts carefully to see how African American writers represent white desire. In some semesters, I ask students to compare Lula to one or more of the following white characters: Mrs. Ellsworth in Langston Hughes's "The Blues I'm Playing" (1934), Mary Dalton in Richard Wright's *Native Son* (1940), or Schoolteacher in Toni Morrison's *Beloved* (1987). *Dutchman*'s subway setting prompts us to consider whether integration has produced racial progress or if whites still act and think in ways that sustain white supremacy even after the end of formal segregation.

Before leaving the play, I interrogate its closing image with my students. For most of them, the dancing conductor is an afterthought and an enigma. The stage directions describe him as follows:

> *Then an Old Negro conductor comes into the car, doing a sort of restrained soft shoe, and half mumbling, the words of some song. He looks at the young man, briefly, with a quick greeting. . . . The conductor continues down the aisle with his little dance and the mumbled songs. Lula turns to stare at him and follows his movements down the aisle. The conductor tips his hat when he reaches her seat, and continues out of the car.*
>
> (37–38)

Students typically pay little attention to him and instead focus on the suggestion that Lula has found her next victim. But I push them to explain why the old African American man is needed here. I want them to see that, through this figure, Baraka once again links the encounter between Clay and Lula to a more expansive historical drama of black modernity. My students see that the word "conductor" links the man to the "conductors" on the Underground Railroad, most notably Harriet Tubman. I hope others will identify the character as a representation of Pullman porters and other African American laborers. We then discuss whether this conductor seems poised to challenge racial inequality or simply to work and maintain the status quo. Most students say that he does not intervene; they note that he "tips his hat" to Lula, as if he regards her as an honorable woman.

Here I connect the description of the "Old Negro" to the Harlem Renaissance's critique of stereotyped imagery of African Americans. For Alain Locke and his peers, the Harlem Renaissance revealed how migration and urban living were transforming the "Old Negro" into the "New Negro" (6). Migration, according to Locke, signified a rejection of the old myths about African American identity and an embrace of a new identity: the New Negro. My students, however, point out that Baraka's play seems to comment or signify on Locke's pronouncements because the "Old Negro" provides the closing image in the play and the "New Negro"—represented by Clay and the unnamed young man—is doomed. Through our discussion, my students realize that Baraka's use of the "Old Negro conductor" suggests that race relations have not been radically transformed and that the old stereotypes still circulate.

Although readers and critics have overlooked it on occasion, *Dutchman*'s train setting and imagery is crucial to its critique of Jim Crow and the civil rights era's progress narrative. The play complicates the idea of trains as symbolic of technological progress and increased social mobility. Sometimes, technology is constrained by existing biases and inequalities. Similarly, migration can mean merely trading one unjust social order for another. Rather than a train leading to freedom, the civil rights movement was in Baraka's eyes a subway car merely circling a city. No progress occurs along this route. Reading *Dutchman* is important for college students because the play rejects the simplistic and triumphalist narrative about the civil rights movement that they learned in high school. In Baraka's subway car drama, developments in technology and trends in migration do not lead ineluctably to a new Eden or promised land of interracial democracy.

NOTES

[1]On occasion, I have screened in class Anthony Harvey's film adaptation of *Dutchman* (1966). While it does emphasize the train, I find that the film does not generate much useful conversation.

[2]See Rose (41–46) for a discussion of how subway trains became key signifiers in early hip-hop culture.

[3]Despite the metaphor of the Underground Railroad, the reality for African Americans after the Civil War was that they were much more likely to work for railroads than they were to ride them to freedom. While railroads rented and owned slaves during the 1840s and 1850s, many African Americans found paid employment with the railroads after the war (Kornweibel 18). In the South, the war had destroyed much railroad track, and African Americans took physically demanding and dangerous jobs rebuilding it, often seeking an alternative to sharecropping (40–41). Other African Americans worked for the railroads under compulsion, as prisoner laborers in convict lease programs. John Henry and his battle against the machine symbolize the harsh reality of railroad work for great numbers of African Americans. Scott Nelson has recently discovered that John Henry was a real person, who was "employed" by the railroad as part of a convict lease program (68–69).

[4]In *Sula* (1973), Toni Morrison describes the humiliations and degradations of riding in a Jim Crow train. The novel reminds us that trains and train stations were key sites in the institutionalization of white supremacy (19–24). Of course, African Americans selected trains as sites of resistance precisely because whites used them to establish racial hierarchy. See Kornweibel's discussion of Ida B. Wells.

[5]Some of my students may draw on the images of trains from jazz and blues songs, which generally provide a more optimistic view. In blues numbers, such as Bertha Henderson's "Leavin' Gal Blues" and Clara Smith's "Freight Train Blues," trains symbolize freedom from oppressive conditions. Many train songs from the 1930s, 1940s, and 1950s revel in the physical journey from pain and misery to freedom. Muddy Waters's "All Aboard" and Louis Jordan's "Choo Choo Ch'Boogie" let listeners imagine how jumping a train might help people forget their troubles. Baraka, as a historian of African American music, was well aware of its reliance on train metaphors. Baraka's *Blues People: Negro Music in White America* (1963) identifies Leroy Carr's "How Long, How Long Blues" as an example of the classic blues impulse, and the song also prominently features trains (119–20).

[6]Baraka may have had in mind the following passage from Ralph Ellison's *Invisible Man* (1952): "Things whirled too fast around me. My mind went alternately bright and blank in slow rolling waves. We, he, him—my mind and I—were no longer getting around in the same circles. Nor my body either. Across the aisle a young platinum blond nibbled at a red Delicious apple as station lights rippled past behind her. The train plunged. I dropped through the roar, giddy and vacuum-minded, sucked under and out into late afternoon Harlem" (249–50).

APPENDIX

Suggested Reading on Trains in African American Life

Bordewich, Fergus. *Bound for Canaan: The Underground Railroad and the War for the Soul of America*. HarperCollins, 2005.

Floyd, Samuel. "Troping the Blues: From Spirituals to the Concert Hall." *Black Music Research Journal*, vol. 13, no. 1, 1993, pp. 31–51.

Kornweibel, Theodore. *Railroads in the African American Experience*. Johns Hopkins UP, 2010.

Maxile, Horace. "Extensions on a Black Musical Tropology: From Trains to the Mothership (and Beyond)." *Journal of Black Studies*, vol. 42, no. 4, 2011, pp. 593–608.

Nelson, Hugh. "LeRoi Jones' *Dutchman*: A Brief Ride on a Doomed Ship." *Educational Theatre Journal*, vol. 20, no. 1, 1968, pp. 53–59.

Nelson, Scott. *Steel Drivin' Man: The Untold Story of an American Legend*. Oxford UP, 2006.

Dutchman, the Black Body, and the Law

Danny M. Hoey, Jr.

> Let no one convince any black man that he is an American like anybody else.
>
> —Baraka, "Black Writing"

I first stumbled on Amiri Baraka's *Dutchman* while I was researching a paper on conflicting ideologies of masculinity in the work of Ralph Ellison and James Baldwin. As I read the play, I came to understand its focus on America's compulsion to imagine and destroy the violent and angry black man. The play also pulsed with a sense of urgency, one that called for someone to do something about this compulsion. I eventually finished my essay, but the trauma of the play stayed with me.

As I progressed in my graduate studies, I was afforded the opportunity to teach an American literature class. Immediately, I decided to include *Dutchman* in this survey. I was excited because I thought that I had a grasp of Baraka's aims and that I could convey these things to a group of willing young people. I approached the text as well as the class with zeal; however, I was all over the place. I did not ground the text in any type of theoretical or historical context. I relied on what I believed to be my natural understanding of what it meant to be a black man in America—my fear of police, my anxiety about possibly dying violently at a young age, my uneasiness about what others (white) felt about my black body. I realize now that this reliance did not do the text or the class any favors: students did not get the text and complained, and I admit that it was not one of my best teaching moments. I thought then that students wanted to believe that racism was dead, that white folks no longer viewed the black male body as a threat and something that could be easily discarded. What I now know is this: I had not prepared students to see the destruction of the black body in *Dutchman* as significant to their thinking about contemporary United States society. I had not given them a historical or critical lens through which to view *Dutchman*.

I decided that I could not teach the play again until I had a critical framework that would allow my students to navigate the complicated intersection of race and masculinity and the tenuous relationship that black men have with the white world. It was not until I read Charlton Copeland's essay "'Fists and the Voices of Sorrowful Women': Race, Gender, Violence, and the Reconstruction of the Word in Toni Morrison's *Jazz*" that I began to conceptualize that framework. Copeland argues that "law and violence stand at the center of *Jazz*'s narrative. . . . The novel examines the history of the violence endured by blacks in the American South and that follows them to urban centers, including East St. Louis and New York City" (132). He further states that "in the face of both organized, interracial violence and intimate, intraracial, gender violence, the law appears silent" (132). I was drawn to this analysis because *Jazz*, like *Dutchman*, takes place in urban New York City and examines the murder of a black man and its implications. I was also drawn to Copeland's conclusion because the "organized, interracial violence" against Baraka's Clay goes unpunished. Copeland's analysis of the law and its silence over violence and the black body gave me a more nuanced way to analyze the play. His argument could also make more concrete the complicated relationship that this society has with the black male body and the ways this relationship shapes our understanding of unequal protection under the law.

I taught the play a second time with a clearer critical framework in which to place it. My goal then became to help students examine how the black male body is constructed as violent and angry, why that constructed black male body goes unprotected in the American judicial system, and how the construction of this black male body elicits the real violence often perpetrated against it. To consider the play in this light, students must understand the ramifications of these constructions and the courts' failure to ensure equal protection. By examining legal texts that outline the history of unequal protection for blacks in America, we can achieve this goal.

I want students to look at *Dutchman* and understand the legal and historical realties that have shaped our consciousness, to articulate the danger in these realities, and, if possible, to leave with different critical perspectives on the black male body and its complicated relation to the world in which it tries to exist.

Historical and Legal Considerations

Before I begin my discussion on the unprotected black male body, I ask students if they have ever been pulled over by the police. Once they have answered the question, I ask them if they were afraid for their lives. This question elicits different reactions. My white students roll their eyes, as if to signal that they are tired of this type of questioning; my black students all chime in, murmuring and shaking their heads in unison, as if to say, "which one of us hasn't?"

I ask these questions because I want students to think about their relationship to the law, as embodied by the police, and how that relationship is constructed and maintained. I am asking students to think critically about their bodies and the safety of their bodies in relation to the police. This line of questioning opens up the conversation about how, historically, the black body has come to be viewed in legal discourse as violent, without value, and easily dismissible. To extend the conversation, I tell them about my own anxiety as a black man when being pulled over by the police. I tell them that I place my hands on the steering wheel so as not to appear aggressive, that I respond with only "yes, sir" and "no, sir," and that I roll my window halfway down to hand my driver's license and car registration to the police because I am afraid of being shot. They are silent, and I tell them these fears are real and grounded in lived experiences. My goal is for students to understand that the violence against black bodies they hear about and see is not a new phenomenon, that the death and violence black people in America have experienced have dictated their relationship to the law, and that this violence has left an ugly scar on the nation's consciousness.

In *Race, Crime, and the Law*, Randall Kennedy explains how the law has constructed a narrative of unequal protection for the black body. I ask students to read the chapter entitled "History: Unequal Protection," in which Kennedy states, "Deliberately withholding protection against criminality (or conduct that should be deemed criminal) is one of the most destructive forms of oppression that has been visited upon African Americans" (29). Kennedy illustrates this point with many cases involving slaves who were maimed or killed by their masters. *State v. Mann*, he argues, "is perhaps the best known of all of the cases relating to slavery and the criminal law" (33). The defendant, John Mann, had a slave named Lydia leased to him, and, according to the North Carolina Supreme Court, Lydia had committed "some small offense, for which the defendant undertook to chastise her." Lydia then tried to run away and was shot by Mann. He was convicted of assault and battery, but the state's supreme court unanimously reversed the decision. Judge Thomas Ruffin wrote an opinion in which he said, "The enquiry here is whether a cruel and unreasonable battery on a slave, by the hirer, is indictable." Ruffin gave this answer: "We cannot allow the right of the master to be brought into discussion in the Courts of Justice. The slave, to remain a slave, must be made sensible that there is no appeal from his master; that his power is in no instance, usurped; but is conferred by the laws of man at least, if not by the law of God" (qtd. in Kennedy 33). I ask students to think about this opinion's consequences for blacks. What does it say about the value of the black body and the importance of protecting it? How has this opinion shaped legal and public opinion about widespread police brutality and systematic failures to punish it? My hope is that students come to understand that the law has long assigned less value and legal protection to the black body than it has to the white body.

Constructing Clay's Demise

In thinking about Clay and his demise, I ask the class to focus on a few major scenes in which he is constructed as predatory, violent, angry, and deserving of his final fate. I ask them to examine critically the desire/contempt relationship between Clay and Lula. How does this relationship figure in his ultimate destruction? Why is Clay and Lula's interracial relationship, or the idea of it, seen as taboo during that time period? How has the perceived relationship between a white woman and black man been viewed historically? To answer these questions, I have students focus on the following exchange from the beginning of the play:

> LULA. Weren't you staring at me through the window? At the last stop?
> CLAY. Staring at you? What do you mean?
> LULA. Don't you know what staring means?
> CLAY. I saw you through the window . . . if that's what it means. I don't know if I was staring. Seems to me you were staring through the window at me.
> LULA. I was. But only after I'd turned around and saw you staring through that window down in the vicinity of my ass and legs. (6–7)

I ask students about the sexual overtones in the conversation between Lula and Clay. Some students nervously point out Lula's aggressiveness; others giggle at the frank mention of her "ass." Other students say Clay seems shocked by Lula's forwardness. I ask if they can tell me why Baraka makes Clay a passive pursuer. They are unable to articulate why, and I tell them that there was a time in the deep South when, if a black man was thought to be interested in a white woman, he was at risk of being lynched or mutilated. I tell my students that *Dutchman* portrays the Jim Crow past's persistence in a nominally integrated present.

Baraka further evokes a feeling of danger through Lula's description of Clay's racial identity, which is meant to indict Clay's assimilation: "Screw yourself, Uncle Tom. Thomas Woolly-head. . . . With old white matted mane. He hobbles on his wooden cane. Old Tom. Old Tom. Let the white man hump his ol' mama, and he jes' shuffle off in the woods and hide his gentle gray head. Ol' Thomas Woolly-Head" (32). Students' typical response to Lula's assault is always interesting and somewhat disturbing. They are usually untroubled by her outburst. They never say they are fine with the way she speaks to Clay, but there is never outrage, never any sense that she has done anything wrong. I reserve my questioning about this until we discuss Clay's response: "Shit, you don't have any sense, Lula, nor feelings either. I could murder you now. Such a tiny ugly throat. I could squeeze it flat, and watch you turn blue, on a humble. For dull kicks. And all these weak-faced ofays squatting around here, staring over their papers at me. Murder them too. Even if they expected it. That man there . . ." (33). Students are outraged by Clay's response. They cannot understand why he is so harsh or why his response to Lula's insulting outburst has to include "murder[ing]" all white folks. I ask them why Lula is afforded the opportunity to aggressively insult Clay and Clay is not afforded the opportunity to protect himself? I ask them why they feel Clay's reaction is worse than Lula's attack. What I hear is disheartening yet honest: students feel that Clay is too aggressive and emerges as a danger to Lula and, by extension, white folks. What takes place in my classroom while we read this exchange underscores what takes place in society: black male bodies, when perceived as predatory, angry, and violent, no longer receive the benefit of the doubt—those bodies have less value because they are dangerous, and they become expendable because they pose a threat, real or imagined.

As Clay unravels, he thus becomes the very thing that justifies his unpunished murder. After Lula stabs Clay, she gives specific instructions about his dead body: "get this man off of me! . . . [O]pen the door and throw his body out" (37). The act of discarding Clay's body is disturbing, yet it does not seem to bother the people who are discarding it. I ask students to recall Kennedy's study and to consider several questions. Why are the passengers willing participants in the disposal of Clay's body? Why does no one call for help? Why does no one restrain Lula? Why is it so important to throw Clay's body from the train? I ask because I want students to come away with a clearer understanding of how all these factors—whiteness, the law, and the unequal protection of the black male body—ensure both the demise of Clay and the silence that follows. The hope is that students become more critical of their own reactions when they encounter black men and black bodies. I also want students to think seriously about the present day black men whose bodies go unprotected and whose murderers go unprosecuted. To be honest, I want them to be as outraged about the violence perpetuated against black male bodies as they were about Clay's aggressive response to Lula.

I understand that my approach to teaching *Dutchman* makes students uncomfortable—my white students because they feel as if it is a personal indictment, my black students because they feel the sting of racism and have experienced it, in some form, firsthand. It is hard for me to teach the play because it forces me to think about my own lived experiences and my precarious relationship to the law and to the police. However, teaching the text against the background of United States jurisprudence offers students, and myself, the opportunity to think critically about the American justice system and its pervasive obsession with the destruction of the black male body.

I now know that framing the discussion within a legal discourse gives students a historical context in which to place the text and offers them new ways to see how the law determines who is afforded equal treatment and protection. I am glad that I found *Dutchman*. I am even more thankful that I get to lead students through a journey of discovery, however painful.

Dutchman's Uncle Tom

Tess Chakkalakal

I teach Amiri Baraka's *Dutchman* in an undergraduate intermediate seminar entitled Reading *Uncle Tom's Cabin* in the Twenty-First Century. The course offers a maximum of sixteen sophomores and juniors a close engagement with the production and dissemination of Harriet Beecher Stowe's *Uncle Tom's Cabin* (1852). I teach the course at Bowdoin College, in Brunswick, Maine, where Stowe wrote the novel in a two-story house that still stands in the heart of the town on Federal Street. The class embarks on many field trips during the first half of the course. We first visit the First Parish Church, where Stowe is said to have had a vision of Uncle Tom's death, which later became one of the novel's most poignant scenes. Our final destination is the Stowe House, where Stowe encountered a fugitive slave, John Andrew Jackson. Stowe harbored Jackson for one night, providing him with food and money to aid him in his quest for freedom. In doing so, she broke the Fugitive Slave Law, which stipulated that escaped slaves should be captured and returned to their masters. Learning about these real-life events complicates and enriches students' understanding of the novel's history and meaning.

The first half of the course focuses on Stowe's novel and the contemporary political debate that informed its scenes, characters, and plot. After a close reading of the novel and several slave narratives that informed it, the class addresses dramatic adaptations that appeared during the novel's serialization in the *National Era* and other adaptations that appeared immediately after. Students read Stowe's own adaptation, *The Christian Slave*, first performed in 1855 by the free black Mary E. Webb to considerable fanfare in London. Students document the changes in Uncle Tom as he is taken out of the historical and generic context of nineteenth-century sentimental fiction and thrust into late-nineteenth- and early-twentieth-century dramatic and cinematic adaptations. Students watch several films, beginning with Edwin Porter's twelve-minute silent motion picture (1903) and clips from Harry A. Pollard's version (1927), turning then to Uncle Tom cameo appearances in such popular films as *Dimples* (1936), *The King and I* (1956), and *The Gangs of New York* (2002). These adaptations of Uncle Tom fall under the rubric of white adaptations. The final section of the course focuses on black adaptations of Uncle Tom. We begin with Amiri Baraka's plays *Dutchman* and *The Slave* (1964), followed by Ishmael Reed's novel *Flight to Canada* (1976), concluding with an examination of Bill T. Jones's *Last Supper at Uncle Tom's Cabin/The Promised Land* (1990) and Robert Alexander's *I Ain't Yo Uncle: The New Jack Revisionist* Uncle Tom's Cabin (1996).

I situate *Dutchman* and *The Slave* in relation to the history of Uncle Tom performances. Baraka's plays help students grapple with the changes to Stowe's

Uncle Tom that were made for stage and screen adaptations. For instance, H. C. Conway's enormously successful version, which appeared at P. T. Barnum's Museum in 1853 and influenced later stage adaptations, depicted slave life as happy and carefree; it omitted Eliza's flight across the ice with her young son, Harry; it accentuated the comic roles; it diminished female ones; it allowed both Tom and Eva to live at the end of the play; and it watered down abolitionist sentiments, rendering them harmless and inoffensive to Southern audiences. These theatrical alterations to Uncle Tom have been well documented by theater historians such as John Frick and Sarah Meer. The political and cultural consequences of these adaptations are somewhat more difficult to assess, however. This history helps students to read Baraka's complex engagement with the Uncle Tom figure and its relation to a modern black identity.

Baraka's engagement with Uncle Tom bears some resemblance to Ralph Ellison's. Though Baraka and Ellison's political and literary outlooks diverge sharply, they converge in their readings of Uncle Tom. Looking back on the success of his novel in his introduction to the 1981 edition of *Invisible Man* (1952), Ellison provided a compelling account of how dramatic adaptations of Stowe's novel affected his own fiction:

> Shortly before the spokesman for invisibility intruded, I had seen in a nearby Vermont village, a poster announcing the performance of a "Tom Show," that forgotten term for blackface minstrel versions of Mrs. Stowe's *Uncle Tom's Cabin*. I had thought such entertainment a thing of the past, but there in a quiet northern village it was alive and kicking, with Eliza, frantically slipping and sliding on the ice, still trying—and that during World War II!—to escape the slavering hounds. . . . No, because what is commonly assumed to be past history is actually as much a part of the living present as William Faulkner insisted. (xvi)

As Ellison observes, Uncle Tom's multiple and varied appearances over time suggest the changing nature of race in the United States. Uncle Tom is one of the racial fictions informing interactions between whites and blacks in the legally segregated America of which Ellison writes. Though less explicit than Ellison's direct reckoning with "blackface minstrel versions" and written at the height of the struggle against legal segregation, Baraka's references to the character raise similar questions about the connections between past and present racial divisions. Like Ellison's *Invisible Man*, *Dutchman* stages the drama of race in the United States through an ambivalent black hero whose words and actions represent what it means to be black in America after slavery's abolition.

Dutchman constitutes a dramatic response to the history of white stage adaptations of *Uncle Tom's Cabin*, those adaptations that changed the meaning of Uncle Tom. I have students examine the references to Uncle Tom in *Dutchman*. The character's appearance in *The Slave* is less explicit than in *Dutchman*. The two plays form a ritual drama symbolizing Baraka's conviction that an

African American identity develops through cycles of violent racial encounters.[1] Although the class focuses primarily on *Dutchman*, I position *The Slave* as Baraka's sequel to *Dutchman*'s Uncle Tom plot, which concludes rather abruptly with Clay's death.

We begin our study of *Dutchman* with a simple question: How have stage adaptations of *Uncle Tom's Cabin* affected black representation? The theater historian Rosemarie K. Bank has observed that stage adaptations are "schizophrenic site[s] in which the character/hero is alternately masculinized and unmanned" (150). But I would argue that *Dutchman* allows students to see precisely how Uncle Tom has been "masculinized and unmanned" through Clay's transformation from a genteel, respectable, middle-class young man to a violent, angry, dead black man. Clay represents a different kind of black hero from Ellison's modern black hero and recalls nineteenth-century ideas of race in his understanding of his present situation. Though Clay bears little direct resemblance to the hero of Stowe's novel, he is similarly caught between his desire for personal freedom and his racial duty. Though Stowe introduced Uncle Tom as "a large, broad chested, powerfully-made man, of a full glossy black" with a "self-respecting and dignified" air, he was depicted on stage as elderly and frail (19). Diminishing Uncle Tom's powerful appearance recasts this tragic hero as the stuff of comedy. Significantly, *Dutchman*, like *Uncle Tom's Cabin*, insists on its hero's death. *Uncle Tom*'s and *Dutchman*'s politics are located in the unpunished murder of a black man. For Stowe, Tom's death is both a personal victory and a spur to action; for Baraka, Clay's death signifies the ongoing racial struggle in the United States. After Lula kills Clay, the other subway passengers "drag CLAY'S body down the aisle" and "throw his body out" (37). His death produces only the appearance of another "young Negro of about twenty" who will meet the same fate (37). For Lula (and the other white passengers), black men are all the same, to be toyed with and disposed of; this realization is key to Baraka's radical black politics.

Dutchman, obviously, is not a typical stage adaptation of *Uncle Tom's Cabin*. Yet, Uncle Tom appears in the play—and is more than just a cameo. He plays a vital role in *Dutchman*. Though Baraka's Uncle Tom differs from his antecedents, this Uncle Tom figures in the development of the play's central black character. My students' task is to determine what form Uncle Tom takes in *Dutchman*. To do this, they must consider what it means for a black man to play him. Our discussion of Baraka's new Uncle Tom role helps clarify the far-reaching effects of the figure in American popular culture. Students read the entire play, but we begin our discussion of it with the explicit appearance of Uncle Tom, which occurs at the play's midpoint, in the second scene, marking the climax of its action. Lula calls Clay an "Uncle Tom" during their already tense conversation, bringing the sexual and racial tension between them to a kind of breaking point: "Screw yourself, Uncle Tom. Thomas Woolly-head. [. . .] There is Uncle Tom . . . I mean, Uncle Thomas Woolly-Head. With old white matted mane. He hobbles on his wooden cane. Old Tom. Old Tom. Let the white man hump his ol' mama, and he jes' shuffle off in the woods and hide his gentle gray head. Ol' Thomas Woolly-Head" (32). What is Uncle Tom doing on this New York subway in a conversation between this modern interracial couple? Students offer several, often divergent, responses to this question. Typically, though, they remark on the contempt with which Lula uses the name. By calling Clay Uncle Tom, Lula moves their playful, sexual banter to a different register, one in which physical violence punctuates the conversation. In response to Lula's labeling, Clay "*slaps her as hard as he can, across the mouth. LULA's head bangs against the back of the seat. When she raises it again, CLAY slaps her again*" (33). In other words, being called Uncle Tom incites violence. Why does Lula call Clay "Uncle Tom"? What does this do to Clay? How does the epithet change him? To answer these questions and help students understand the connections (or disconnections) between Clay and Uncle Tom, I lead students back to the beginning of the play.

According to the opening stage direction, Clay is a "twenty-year-old Negro" sitting alone and staring out the window of a New York subway. Much of the additional information about Clay comes from an entirely unreliable source, a thirty-year-old white woman who appears, from her aggressive behavior, to be mentally unstable. Yet the details she provides are, at first, all we have to get a sense of his character: "You look like you been trying to grow a beard. That's exactly what you look like. You look like you live in New Jersey with your parents and are trying to grow a beard. That's what. You look like you've been reading Chinese poetry and drinking lukewarm sugarless tea" (8). We learn later that Clay is wearing a jacket and tie, that he has attended a "colored college," that he enjoys reading French poetry, that his mother was a Republican, and that his grandfather was a night watchman (10). What is the significance of these details, and why does Lula know them when she claims not to really know Clay ("I told you I didn't know anything about *you*. . .")? The reason is because Clay is "a well-known type" (12). According to Lula's logic, he is the type of man who "never once thought [he was] a black nigger" (19). Lula uses the N-word twice in the play, but she does not employ it as an insult. Rather, she uses it to point out what Clay is not, certain racial qualities that he lacks. Clay is "no nigger" but "just a dirty white man" (31). Instead of being "a black nigger"—a figure Lula respects—Clay is an "Uncle Tom," someone who is not *really* black and therefore a figure of contempt. According to Lula, his outward appearance suggests a lack of certain internal qualities that would make him "a black nigger," and like the original Uncle Tom, Clay submits to white authority. For her, Clay descends from a long line of black men who are "afraid of white people." He is an "Uncle Tom Big Lip!" tripping over his words as he acquiesces to white power (33). By calling Clay an Uncle Tom, Lula connects Clay to a legacy of black submission, not resistance. That Clay's grandfather was "a night watchman," a man who was employed to protect (white people's) property from (black) trespassers, and that his mother voted Republican make Clay an "Uncle Tom." By indicating that Clay appears to be black but thinks and acts in the interests of the white majority, Lula incites him to assert his racial difference.

Although Lula taunts and mocks him for much of the play, the unassuming Clay takes offense and asserts himself only after she calls him Uncle Tom. After he slaps her, he says, "Now shut up and let me talk." He proceeds to explain that he could murder her:

> For dull kicks. And all these weak-faced ofays squatting around here, staring over their papers at me. Murder them too. Even if they expected it. That man there. . .
> [*Points to well-dressed man.*]
> I could rip that *Times* right out of his hand, as skinny and middle-class as I am, I could rip that paper out of his hand and just as easily rip out his throat. (33)

But why, my students and I ask, does being called "Uncle Tom" incite such violence from Clay, who previously showed little capability of such violent acts?

In calling Clay Uncle Tom, Lula pulls off his mask of middle-class respectability and reveals a black man, a man who "could easily rip out [a white man's] throat." The unexpected appearance of this stereotyped black man is what prompts Clay to play the role of the black murderer, to assail white cultural and social authority. Clay wants to show Lula, through his violent actions, that he is still black on the inside, even though he does not act black on the outside. In *Dutchman*, Uncle Tom invokes how white people see black men like Clay who have conformed to the majority. By calling Clay an Uncle Tom, Lula has set in motion a personal black revolution but one that is fated to fail.

By considering the connections that Baraka makes between Clay and Uncle Tom, students come to terms with what Uncle Tom means over a century after the publication of Stowe's novel. The most common understanding of the term *Uncle Tom* is a black man considered by other blacks to be subservient to or to curry favor with whites. *The Oxford English Dictionary* traces the term's etymology to "the name of the hero of *Uncle Tom's Cabin*" and reports that the term is in "extended use" ("Uncle Tom"). After listing several uses of the term, the *OED* provides variations that have resulted from its "extended use": "Uncle Tommery," "Uncle Tomming," "Uncle Tommish," and "Uncle Tomism." *Dictionary.com* defines "Uncle Tomism" as "a policy of relationship between whites and blacks involving a benevolent and patronizing attitude on the part of the whites and a willingly submissive attitude on the part of the blacks" ("Uncle Tomism"). None of these standard definitions are particularly helpful for my students. What does Uncle Tom, a nineteenth-century fictional character, signify for them in the twenty-first century? But Baraka's play helps students see the character's transformation. He was once the hero of a popular antislavery novel written in the mid–nineteenth century by a white woman. Today, Uncle Tom is the name given to African Americans who have entered the middle class, who have given up on being part of the black community. It can be embraced, as Clay ultimately does, or rejected. Either way, it evokes the tension underlying the existential condition of being a black American. Moreover, it is through Uncle Tom that the audience sees Clay's new impulse to define blackness for himself: "Let me be who I feel like being. Uncle Tom. Thomas. Whoever. It's none of your business. You don't know anything except what's there for you to see. An act. Lies. Device. Not the pure heart, the pumping black heart. You don't ever know that" (34). Ceasing to be the black man who conforms to white perceptions of bourgeois virtue and rejected by both blacks and whites, Clay becomes "who I feel like being." Being black, in *Dutchman*'s terms, has to do with a "black heart." As Clay makes clear, this heart cannot be seen or known by whites; it can only be known by those who have one. What makes him black is his "pumping black heart." It is worth noting, as I do in class, that the terms by which Clay defines his blackness are both literal and figurative. Clay is black because he feels black and because his heart is black. This rhetoric of feeling and the heart echoes the sentimentality of the original *Uncle Tom*, a novel that urges its readers "*to feel right*" (404).

The 1964 production of *Dutchman* marks an important intersection between the history of Uncle Tom and definitions of blackness. The passage of the Civil Rights Act of 1964 changed what it meant to be black in America. What were the effects of the law on how blacks and whites felt about one another? Baraka's play stages an answer to that question through the figure of Uncle Tom and the history of racial violence it symbolizes. In many respects, the way Baraka employs Uncle Tom in *Dutchman* remains salient and continues to exert enormous influence over how Uncle Tom is employed (and performed) in political and cultural discourse today. To call someone an Uncle Tom is to call into question that person's commitment to a racial community. An Uncle Tom is an individual who is more committed to personal success than to belonging to a racial community. While Baraka's Uncle Tom is historically and rhetorically far removed from Stowe's Uncle Tom, the play's explicit allusion to Uncle Tom stages a political commentary on the possibilities and constraints of racial classification in the United States.

Uncle Tom's death in Stowe's novel is inevitable. It is his death that moves the novel's readers. But it results in a heavenly transcendence that is supposed to save the souls of the white characters. This, for my students, is one of the novel's most troubling features, while Clay's death in Baraka's play comes as something of a shock. Yet, read in relation to Uncle Tom, it makes sense. Both black men are killed to protect the interests of the white majority, and their inevitable deaths allow us to grasp the limits placed on black freedom. As one of my students formulates the problem, black men pose a real or imagined threat to the structure of American society. I conclude our study of Baraka with a short writing assignment (three pages) in which students examine the impact of Baraka's mid-1960s Uncle Tom on contemporary American culture and social values. Students find examples of Uncle Tom in media sources—newspapers, magazines, films, novels, plays, and the like—and make sense of how the figure is invoked. The contexts of these examples range from the Clarence Thomas–

Anita Hill hearings to the documentary *The Fab Five*, in which the basketball player Jalen Rose calls members of the Duke University basketball team "Uncle Toms." On the whole, these examples show how the figure of Uncle Tom diminishes the legitimacy of black men who, like Clay, attempt to re-create their identities apart from a singular black community. They help students grasp how race continues to limit the rights of some American citizens. Drawing on the violent death of Stowe's Uncle Tom, Baraka's *Dutchman* (like Ellison's *Invisible Man*) enables students to grapple with the difficulty of being at once black and "who I feel like being." As Walker Vessels reveals in *The Slave*, being "who I feel like being" is only possible if one rejects the history of slavery embodied by Stowe's fictional Uncle Tom.

Vessels presents students with an example of a modern Uncle Tom. Unlike his precursor Clay, Vessels repudiates, from the start of the play, the conventions regulating black-white encounters. He explains to the audience the consequences of Uncle Tom roles on the lives of actual black men: "A stupid longing not to know . . . which is automatically fulfilled. Automatically triumphs. Automatically makes us killers or foot-dragging celebrities at the core of any filth" (43–44). Vessels reveals Clay's mistake. Clay's unconscious commitment to convention and respectability recalls the virtues of Uncle Tom, a slave who sacrifices his own freedom to comply with a moral structure that rewards his goodness with death. While there is no explicit reference to Uncle Tom in *The Slave*, Vessels's opening monologue, delivered before the action begins, draws implicitly on the character's history, giving Clay's middle-class respectability a rebirth through the figure of a violent black revolutionary. I encourage students to read *The Slave* as a sequel to *Dutchman*, with which it was published, extending Clay's life beyond the short and volatile subway ride with Lula. By doing so, students can see the extent to which Baraka develops black male identity on stage by playing his characters off of "Old Uncle Tom."

NOTE

[1] Many critics remark on *Dutchman*'s numerous mythological and literary sources. Typically, such readings focus on classical references in relation to Lula. I shift the conversation to the play's allusions to Uncle Tom in order to have students consider its specific United States historical and social context. For a good account of the play's classical allusions, see Christopher Baker, "A Trip with the Strange Woman: Amiri Baraka's *Dutchman* and the Book of Proverbs."

Dutchman, A Raisin in the Sun, and the History of Minstrel Theater

Roland Leander Williams, Jr.

Masks were all the rage in the national theater before the Civil War. White minstrels in blackface packed music halls. Playing for laughs, the performers acted out racial stereotypes formed in the surrounding slave system. Their routines portrayed blacks as flat characters who were either obliging or offensive. The minstrels launched a mainstream tradition rendering dark complexion into a mask that signified a one-dimensional figure. From the mid–nineteenth century to the present, African American drama has almost inevitably come into conflict with this body of theatrical convention. Indeed, the minstrel tradition is one of the American histories from which Clay and Lula, in Amiri Baraka's *Dutchman*, hopelessly "pretend" to be "free" (21).

In my undergraduate introduction to African American literature, students compare *Dutchman* and Lorraine Hansberry's *A Raisin in the Sun* (1959), another major mid-century African American play that responds to the minstrel tradition. This comparison reveals African American drama's recognition of blacks' moral and psychological complexity, invisible in the minstrel theater and much subsequent mainstream theater. At first sight, Baraka's Clay and Hansberry's Walter resemble antebellum-era characters portrayed onstage by blackface minstrels. Clay appears obliging. Walter seems offensive. Yet, ultimately, they transcend minstrelsy's taxonomy of black types.

My classroom work with *Dutchman, A Raisin in the Sun*, and the minstrel tradition is informed by recent scholarship on both minstrelsy and African American drama, some of which I cite below. But the account of minstrelsy that I offer my students places considerable emphasis on Sterling Brown's foundational analysis of minstrel types and their social origins. According to Brown, the slave system ingrained in popular culture offers two images of African Americans. One figure, which he labeled the "contented slave" (180) was pious and considerate. The other one, tagged the "wretched freeman" (186), was profane and contentious. Brown surmised that both figures made African Americans look unfit to live by their own designs (179–86).

In *Demons of Disorder: Early Blackface Minstrels and Their World* (1997), Dale Cockrell follows earlier scholars in identifying a 1769 staging of Isaac Bickerstaffe's *The Padlock* (1768) as one of the earliest American blackface performances. Lewis Hallam, Jr., donned the mask to play Mungo, an outrageous black servant, who croons on impulse and drinks to excess in this comic opera. At around the same time and for the subsequent half century, white actors blackened their faces to assume the lead roles in William Shakespeare's *Othello* (1603) and Thomas Southerne's *Oroonoko* (1696) or to provide comic relief as clowns between acts in other dramas. But the minstrel tradition is usually said to begin in the early nineteenth century. By the middle of the century, minstrelsy was a tremendously popular entertainment form, and, as contemporary scholars generally acknowledge, it has exerted great influence on American culture ever since.

Histories of minstrelsy often trace its beginnings to Thomas Dartmouth Rice's classic blackface routine, which took the country by storm in the early 1830s. Rice assumed the guise of a black slave who is happy with his lot. He wore a floppy hat and a ragged suit. Billing himself as Jim Crow, Rice sang and danced a jig that excited a national dance craze. Legend holds that he copied the shtick from a crippled black farmhand who tended horses with a song and dance.

In 1834, George Washington Dixon caused a similar stir when he pranced on stage as a free black dandy. Dixon wore a top hat, embroidered vest, and fancy coat. He had a gold watch on a chain and waved a chic pair of spectacles. Dubbed Zip Coon, he acted brash and boastful. According to Monica Miller, Dixon appropriated a black dandy aesthetic, transforming the figure into an imaginary scoundrel who lived for his own pleasure with an abandon that destined him for trouble.

Characters akin to Jim Crow and Zip Coon were featured acts in the minstrel show, a production born on a cold winter night in 1843, when Dan Emmett played a fiddle in the Bowery, accompanied by an ensemble that played a banjo, tambourine, and bones. Three years later, on Broadway, Edwin Pearce Christy brought a big band onstage in an arc and introduced himself as Mr. Interlocutor; in so doing, he established the standard format of the minstrel show. Every performer but Christy appeared in blackface, while he opened the show with a monologue interrupted by mutters and malapropisms from Mr. Tambo or Mr. Bones, inane characters situated at opposite ends of the arc. In the second part of the show, he orchestrated a parade of acts by fictive blacks; and, for the grand finale, Christy staged a party of plantation slaves singing and dancing in glee.

The minstrel show prepared the stage for the Tom Show, a drama adapted from Harriet Beecher Stowe's *Uncle Tom's Cabin* (1852). As Sarah Meer demonstrates in *Uncle Tom Mania: Slavery, Minstrelsy, and Transatlantic Culture in the 1850s* (2005), the Tom Show became a main attraction across the country in the 1850s. In *Uncle Tom's Cabin and American Culture* (1985), Thomas Gossett reveals that the play reigned until 1903, when the director, Edwin Porter, turned it into a silent movie.[1] In the stage iterations, the principal black male characters conform to the outlines of Jim Crow and Zip Coon. Uncle Tom, the bashful slave who looks after others, favors Jim Crow in temper. George Harris, the bold fugitive who looks after himself, resembles Zip Coon. Like the older figures, Tom and George are flat characters. Neither one changes his disposition.

George enters the Tom Show in a fit of rage. His wife is unable to calm him down. He is tired of having white men tell him what to do, since, he feels, he is twice as bright as them. George tells his wife that he plans to run away, and then he hits the road in flight to Canada. A light-complexioned mulatto, he assumes the guise of a Spaniard to facilitate his getaway. George pours scorn on whites, save some Quakers, who advance his cause. He flees, armed with pistols. When a posse corners him, he backs the mob off with gunfire. From the posse's point of view, George represents a social menace whom the country needs to expel or execute.

Unlike George, Tom puts the interests of others ahead of his own. For the benefit of Mr. Shelby, Tom accepts being separated from his wife and sold down the Mississippi River. On the steamboat after leaving his old Kentucky home, he sees Little Eva, a curly-haired blonde child, fall overboard and dives headlong in the water to save her. His personal welfare is never a matter of concern. In time, he refuses to foil the escape of dear Cassy from the clutches of lascivious Simon Legree. Consequently, Tom suffers a fatal beating, ordered by the slaveholder, which costs society a helping hand.

But the Tom Show and the minstrel theater were not the only theatrical representations of blacks, and African American playwrights and actors certainly took part in the portrayal of black lives. As Mel Watkins observes in *On the Real Side: A History of African American Comedy* (1999), black bondage not only brought blackface to the stage but also shaped the development of African American theater. While in the dusk of the nineteenth century blackface faded from the stage, patrons of drama continued to associate black faces with deference or defiance. Grasping the situation, African American playwrights lured audiences with figures that at once recalled and ironized minstrel stereotypes.

African American playwrights have generally resisted the convention of obliging or offensive flat black characters akin to Uncle Tom or George Harris, and one finds many complex, dynamic black characters in the history of black theater. The protagonist of William Wells Brown's *The Escape; or, A Leap for Freedom* (1858) turns from stoic suffering to scheming and fighting to get out of the country. In Pauline Hopkins's *Peculiar Sam; or, The Underground Railroad* (1879), the title character shifts from meekness to militance and smuggles a band of slaves into Canada. For better or worse, the protagonists created by African American playwrights undergo transformations. In Angelina Weld Grimké's *Rachel* (1916), a dashed dream to know more than a servant's fortunes fills amiable John Strong with a murderous rage. The hero in Louis Peterson's *Take a Giant Step* (1953) stews with anger in a white suburb until he cooks up a plan to win the goodwill of his neighbors.

After I present to my students this brief history of both minstrelsy and the beginning of its unmaking, we turn to *A Raisin in the Sun* and *Dutchman*. These plays initially seem to follow minstrel conventions but ultimately depart decisively from them. At the beginning of the play, Walter's wife has to call him out of bed. The man drags himself into view wearing "pajamas, which are rumpled and mismatched." Walter here stands closer to a wretched freeman than he does to a contended slave. Hansberry informs us that Walter "is a lean, intense young man in his middle thirties, inclined to quick nervous movements and erratic speech habits—and always in his voice there is a quality of indictment" (25). He is loath to oblige others and questions his fitness to live by his own designs.

In the middle of *A Raisin in the Sun*, when Walter is drunk at home, he sounds like George in the Tom Show. He is indignant because he is past thirty years old, has "been married eleven years," and has "a boy who sleeps in the living room." He complains that, as a chauffeur, all he has to give his son "is stories about how rich white people live" (34). He yearns to have the wherewithal of a wealthy white man. His wife endeavors to change his attitude, but to no avail. He complains that "ain't nobody" with him (85), not even her.

Whereas Walter initially recalls the Tom Show's George, Baraka's black male protagonist is at first reminiscent of Tom. At the beginning of *Dutchman*, Clay, a "twenty-year-old Negro," appears mild-mannered, even meek. In the subway car, coursing through the "underbelly of the city" (3), he sits alone by a window. His attire is neat and clean; his expression is idle. He holds a magazine of "wilting pages" (3) and stares into space above it. Clay stays idle until the train pulls into a station and he catches the face of a "thirty-year-old white woman" (3), Lula, staring from the platform. She smiles, and Clay smiles back, "almost an instinctive though undesirable response" (4). Feeling wrong, he averts his eyes from the woman. It looks unlikely that he will act in a profane and contentious manner.

When Lula prepares to sit beside Clay, he further projects the accommodating air of Tom. She says, "I'm going to sit down. . . . O.K.?" Clay answers, "Sure." She "[*s*]*wings down onto the seat, pushing her legs out as if she is very weary.*" Lula blames her apparent fatigue on "too much weight." In an effort to flatter her, Clay replies, "Ha, doesn't look like much to me" (6). I want my students to see, though, that both *Dutchman* and *A Raisin in the Sun* throw off the representational burdens imposed by the minstrel tradition. I discuss the way Hansberry challenges these conventions and how she ultimately conveys the human complexity of African Americans. The plot of *A Raisin in the Sun* revolves around Walter's conversion from a hothead to a cool cat. Three speeches highlight his transformation. The first one occurs when Walter comes home drunk from work in the middle of the afternoon. Besides feeling sick of being a chauffeur and tired of having a boss, he is dying for his family to support his moneymaking scheme. Wishing to get a rise out of his wife, his sister, and her date, he dances atop the dining table. In his drunken state, Walter ridicules and scoffs at the others, but they turn a deaf ear to him. Their disregard causes him to proclaim himself a volcano surrounded by ants, before he feels queasy and lurches to the washroom down the hall.

Walter is a wretched freeman after his friend Willy swipes the money that Walter has invested in their liquor store partnership. Then, he seems good for nothing but wild schemes. Walter takes the offer from the Clybourne Park Improvement Association to buy the suburban property on which his mother has put a deposit. He explains to his mother that the world's "all divided up. . . . Between the takers and the 'tooken'" (141). Walter thanks Willy for teaching him to forget fretting about "the wrong and right of things" (142). He swears, "there ain't nothing but taking in this world, and he who takes the most is the smartest—and it don't make a damn bit of difference *how*" (143).

His attitude changes, however, when Karl Lindner, the neighborhood association's agent, returns to the Youngers' apartment. Lindner comes to seal the deal that would pay the family to forgo the chance to live in Clybourne Park. Walter acknowledges that he is a chauffeur and that his wife and mother are domestics. "We are very plain people," he says (147). Walter counts his son as the sixth generation of a family with "a lot of pride" (148), and he recalls that his father, who was "a laborer most of his life" (148), just about "beat a man to death once because this man called him a bad name" (148). Walter also muses about his sister's future as a doctor.

This train of thought prompts him to forgo his bid for easy money. He takes the Clybourne buyout off the table. Walter informs Lindner that his family will occupy the property to which they have the title. But, he assures the agent, "We don't want to make no trouble for nobody or fight no causes, and we will try to be good neighbors" (148). His new attitude opens him to accusations that he has fallen into a class of "assimilationist Negroes" or "Uncle Toms" anxious to enter the mainstream (81). But his turnaround actually uncovers a discreet side of the man that peeps out like the face of an actor during a quick change of masks. Lindner leaves without prevailing over Walter.

Like Walter, Clay ultimately transcends minstrel type. At the beginning of *Dutchman*, Lula has Clay in the palm of her hands in the twinkling of an eye. Wearing "loud lipstick" (5) and a daring dress, the woman arrests his attention. With the air of a *fille de joie*, she flirts with the black man. Lula causes Clay to wonder if the two have a friend or acquaintance in common. In short order, Clay resembles an actor slipping out of character. Catching himself, he attempts to reassert his prior persona. He begs Lula to be "cool." She apes him. "Be Cool," she sneers. Then, she declares, "That's all you know" (31).

Lula assails him with digs and barbs. She calls him "an escaped nigger" who has "crawled through the wire" on his old plantation. Lula fancies that Clay lives at large behind the mask of a contented slave. She christens Clay "Uncle Thomas Woolly-Head" (32) and predicts that he is destined to hobble on a "wooden cane" (32) in fear of "white people" (33) for the rest of his days. "You fool!," she screams (33).

Clay is outraged. It is not enough that he slaps, shakes, and curses Lula. He wants to rip her up. Clay says, "Let me be who I feel like being." He gives her a piece of his mind. All she sees of him, he insists, is a lie about his skin. She is blind, he says, to his "pumping black heart." Clay brings to mind Nat Turner as he explains that blacks repress their urge to cut white throats: "If Bessie Smith had killed some white people she wouldn't have needed that music" (35). He goes on until Lula exclaims, "I've heard enough" (36).

Clay blows the cover that has secured him safe passage in the past. He drops the mask of a one-dimensional figure and bares the face of a soul with multiple parts. Clay forgets to exercise discretion, the quality cultivated in blacks by bondage. It is a blunder that puts his welfare at risk. Realizing the error, he decides to "get off this train." Sadly, it is too late. A taboo is broken. His fate is sealed. Clay has lost his cool and boiled the blood of Lula. Standards articulated under black bondage say it is wrong for a black man to incense a white woman. Instead of observing the code, Clay has violated it. He tries hard to regain his composure, to recover his charm, hoping that Lula will pardon his transgression. But Lula will not allow him to recant. Once he goes to leave, she "brings up a small knife and plunges it" into his breast (37).

Clay's encounter with Lula exposes his habit of hiding his feelings from whites. Of course, white supremacy has long demanded this. The fact is underscored by the last black figure to appear in *Dutchman*, "an old Negro conductor" (37). The man "comes into the car, doing a sort of restrained soft shoe, and half mumbling the words of some song" (37–38). Evoking Jim Crow, he "tips his hat" to Lula "and continues out of the car" (38), leaving the white woman unfazed. The implication is that the conductor, a representative of an earlier generation, keeps his act together in the public arena.

Examined together against the backdrop of blackface minstrelsy, Clay and Walter reveal that African American playwrights have endowed their heroes with breadth and depth and have thus challenged the mainstream stereotypes that emerged from minstrelsy. Clay's and Walter's complexity challenges Jim Crow and Zip Coon, along with Uncle Tom and George Harris. The protagonists of Baraka's and Hansberry's plays signify that the souls of black folk dwell behind a mask cast in part by the minstrel theater.

NOTE

[1] Instructors may also want to consult the studies by Toll; Lott; Lhamon; and Mahar.

Dutchman and Black Vernacular Culture

Jean-Philippe Marcoux

I teach Amiri Baraka's *Dutchman* as part of a second-year undergraduate course on twentieth-century American drama. The course is interested in American playwrights' responses to the elusiveness and fallibility of the American dream. Our reading list also includes Eugene O'Neill's *The Emperor Jones*, Thornton Wilder's *Our Town*, Arthur Miller's *All My Sons*, Tennessee Williams's *The Glass Menagerie*, and Sam Shepard's *True West*. The course unit on *Dutchman* requires two weeks (six hours). During the first week, I lecture on some of the historical and cultural contexts from which *Dutchman* emerged. The second week is devoted entirely to group discussion of the play's specific engagements with the vernacular. In this essay, I explain how Clay employs black vernacular culture to confront the history of race relations in the United States as well as the stereotypes it generated.

I begin my lecture by pointing out that the play was first produced in 1964, one year after the publication of Baraka's *Blues People*, which is a sociological study of how black music has narrated and responded to racial oppression. I underscore African Americans' development of a rich "slave culture" (Stuckey) to transcend the limitations enforced first by slavery and then by a society that refused to make good on its constitutional promises. This culture consists of vast vernacular forms that affirm blacks' humanity and keep their history alive. Before going any further, it is necessary to define our main terms, beginning, of course, with "vernacular."

I direct the students to the very accessible description of *vernacular* that Henry Louis Gates, Jr., and Nellie Mckay offer in *The Norton Anthology of African American Literature*: "[African American vernacular] consists of forms sacred—songs, prayers, and sermons—and secular—work songs, secular rhymes and songs, blues, jazz, and stories of many kinds. It also consists of dances, wordless musical performances, stage shows, and visual art forms of many sorts" ("Vernacular Tradition" 6). Gates further states that "[r]efusing to subscribe wholly to the white American's ethos and worldview, African Americans expressed in these vernacular forms their own ways of seeing the world, its history, and its meanings" (4). Building on this foundation, I point out that, in *Dutchman*, the vernacular is contained in "the pure heart, the pumping black heart" (34), which Baraka imagines as a locus of black cultural resistance.[1]

I then explain the cathartic function of black music: while slaves faced daily oppression and dehumanization, they also resisted these forces. They developed, for example, musical rituals that allowed them to exorcize the demons of slavery. Moreover, slaves often encoded their songs in ways that the enslavers could not fathom (e.g., as mockery of overseers). Lawrence Levine and Lauri

Ramey have shown how spirituals like "Steal Away to Jesus" signaled the imminent arrival of the Underground Railroad. Therefore, black music and its performance became ways to resist oppression, to survive the conditions on plantations, and to uphold the humanity denied to African Americans.

To emphasize that last point, I use James Cone's account of the music's meaning for blacks: "Whatever form black music takes, it is always an expression of black life in America and what the people must do to survive with a measure of dignity in a society which seems bent on destroying their right to be human beings. The fact that black people keep making music means that we as a people refuse to be destroyed" (130). Cone also believes that "[t]he blues tells us about black people's attempt to carve out a significant existence in a very trying situation. The purpose of the blues is to give structure to black existence in a context where color means rejection and humiliation" (114). I find that these explanations summarize the music's many definitions.

To demonstrate how Baraka viewed black music, I then employ Kimberly Benston's *The Renegade and the Mask*. Benston's conceptualization of the music as a continuum of cultural resistance forces the students to look beyond Clay's apparent rejection of ethnic ties with blacks. Benston expands on Baraka's *Blues People* to propose a theory of roots (84–87). For Benston, roots music reinvokes and iterates elemental black identity; it shares the history of the black experience in speaking to African American ontology. Essentially, roots music is pure black music whose ritualization whites cannot fathom. Benston's theorization of roots helps students to understand Baraka's allusion to Bessie Smith and Charlie Parker, two representatives of roots musical forms, namely, the blues and bebop. Though it is "the first native American musical expression" (Benston 84), blues "finds its source in African spirit" (85), in "a kind of ethno-historic rite as basic as blood" (Baraka, *Blues* 148). These definitions highlight the music's assertions of black being. Likewise, Benston considers bebop "the second great moment of black music," for it "set out to restate the 'basic blues impulse' in black music." "Yet Baraka designates it as 'roots,'" Benston adds, "because it also initiated a true advance and this was again more a matter of cultural than of specifically musical statement" (86). I explain to students that such statement suggests that bebop speaks to black creativity and identity in ways similar to blues. Here Benston sees bebop as black innovation, as one of the ways blacks adapted their vernacular culture to their contemporary predicament.

Such descriptions of bebop foreground most of the ideas, contexts, and themes I wish to convey when evoking black music. For instance, I point out that the beats adopted bebop to sound their rejection of the great American way and of the mainstream culture of conformity. They identified with the fury of jazz performers like Charlie Parker and Dizzy Gillespie, linking them to such *poètes maudits* as Rimbaud and Baudelaire. The beats heard in bebop the same countercultural statements uttered in their own works. More tellingly, perhaps, beats appropriated black music because it expressed, they believed, their own isolation from conservative America; they equated their desolate yet hopeful states to those of disenfranchised blacks who used their culture to survive.

To introduce students to the late 1940s and early 1950s contexts that gave birth to both bebop and beat philosophy, I use Ross Russell's essay "Bebop," which defines this jazz style as "[the] music of revolt: revolt against big bands, arrangers, vertical harmonies, soggy rhythms, non-playing orchestra leaders, Tin-Pan Alley—against commercialized music in general" (202). Bebop's resistance is often defined more aesthetically—a jagged rhythmic structure, a preference for complex improvisatory solos, and a rejection of swing and commercial co-optation—than politically. Still, because of bebop's aesthetic complexity, black cultural commentators and poets have often spoken about bebop in political terms. When Baraka has Clay allude to "Bird" (i.e., Charlie Parker), he certainly points in the direction of a politicized view. It might be helpful to refer to Baraka himself, who, in *Blues People*, notes how "[s]wing had no meaning for the blues people, nor was it expressive of the emotional life of most Negroes after the war" (181). Also, Baraka hears in the "willfully harsh, *anti-assimilationist*, sound of bebop" (181) the rejection of and resistance to swing, which is perceived as a symbol of white commercialization of black culture; such rejection can be interpreted politically.

Clay's allusion to root forms reclaims not only the black tradition of using art as coded resistance but also the history of black suffering that the music has sought to exorcize (Heble 60). I try to convey to my students how Clay, during his long monologue, "steps back into *real* history" (Benston, *Baraka* 171). Clay's allusion, I show, is a performance of black cultural memory that brings him back to a positive assertion of identity meant to defeat Lula's reductive definition of blackness and black culture.

Once I have defined my terms, I provide examples of black misrepresentation that Clay confronts using vernacular music. Since students in the course have usually taken an introductory course in American literary and cultural history, which includes two class sessions (or six hours) on the African American experience from the antebellum period to the civil rights era, they are generally aware of post–Civil War interracial dynamics, especially those between black men and white women. These dynamics formed the basis of the myth of the black rapist.

To contextualize the myth further, I show what is perhaps the most famous visual example of such interracial taboo: the "chase" scene from D. W. Griffith's *Birth of a Nation*, a scene that that ends in a white woman's death and becomes a prelude to the formation of the Ku Klux Klan. This context helps the students frame Baraka's opening stage directions. I highlight the stage directions that precede scene 1 both to foreshadow the play's conclusion and to begin to explain why Clay will invoke black vernacular music to resist the history he seems to be reenacting:

> *The man looks idly up until he sees a woman's face staring at him through the window; when it realizes that the man has noticed the face, it begins*

> *very premeditatedly to smile. The man smiles too, for a moment, without a trace of self-consciousness. Almost an instinctive though undesirable response. Then a kind of awkwardness or embarrassment sets in, and the man makes to look away, is further embarrassed. . . .* (4)

Clay, realizing the historical meaning of his gaze, feels "embarrassed"; he finds himself involved in a history of lynching that even his acting as a white man cannot restrain. For Lula, Clay has revived the black rapist stereotype in the subway, a setting already "heaped in modern myth" (3). My students and I discuss how the modernization of the black rapist myth speaks to the relentless demonization of blacks by a racist system that constantly seeks to deprive them of their humanity. Lula is right, then: she is an "actress" (19), and her stage is the history of racial violence symbolized by Clay's inevitable murder at the end. This inevitability is prefigured in the myth of the Flying Dutchman.[2] The goal is, in fact, to show that she needs to re-enslave the "escaped nigger" (29) to a historical narrative she authors. Her use of the racial epithet reveals her need to control the replaying of history. In short, I point out that Clay is trying to claim his freedom in a world that wishes to re-enslave him to a history his white oppressors never wanted him to escape. To exorcize this oppressive history, Clay will conjure up black music, which will allow him to reject the demonizing epithet and prevent him from capitulating under its historical weight.

Subsequently, I can point to another instance of cultural misunderstanding and misrepresentation, which, this time, catalyzes Clay's monologue: Lula's misguided conception of "the belly rub." For Clay, the belly rub is part of the cultural continuum of ritualized black art. I refer to Melvin Dixon who, in simple but pertinent words, contends that the dance is part of the "hidden culture which remains invisible to Lula" (78)—mostly because she reduces her conception of black rituals to sexual acts in "dark places" (Baraka, *Dutchman* 34). Since misrepresentation of black dance leads to Clay's affirmation of blues and bebop as resistance, it is pertinent to identify the belly rub as a dance that accompanied ragtime and blues performance and thus as a dance firmly ingrained in black vernacular traditions. I want my students to grasp the importance of black dance as a form of ritualized performance and vernacular resistance similar to music, and not primarily in terms of the explicit, primitive sexuality that Lula perceives.

For Lula, the dance and the music enact the stereotype of oversexed black men (Clay's "manhood," 25) that is part of white Southern mythology. Lula proposes a tryst at her "hovel" (24), a space created from stereotypes of debasement that Lula associates with primitive black sexuality. Lula's strategy is important to explain to students, for it evokes the previously mentioned interracial dynamics.

To counter these reductive perceptions of black vernacular performances, Clay speaks of their coded nature. Blacks employ the music to communicate, to resist oppression, and to raise consciousness; this use is the crux of Clay's message in the final monologue. Again, the goal is to prompt students to engage critically with the notion that the vernacular culture Euro-American oppressors sought to negate, erase, and debase is the means by which African Americans have upheld their humanity. Students thus understand that behind "what's there to see," behind the "act," lies a coded "device" (34) that blacks, since slavery, have used to transcend daily oppression and racism. That "device" is a cultural ritual of exorcism capable of alleviating the burden of stereotypes and misrepresentation.

Likewise, Clay understands the language encoded in Bessie Smith's and Charlie Parker's musical performances:

> Old bald-headed four-eyed ofays popping their fingers . . . and don't know yet what they're doing. They say, "I love Bessie Smith." And don't even understand that Bessie Smith is saying, "Kiss my ass, kiss my black unruly ass." . . . Charlie Parker? Charlie Parker. All the hip white boys scream for Bird. And Bird saying, "Up your ass, feeble-minded ofay! Up your ass." (35)

My class comes to see that Baraka's use of "saying" expresses the black vernacular's encodedness. Like the slaves mocking the overseer or enslaver through song, Parker and Smith taunt their audiences (even as the audiences sing their praises). These musicians "sing curses in codes" (35) to oblivious white audiences who symbolize the "great intellectual legacy of the white man" (35), a tradition that the play regards as incompatible with black humanity.

To get students to think about the potential of such coded double-talk in music, I ask them if other words in the play have more than one relevant meaning. Students like to work with the word "murder"; Baraka's use of the word tends to polarize students according to how they perceive Clay (as either assimilationist or emergent cultural nationalist, or, as students say, as either "white" or "black"). To initiate the debate, I explain the idea of "murder" as subversion using William J. Harris's analysis of Baraka's "jazz aesthetic."

Harris states that "[a]s a black artist, [Baraka] is obsessed with white images because they create and control the nature of reality for both whites and blacks" (*Poetry* 24). Though focused on Baraka's poetry, Harris's study offers a very interesting way of reading Clay's subversion of white misrepresentation and the humiliating roles Lula ascribes to him. Harris uses a musical metaphor in order to underscore the subversive potential of black culture. Citing John Coltrane as exemplar of the "jazz aesthetic process" (14), Harris writes,

> Coltrane takes a weak western form, a popular song [e.g., "My Favorite Things"], and murders it; that is, he mutilates and disembowels this shallow but bouncy tune by using discordant and aggressive sounds to attack and destroy the melodic line. . . . Baraka also wants to take weak western forms, rip them asunder, and create something of the rubble. He trans-

> poses Coltrane's ideas to poetry, using them to turn white poetic forms backwards and upside down. This murderous impulse is behind all of the forms of Baraka's aesthetic and art. (14–15)

If we accept the premise of Harris's study, it is possible to state that Clay "murders" the Baudelaire in "black Baudelaire" (19), that Clay takes off the mask of the beat bohemian and adopts a more cultural nationalist identity. Moreover, by invoking Parker's subversive sound, Clay asserts his own culture and ontology.

The revolution to which Clay alludes at the end of his monologue is also subversive; it becomes an enactment of a revolutionary black consciousness. Free from the stereotypes that have been "murdered" by vernacular performances of blackness, African Americans, led by artists like Parker, Smith, and Clay, will confront racism and inequality using their history and culture as weapons.[3] For Clay, then, music is a sublimation (Heble 59; Olaniyan 79; Lindberg 143) of literal "murderous impulse[s]" (Harris 15). Clay suggests the "murder" of an assimilating Eurocentric culture through a revolution of black consciousness expressed in vernacular forms.

Moreover, sublimation speaks to the ways slaves used their culture to challenge the dehumanization that they faced daily on the plantations. To reject the definitions of black humanity forced on slaves through the means of cultural performances is, in many ways, the first instance of black cultural nationalism. In the 1960s, cultural nationalists like Baraka worked in conjunction with militant political organizations to catalyze the black revolution; they heard political messages in the music of Curtis Mayfield, Martha and the Vandellas, and James Brown—all descendants of blues singers like Leadbelly, Blind Lemon Jefferson, and Bessie Smith. Likewise, Baraka and many of his contemporaries heard in the free jazz of John Coltrane—a descendant of Charlie Parker—a musical corollary to the teachings of Malcolm X. Critics like Howard Rambsy II, Meta DuEwa Jones, and Scott Saul have argued that the Coltrane–Malcolm X association permeates the artistic production of black arts intellectuals in the 1960s.

In many ways, Baraka sees these performers' artistry as a politicized rejection of oppression and a positive assertion of black identity. When Clay alludes to Parker and Smith, he highlights these performers' use of their music to fight off the oppressors; black artists like Parker and Smith provided black audiences with the means to revolutionize their individual and collective consciousness. Essentially, the music, according to black cultural nationalists, could guide and lead the black masses to self-determination.

Most students are initially inclined to read *Dutchman* as political commentary or as an allegory of race relations, but I try to call their attention to Baraka's vernacular practice. In the context of the emergent black cultural nationalism of the mid-1960s, artists like Baraka (re)turned to vernacular traditions in order to highlight the ways in which African Americans have maintained their humanity and kept their history alive by claiming the vernacular as cultural memory.

NOTES

[1] A Yẹmisi Jimoh states that "the oppressive conditions of slavery, and similar attempts in later years to shatter the spirit of black people, create a body of shared experiences that have shaped the construction of an aesthetic and life philosophy located in the music of African Americans" (25–26).

[2] I find it helpful to provide students with a succinct explanation of the myth. Jerry Gafio Watts explains that the Flying Dutchman "was condemned to sail forever with a crew of the living dead" (493n66). Heble sees the Flying Dutchman as a "ghostship . . . without hope of reaching the shore." He likens the vessel to the subway, another "ghostship, with Lula, its captain, condemned to commit a ritual act of murder, and Clay, in this case, condemned to be the victim" (57).

[3] According to James Smethurst, "Clay advances the view that jazz is a displacement of black rage that, if one is able to hear it, is a truer account of black experience in the United States than any formal history or than actual events themselves" (83). Clay seems to be following Malcolm X's dictum that "Afro-American history and culture [are] indispensable weapons in the Black quest for freedom" (Van Deburg 5).

"And That's How the Blues Was Born": Baraka's *Dutchman* and Baldwin's *Blues for Mister Charlie* in Conversation

D. Quentin Miller

The similarities between Amiri Baraka's *Dutchman* and James Baldwin's *Blues for Mister Charlie* are striking. Both plays were produced in 1964, both were written by experimental writers best known at that time for other literary genres (Baraka for poetry and criticism, Baldwin for essays and fiction), and both were controversial and provocative. In both plays, a volatile, neurotic white character murders a young black man. Indeed, the same actor, Al Freeman, Jr., played Richard Henry in the Broadway debut of Baldwin's play and Clay in the 1966 film version of Baraka's. The differences between the plays are also significant. *Dutchman* is surreal and nightmarish whereas *Blues* is moody and allegorical. Baraka's short play centers almost entirely around two characters, while Baldwin's expansive drama contains multitudes. The setting of Baraka's is a subway car, a distinctly public space; Baldwin's has a variety of settings, ranging from the public (a juke joint, a church, a courtroom) to the private (a desolate country road, a kitchen). Baraka's play shows the transformation within one black man from repression and accommodation to rage; Baldwin's shows the same transformation, but it is distributed among a number of characters. The two plays together provide an excellent opportunity to highlight the ambivalence and tension surrounding integration in the early 1960s.

Such observations can serve as starting points for discussions about the relation between social issues and theater, about the persistence of history and the value of pessimism with regard to progress, and about the power of rage as a response to racism. Yet no understanding of the two plays can be complete without a discussion of the blues. Baraka's *Blues People* underscores what I consider the pivotal line in *Dutchman*: when Clay ruminates on the history of plantations and the songs that came from them,[1] he says, "And that's how the blues was born" (30). Lula's eccentricity erupts into all-out madness at this moment as the play builds toward its violent crescendo. Similarly, in Baldwin's play, the blues dually function to express black identity and elicit a reaction from white auditors. As Meridian tells Parnell, "*All* white men are Mister Charlie," and he wonders what will happen "if Mister Charlie can't change" (40). The "for" in Baldwin's title indicates that the blues are played on behalf of white people who don't have the capacity to sing them but also that they are played so that white people might hear them. The plays encourage reading strategies similar to the listening strategies one should use when encountering the blues. To appreciate them, one must make broad connections and be willing to listen rather than be content merely to hear. This concept is key to a survey course I teach on African American literature but applied broadly to many situations and different modes of perceiving. Double consciousness and invisibility (found in W. E. B. Du Bois and Ralph Ellison, respectively) are related to distorted vision. A crucial parallel occurs when one fails to hear the sorrow or weariness in the blues (the former found in Frederick Douglass and the latter in Langston Hughes). Students need to see and hear clearly in order to appreciate the literature we study. As Houston Baker argues, "[The blues] are the multiplex, enabling *script* in which Afro-American cultural discourse is inscribed" (*Blues* 4).

The blues were a site of contention in the early 1960s because the form had been overshadowed by its popular descendent, rock and roll. Baraka and Baldwin were both sensitive to the dangers of cultural appropriation as an essential African American expression was converted into dance music by wildly popular white performers like Elvis Presley. Baldwin and Baraka were also concerned that desegregation would bring the loss of original black forms of expression. As Baraka argues in *Blues People*, white Westerners frequently misread the blues—and misread black people more generally—because they apply evaluative standards that exclude both Africans and African Americans. In discussing the origins of the blues, Baraka writes, "If we think of African music as regards its intent, we must see that it differed from Western music in that it was a purely *functional* music. . . . 'Serious' Western music, except for early religious music, has been strictly an 'art' music [and thus] has never been an integral part of the Westerner's life; no art has been since the Renaissance" (*Blues People* 29). Baraka plays with the term "art" to demonstrate the difference between what is considered art in the Western world—something beautiful—and African art, which connects "music, dancing, song, the artifact, and a man's life or his worship of the gods. *Expression* issued from life, and *was* beauty" (29). The blues are the intersection of the two sensibilities and the origin of African American identity; Baraka writes, "I cite the beginning of blues as one beginning of American Negroes. Or, let me say, the reaction and subsequent relation of the Negro's experience in this country in *his* English is one beginning of the Negro's *conscious* appearance on the American scene" (xii). The moment in *Dutchman* when Clay announces, "And that's how the blues was born" is thus the moment when Clay's black consciousness is born, in his English ("blues was") as opposed to the standardized English he employs elsewhere in the play. It is a violent birth that challenges Lula's sensibility as the representative of white America.

The blues not only express the identity of African Americans but also disturb or unsettle white auditors who haven't understood them properly. Clay, in his ranting monologue toward the end of the play, tells Lula that Bessie Smith—nicknamed "the Empress of the Blues"—was telling white people to "kiss [her] black unruly ass" (34) and that Charlie Parker could have as easily "killed the first ten white people he saw" as played "a note of music" (35). Here, the blues become both an affirmation of identity and an artistic sublimation of aggression or violence. Clay admits that his attempt to assimilate into the "middle-class fake white" world is also a way to avoid violence: "I sit here, in this buttoned-up suit, to keep myself from cutting all your throats" (34). But his fatal flaw is that he is not an artist, only a "would-be poet" who lacks a blues singer's commitment to craft; he tells Lula, "[I]f I murdered you, then other white people would begin to understand me. You understand? No. I guess not. If Bessie Smith had killed some white people she wouldn't have needed that music" (35).

Baldwin's title names the blues, but there is no content parallel to Clay's discussion of Bessie Smith or Charlie Parker, though Baldwin does discuss these figures at length elsewhere.[2] The blues music in Baldwin's title is analogous to his act of writing the play. As he says in his introduction, "We are walking in terrible darkness here, and this is one man's attempt to bear witness to the reality and the power of light" (xv).[3] Like Baraka, he is interested in the blues as an expression of black identity and experience,[4] and he is interested in the way the blues affect white audiences and listeners. His 1964 essay "The Uses of the Blues" begins:

> The title "The Uses of the Blues" does not refer to music; I don't know anything about music. It does refer to the experience of life, or the state of being, out of which the blues come. Now, I am claiming a great deal for the blues; I'm using them as a metaphor—I might have titled this, for example, "The Uses of Anguish" or "The Uses of Pain." But I want to talk about the blues not only because they speak of this particular experience of life and this state of being, but also because they contain the toughness that manages to make this experience articulate. I am engaged, then, in a discussion of craft, or, to use a very dangerous word, art. (57)

Baldwin's essay links his art (writing) to the blues and focuses on the lyrics of two prominent blues singers—Bessie Smith and Billie Holiday—whose lives, like that of *Blues*'s Richard Henry, were filled with suffering, tragedy, and addiction. Baldwin writes:

> [A] Negro has his difficult days, the days when everything has gone wrong and on top of it, he has a fight with the elevator man, or the taxi driver, or somebody he never saw before, who seems to decide to prove he's white and you're black. But this particular Tuesday it's more than you can take. . . . and God knows what will happen. I have seen it all, I have seen that much. What the blues are describing comes out of all this. (58–59)

The situation Baldwin describes occurs in the climactic scene in *Blues for Mister Charlie* in which Richard confronts (some would say provokes) his racist murderer, Lyle Britten. It also describes Clay and Lula's interaction in *Dutchman*.

It is important to underscore that Clay and Richard are unlike the blues singers Baraka's and Baldwin's nonfiction describes because they have no outlet to express their anguish in a socially beneficial or acceptable manner. Clay has forsaken poetry in favor of an automatic, unexamined middle-class existence, and Richard has suffered through drug addiction, engaged in joyless affairs, and descended into a nihilistic bitterness (in contrast with his peers, who engage in social activism). In "The Uses of the Blues," Baldwin borrows verbatim a line from his famous story "Sonny's Blues": "There is no way not to suffer" (59). In "Sonny's Blues," this truth is affirmed by Sonny, who, like Richard, has struggled with addiction. But Sonny has a lifesaving outlet in his music. Baldwin speaks of the "triumph" of blues singers: "the person to whom these [painful incidents] happened watched with eyes wide open, saw it happen. So that when Billie or Bessie or Leadbelly stood up and sang about it, they were commenting on it, a little bit outside it" (59). The blues provide a way to cope with suffering, to "comment on it" in order to experience not only despair but also "joy" (57). Both Clay and Richard are eventually pushed to express their rage, but they do so in a diatribe of invective. Had they found their blues voices, they might have purged their rage and discovered the joy that would keep them alive. Since they did not, their deaths can benefit only the plays' audiences. It is difficult to regard Clay and Richard as heroic. Both young men attack dangerous white people who murder them in turn. Both objectify women and threaten them with sexual violence. Neither has accomplished anything worthwhile, and neither expresses hope in the future. In fact, they are not heroic, and they are doomed to a premature death because they are not in touch with their blues sensibility. It takes artists like Baldwin and Baraka, a "little bit outside" of their tragic lives, to contextualize them and to make them, in a sense, the subjects of blues songs.

This observation is key to a principle I impart to students in my African American literature survey: understanding the blues for what the music really expresses is akin to understanding the stories of blues people that we encounter in African American literature. Many of these stories are filled with suffering that does not lead to conventional redemption. Baldwin intends his play as this kind of lesson; as he says in "The Uses of the Blues," we must all be willing to "go into the chaos out of which and only out of which we can create ourselves into human beings. . . . You can't know anything about life and suppose you can get through it clean" (64–65). Similarly, in "Jazz and the White Critic" (1963), Baraka writes, "The blues and jazz aesthetic, to be fully understood, must be seen in as nearly its complete human context as possible. People made bebop. The question the critic must ask is *why*? But it is just this *why* of Negro music that has been consistently ignored or misunderstood" (16). Both authors make sure their audiences cannot ignore or misunderstand the circumstances from which the blues arise, the troubled lives of people like Clay and Richard. Both plays insist, despite their breaks with realism, that the characters at the heart of the drama are real people. Baraka's plea is for the audience to understand "blues people" just as we must strive to understand the blues. Clay echoes the title of *Blues People* during his rant to Lula.[5] He cautions her to tell the white world to stop "preach[ing] so much rationalism and cold logic to these niggers" because

> maybe they'll begin to listen. And then, maybe one day, you'll find they actually do understand exactly what you are talking about, all these fantasy

> people. All these *blues people*. And on that day, as sure as shit, when you really believe you can "accept" them into your fold, as half-white trusties late of the subject peoples. With no more blues, except the very old ones, and not a watermelon in sight, the great missionary heart will have triumphed, and all of these ex-coons will be stand-up Western men, with eyes for clean hard useful lives, sober, pious and sane, and they'll murder you. . . . and have very rational explanations. (36; emphasis mine)

This pronouncement causes Lula to drop her insane persona and to dispatch Clay efficiently. He is essentially describing himself: a blues person with "no more blues" but with the sort of simmering rage that produced the blues in the first place. Without an artistic outlet, he might have murdered Lula. She recognizes him as a real threat, liable to kill the first white person he sees, like Charlie Parker or Bessie Smith would have if they didn't have music. Blues people, in this sense, are not necessarily blues performers but people who have suffered and struggled in a racially oppressive society.[6] Their stories constitute the majority of the figures in African American literary history. An expansive definition of "blues people" suggests that music and art are not the only socially constructive ways for black people to channel rage. The blues can be the spark that ignites speechmaking, political organization, community activism, or many other forms of activism.

I continually rearrange the syllabus of my African American literature survey course and make substitutions annually to ensure a fresh approach to this important tradition. I generally organize the course chronologically, but, in a recent iteration, I divided it into three thematic units to move discussions back and forth across the tradition nimbly, making connections as the semester progressed. In this version, Baldwin's and Baraka's plays were the final two works, so students had a wealth of material to refer back to. I used this opportunity to play some blues songs and to discuss their relation to more contemporary popular musical forms: rock and hip-hop. I began with Bessie Smith's "Back-Water Blues" and Charlie Parker's "Blues" to illustrate what Clay was saying about them (that their music is rage, channeled and translated into music). I supplemented these works with excerpts from Baldwin's "Uses of the Blues" and Baraka's *Blues People* in order to demonstrate the authors' emphasis on pain, suffering, and the history that produced the blues. I then played a song roughly contemporary to the two plays—Les McCann's 1969 soul-jazz masterpiece "Compared to What?" Finally, we listened to a contemporary rap song, "My Pen & Pad" by Blackalicious, about the redemptive potential of creating music and the importance of sensitive listening.[7] This music highlighted a central issue in the plays: the vital importance of expressing rage artistically so that one can avoid pointless deaths like those of the plays' antiheroes. We also talked about the hard work of careful listening and about the possibility of misinterpretation: is it possible to hear the joy and the exuberance in these songs without understanding their relation to pain and suffering? Can we see Clay and Richard in this tradition, or are they excluded from it because their voices have no outlet, musical or otherwise? The inventive lyrics we heard encouraged us to look at Clay's and Richard's language: both have a tremendous linguistic facility once they allow themselves to speak, and we might regard their oratory as a blues form that goes unrecognized as art.

Following this discussion, students began to see the rich complexity of the blues: music that is at once redemptive and purgative, expressive and creative, inventive and based firmly in reality. Given that this discussion came at the conclusion of our semester, we were able to consider the ways the literature we previously read could be described similarly. First, though, we discussed the music. Challenging though it might be to link these four somewhat disparate songs, my students rose to the occasion and added original insights. One student, for instance, spoke of the way the rap lyric we listened to simulated drums more than any other instrument. This student felt that, by integrating blues music into the African American literature curriculum, the course made more audible the African beats that sound in the English language. Baraka, of course, leads us in that direction in *Blues People*, but my students arrived there on their own. Once they had done so, we returned to a discussion of Langston Hughes, who highlighted that rhythm and merged the "tom-tom beating in the Negro soul" ("Negro Artist" [Lewis] 94) with the external world.

Other examples from the semester flooded forth. One student recalled Frederick Douglass's moving description of plantation work songs, which reveal "at once the highest joy and the deepest sadness" (Appiah 26). Another recalled how Claudia, the narrator of Toni Morrison's *The Bluest Eye*, feels a bond with her mother when the latter is "in a singing mood. . . . She would sing about hard times, bad times, and somebody-done-gone-and-left-me times. But her voice was so sweet and her singing-eyes so melty I found myself longing for those hard times" (25). A lengthy discussion ensued about Ellison's *Invisible Man*, how the progression of blues people in that novel—embodied by Louis Armstrong, the disgraced Jim Trueblood,[8] the amusing slick talker Peter Wheatstraw, and the yam-seller—collectively teach the narrator most of what he needs to know about his identity so that he can learn to sing the blues in his own way: by narrating one of the most important and ambitious novels in the tradition.

In a sense, we concluded, we had been studying variations of the blues all semester long. The blues are a dynamic art form, as Baraka makes clear, and artists must be willing to update them so that each new iteration can be fresh and unique while still connected to history. The same principle applies to African American literature, which can be viewed as contiguous with the blues. In both plays, written at a time when the triumphs of the civil rights movement were compromised by the persistence of racism (glaringly manifested in such incidents as the 1963 assassination of Medgar Evers or the bombing that same year of the Sixteenth Street Baptist Church in Birmingham, Alabama), the blues have the potential to be violent, consciousness-changing songs, not just mood-altering sorrow songs. Like these plays, they can be both at the same time, depending on how we hear them.

NOTES

[1] It is important to point out that Clay's first comment about the origin of the blues is naive and lazy, if not satirical; as Baraka says in *Blues People*, "The stereotyped pictures that many of the apologists for the Southern way of life used as flyleaves for their numerous novels after the Civil War, depicting a happy-go-lucky black existentialist strumming merrily on his banjo while sitting on a bale of cotton, were, I'm sure, more romantic fiction than fact. The slave would hardly have had the time to sit on his master's bale of cotton during the work day, and the only instruments that were in common usage among the slaves were drums, rattles, tambourines, scrapers . . . and the like; even such an African instrument as the banjo was very scarce" (69). Still, Clay's acknowledgment of the blues is an unconscious attempt to connect to his origins, and it gives way quickly to his much more sophisticated interpretation of the blues, an interpretation in line with his author's beliefs.

[2] In Baldwin's story "Sonny's Blues" (1957), Sonny worships Charlie Parker and cannot believe his older brother, the story's narrator, has not heard of him. Baldwin talks about Bessie Smith in "The Uses of the Blues" and also claims that he was listening to her repeatedly as he finished writing his first novel *Go Tell It on the Mountain* in Switzerland. See his 1959 essay "The Discovery of What It Means to Be an American." See also D. Quentin Miller's "Using the Blues."

[3] Quotations of *Blues for Mister Charlie* are taken from the 1992 Vintage edition of the play.

[4] This idea is also central to H. Baker's argument in *Blues, Ideology, and Afro-American Literature* (1984); he writes, "The blues are a synthesis. . . . [T]hey constitute an amalgam that seems always to have been in motion in America—always becoming, shaping, transforming, displacing the peculiar experiences of Africans in the New World" (5).

[5] Coincidentally, Baldwin wrote a pamphlet for the actors in the original production of *Blues for Mister Charlie* entitled "The Blues People" (Leeming 235–36).

[6] H. Baker's study recasts many protagonists of classic African American literature as blues singers (*Blues* 13–14).

[7] Albert King's "Born Under a Bad Sign" would also work here to suggest the connections among classic blues, bebop, and hip-hop. In fact, the late 1960s were filled with great electric blues performances by B. B. King, Buddy Guy, Taj Mahal, and Jimi Hendrix, to say nothing of white rock performers like The Rolling Stones or Led Zeppelin, who directly appropriated the blues idiom and placed it in a rock context. I deliberately choose "Compared to What?" because of its departure from the classic twelve-bar blues sound, but instructors have almost limitless choices to illustrate the classic blues and its variations, both pre– and post–*Blues People*. Rap and hip-hop choices are also limitless, and instructors might reach for a socially conscious, outraged act like Public Enemy, but my selection of "My Pen & Pad" was deliberate here, too, as its bouncy beat and dizzying wordplay forces careful and repeated listening. See Bradley and DuBois, *The Anthology of Rap* (2010).

[8] See H. Baker, *Blues* 172–99.

"No Metaphors," "No Grunts": *Dutchman*, Black Art, and Authenticity

Molly Hiro

In my African American Writers survey, an upper-division course I offer every two years or so at the small, private, majority-white college where I teach, one of the most popular readings is always Audre Lorde's short 1977 piece, "Poetry Is Not a Luxury." I've never known why this is, but I suspect that Lorde's open, optimistic tone comes as a relief to students accustomed to the guardedness that is characteristic of many of her predecessors in the African American literary tradition, few of whom could have uttered anything as sanguine as "I feel, therefore I can be free" (645). But perhaps as moving to student readers, I suspect, is the power and urgency Lorde ascribes to art (the very thing, of course, that these students have signed on to study for four years). Rather than "sterile word play," the meaning that "the white fathers" have assigned the term, "poetry" for Lorde is "a *revelatory* distillation of experience" (644; emphasis mine). Art, in this understanding, peels away the surface and reveals the truth of one's experience. For Lorde, such a truth and the art that reveals it are racialized. An antidote to "living in the European mode," poetry allows access to the "dark place within" (644).[1]

I teach Amiri Baraka's *Dutchman* just after Lorde's essay, for the play unsettles the easy "relatability" (to use a neologism abhorred by many a fellow professor) "Poetry" invites by severing the latter's linkage of art and authenticity. Whereas "Poetry Is Not a Luxury" ascribes to art a unique power to reveal racial truths, *Dutchman*'s disquieting claim, as stated by Clay at the play's conclusion, is that art simply represses the actual truth: blacks' desire to murder whites. Reading Lorde before Baraka makes for an admittedly anachronistic pairing (since *Dutchman* comes more than a decade before "Poetry"), but the sequencing is justified by *Dutchman*'s critique of art as "revelatory," which challenges the promises of Lorde's essay. Moreover, teaching *Dutchman* late in the semester, as I do, enables me to sharpen larger questions we've raised about race and representation throughout the term. In demonstrating how a white woman's power scripts and ultimately destroys a black subject, Baraka's play exposes the complicity of readers—particularly of white readers—in preserving a myth of universally accessible and palatable racial authenticity. In what follows, I will explain how I introduce students to the discourses of racial representation and racial authenticity in African American literature; then I will show how *Dutchman* can provide a new and challenging perspective on these issues.[2]

In my survey, we discuss authenticity and self-representation from the start of the term. Early black American authors published their life stories for a reading public whose limited understandings of blacks were likely fed by well-worn biblical passages or racist pseudoscience. It always fascinates students how former slaves' rich and subtle narratives needed to be bookended by the authenticating documents and signatures of whites who had previously held the sole authority to represent blacks. Even the format of the second edition, single-volume *Norton Anthology of African American Literature* foregrounds issues of authenticity. The volume opens with a 150-page sheaf of folk tales and songs, from "Go Down Moses" to Public Enemy's "Don't Believe the Hype." To begin an otherwise rigorously chronological anthology of African American writing with examples of what, in their opening essay, the editors call "the vernacular tradition" privileges the "recognizably black" (Gates and McKay, "Introduction" 5) over the "white" stylings of, say, a Phillis Wheatley.[3]

The texts I assign often feature a particular trope of authenticity, found in authors' representations of those moments in which they or their narrators "discover" that they are black. In these primal scenes of realization, a white interlocutor's designation of them as other creates an inner turmoil that is eventually followed by an embrace of the newly discovered racial identity. James Weldon Johnson's novel *The Autobiography of an Ex-Colored Man* (1912)—a story of a young mixed-race man who grows up thinking he is white, later takes on a black identity, and finally passes for good as white—provides a powerful example of this trope. The text advances the deep, psychological truth to the black subject's blackness as early as its preface, which promises the reader an "initiat[ion] into the free-masonry . . . of the race," "a view of the inner life of the Negro in America" (xl). The dramatic moment in which the school principal publicly calls out the narrator as black becomes even more powerful when retold as the moment whereafter all his "thoughts were coloured . . . by one dominating, all-pervading idea which constantly increased in force and weight until [he] finally realized in it a great, tangible fact" (20–21).

That all-consuming fact is his authentically black racial identity, and it becomes all-consuming for my students as well. Even though this text and others that we read throughout the term condition students to think of racial identity as fundamentally fluid and constructed, most nonetheless accept the narrator's blackness as fact. They frequently express disapproval of his ultimate decision to live life as a white man. Though his skin is light enough to allow him to pass for white, my students typically (cued as well by his own expressions of guilt) want him to attend to his "true self" and remain black. Texts like Johnson's therefore showcase the way in which authenticity turns inward in modern black writing. In the twentieth century, as Shelly Eversley points out, "The outward signs of a 'negro' identity became less crucial, and as the subtle characteristics of a racial ideal assumed prominence, psychology and narrative interiority helped to define black writing and black identity" (xiii).

If, as in *Autobiography*, narrative art becomes a means of demonstrating the arrival at one's authentic blackness, then, in other readings on my syllabus, music becomes a catalyst for rediscovering that truth, or for distinguishing black selves from white. Langston Hughes's description of the "eternal tom-tom beating in the Negro Soul" ("Negro Artist" [Gates and Smith] 1323) is echoed when

Nella Larsen's protagonist Helga Crane, in *Quicksand* (1928), feels "drugged, lifted, sustained, by the extraordinary music, blown out, ripped out, beaten out" in a jazz club (61). And when, moments later, she corrects herself, insisting that "[s]he wasn't . . . a jungle creature" and "harden[ing] her determination to get away," Larsen represents this moment as an evasion of something deep and true that the music had brought out in Helga (61). In the essay "How It Feels to Be Colored Me" (1928), Zora Neale Hurston describes her experience of attending a show at the "New World Cabaret" with a white person: "I dance wildly within myself; I yell within, I whoop. . . . I am in the jungle and living in the jungle way." Her companion merely remarks that the music is "good," while "drumming the table with his fingertips" (1042). Their different responses to the same music place a great expanse between them: she can see the man "but dimly across the ocean and the continent that have fallen between us" (1042). Moreover, this gap demonstrates that "[h]e is so pale with his whiteness then and I am *so* colored" (1042). Hurston's equation of "colored" with something fundamentally primitive does often strike contemporary student readers as uncomfortably stereotypical. Yet her characterization of whiteness as comparatively cold, dull, and remote, contrasted with her own engaging, open, confessional tone in the essay, work together to affirm and make accessible even such potentially problematic black authenticity.[4] Studying *Dutchman* soon after these discussions can work to unsettle any such comfort with racial authenticity, as we shall see next.

Having discussed the relations between art and authenticity in early-twentieth-century African American literature, we encounter the 1960s and 1970s black arts movement, only to discover that one of its founding presumptions is that most of the previous art was not wholly true to the black experience. For proponents of the black aesthetic, poetry and music do not simply reveal racial truth—they constitute racial truth. Moreover, this true blackness is antithetical to whiteness (as well as to faux blackness) and as such, antagonistic toward white—or nonblack—audiences. We could add "nonmale" and "nonstraight," since two of the most troubling aspects of black arts texts and manifestos are the sexism and homophobia that predominate. But the way black arts reframes the relations between art and authenticity is so compelling that these texts demand our consideration.

If the earlier writers I've mentioned promise access to the truth of race through revelatory glimpses into characters' interiors, black arts keeps such glimpses to itself while moving the locus of racial authenticity from individual psychology to group identification and politics. So, for instance, when the artist Tom Lloyd was asked, in a 1968 debate among visual artists about the definition of "black art," he insisted that it was "art relevant to the Black community"; pressed to define it more precisely, he responded, "I'm Black and I know where my feelings lie" (qtd. in Lennon 99). Lloyd's response implicitly rejects the demand to reveal one's deepest feelings as a testimony to an authentic blackness; true black art becomes simply art that is relevant to those who identify as such.

Moreover, black arts gets aligned by its spokespersons with palpable action; we thus see Addison Gayle, in the introduction to his collection *The Black Aesthetic* (1971), argue that "[t]he question for the black critic today is not how beautiful is a melody, a play, a poem, or a novel, but how much more beautiful has the poem, melody, play, or novel made the life of a single black man?" (Introduction xxiii).

These ideas about black arts inform the hypermateriality of poems such as Baraka's famous "Black Art" (1966), which opens aggressively: "Poems are bullshit unless they are/teeth or trees or lemons piled/on a step" ([Gates and McKay] 703). What do teeth, trees, and lemons have in common apart from their status as everyday, real things? Poems are things; and they do things, as in the line "We want Poems that shoot guns" (703). Baraka's conclusion sustains this emphasis on stripped-down aesthetics:

> We want a black poem.
> And a
> Black World.
> Let the world be a Black Poem
> And Let All Black People Speak This Poem
> Silently
> or loud. (704)

For writers such as Johnson and Hurston art functioned to reveal the truth of blackness; in Baraka's poem, art functions to "shoot guns" or to accomplish the truth of blackness through action that repels, rather than engages, the other. And if art previously served as a catalyst to reveal racial authenticity, now it aims to move beyond such mediation, instead becoming authenticity—Baraka says, "Let the world be a Black Poem," not "let the poem show the world." Nikki Giovanni's "For Saundra" (1968) engages similarly with questions of poetry's use; the poem concludes:

> maybe I shouldn't write
> at all
> but clean my gun
> and check my kerosene supply
> perhaps these are not poetic
> times
> at all. (881)

We can recognize in these lines the black arts movement's lingering anxiety that—despite its revolutionary claims for artistic production—art might compromise the political engagement and black separatism for which the era called.

Amid this constellation of concerns—set up throughout the term, and in a more focused way with respect to black arts just before we read the play—my students encounter *Dutchman*. Even though it is brief, I teach it over two class meetings, in order to make room for discussion of Lorde's "Poetry Is Not a Luxury" on the first day and to watch excerpts from the 1966 film adaptation on the second. On day one, we focus on scene 1, tracking the attraction and tension between Lula and Clay in the subway car. Because Lula claims to know so much about Clay, he deduces that they must have a friend in common. Since they do not, the question emerges: Is Lula figuring Clay out? To use our familiar trope, is she peeling away a surface to reveal his true self? Or is she scripting him—describing him in a way that suits her notion of what a young black man really is? While on the surface Clay appears the type of a black hipster, Lula exposes what's underneath by saying, "You look like you live in New Jersey with your parents and are trying to grow a beard" (8). Later, she dismisses even this self as somehow false when she says, "What right do you have to be wearing a three-button suit and striped tie? Your grandfather was a slave, he didn't go to Harvard" (18). Becoming even more provocative, she adds, "I bet you never once thought you were a black nigger" (19). In these moments, Lula's social taxonomy reflects a larger presumption about the accessibility of blackness's inner truth. But, elsewhere, she scripts Clay's lines—with demands such as "Now you say to me, 'Lula, Lula, why don't you go to this party with me tonight?' It's your turn, and let those be your lines" (16). At this moment, Baraka's central white character is engaged not in discovering some submerged racial truth within her black interlocutor but in creating that truth. Scene 1 dramatizes white authority's mastery over the representation of racial authenticity.

To further expose or script Clay's authentic blackness, Lula turns to music, an art form that, as we have already seen, is thought to offer privileged access to the truth of racial identity and difference. When Clay refuses to dance with Lula (to "rub bellies," as she puts it) before the subway onlookers, she calls him out as counterfeit: "You ain't no nigger, you're just a dirty white man" (30, 31). Lula's relentless public shaming pushes Clay to an explosive reaction, an angry rejection of the way she has represented him and a lengthy manifesto of his own. Students quickly recognize that, through this speech, Clay reasserts his prerogative to represent his racial identity, about which people like Lula know nothing. In this instance he uses his heart, a familiar idiom of authenticity and a deep and vital part of himself, to tell the truth of his identity: "You don't know anything except what's there for you to see. An act. Lies. Device. Not the pure heart, the pumping black heart" (34). Next, he reclaims blues and jazz as belonging to and meaningful for black folks only. White folks who proclaim "'I love Bessie Smith' . . . don't even understand that Bessie Smith is saying, 'Kiss my ass, kiss my black unruly ass.' . . . And if you don't know that, it's you that's doing the kissing" (34–35).

James Edward Smethurst has argued that this crucial moment reveals Baraka's conviction that jazz forms "a truer account of black experience in the U.S. than any formal history" might offer (83). According to this reading, Clay's defense of jazz privileges the equation of art and authenticity that the black arts movement affirmed. When first encountering the play, students often arrive at this point as well. But I push them to recognize the way Clay's next words actually turn that equation on its head:

> If Bessie Smith had killed some white people she wouldn't have needed that music. She could have talked very straight and plain about the world. No metaphors. No grunts. No wiggles in the dark of her soul. Just straight two and two are four. Money. Power. Luxury. Like that. All of them. Crazy niggers turning their backs on sanity. When all it needs is that simple act. Murder. Just murder! Would make us all sane. (35)

Here Bessie Smith's music is simply a cover for the real truth, which is the universal drive among long-oppressed black people to kill white people. Through Clay's phrasing, moreover, Baraka implies that black art forms are too highly mediated ("metaphors"), and therefore inarticulate ("grunts"), to convey the truth of black experience, to "talk very straight and plain about the world." And while Clay's manifesto ultimately agrees with Lorde's argument that "poetry is not a luxury," art, in his terms, is a necessity for black folks not because it enables truth (racial and political self-expression) but because it represses a truth that is taboo (the fundamental black desire to kill whites). We have seen, in Giovanni's "For Saundra," the worry that no art might be radical enough to convey the proper black separatist message; Clay's way of seeing the relations among art, truth, and politics clearly goes beyond even this.

What's more—and what becomes especially unsettling in my African American literature classroom—is the way this new articulation of black art's purpose both shuts out and implicates its readership, especially white readers. A generation earlier, Richard Wright's *Native Son* aimed to repel mainstream white audiences with a similar portrayal of black murderousness, but the reader who sticks with the novel gets rewarded with a view into the truer, troubled interior of Bigger Thomas. Taking *Dutchman* seriously requires acknowledgment that it short-circuits the process by which a sensitive and patient reader can find a redemptive authenticity beneath even such psychologically troubled surfaces, since the play suggests that what lies beneath might instead be even more fundamentally violent. And the fact that the play ends not with Clay's murder of Lula but with Lula's killing Clay shows how such probing reading can have destructive results. If Clay has vigorously rejected Lula's representation of black folks and their art by claiming a more authentic understanding of the relation between art and action, Lula, by killing Clay, is the one to move beyond representation and actually act. In the end, the white character wrests control, once again, of the script.

In our historical moment, when some critics question whether there even remains an African American literature, it is certainly hard to imagine a contemporary black-authored text that would describe black art in Clay's aggressively separatist way.[5] Yet it seems especially vital in an age that idealizes color-blindness to keep the play's lessons at the forefront. In teaching the play as I do, I hope to model a reading practice that puts before any identification with a narrator or character's racialized true self just a moment of self-conscious hesitation.

NOTES

[1] Lorde's notions of truth and art are also gender specific. She ascribes that "dark place within" to women's experiences in particular.

[2] In my course, I develop the concept of authenticity through the primary texts I discuss in this essay. However, instructors interested in the issues that I take up here may wish to consult Chinitz; Jarrett; E. Johnson; Lewis; Retman; and Schur.

[3] I refer here to the single-volume second edition (2004) of the *Norton Anthology of African American Literature*, from which I have long taught. The newer third edition (2014) divides the materials from "The Vernacular Tradition" between its two volumes, but the fact remains that inclusion of twenty-first-century hip-hop at the front of an otherwise chronological anthology (in the second volume) disrupts the typical chronological ordering of Norton editions.

[4] Indeed, a few years ago, one of my more outspoken students, a white woman, admitted in our discussion that she sometimes felt strangely envious of the richness of the African American experience described in Hurston's essay. Her comment's well-meaning but myopic idealizing of black experience unsettled me and others in the group (and a brief discussion about the possibilities and limits of our identification with the voices of racial others ensued), but it indexes my point about the cross-racial appeal of African American authenticity.

[5] Among the recent critical works that question or reaffirm the existence of African American literature are John Ernest's *Chaotic Justice* (2009), Kenneth Warren's *What Was African American Literature?* (2011), and Gene Andrew Jarrett's *Representing the Race* (2011).

Amiri Baraka and Philip Roth: Passing, Place, and Identity

James D. Bloom

Since 1990, *Dutchman*'s place in my teaching repertoire has expanded beyond my African American literature class into other United States literature courses and my first-year seminar Civiliation As (We Think) We Know It. In all these classes, students read *Dutchman* as an exploration of identity construction and cultural heritage. Pairing Baraka with the novelist Philip Roth can facilitate such explorations. Nearly exact contemporaries, Baraka and Roth wrote repeatedly about their heritage as natives of Newark, New Jersey. This biographical coincidence enables students to discover how a sense of place informs both writers' interrogations of identity construction.

The question of identity formation dates back to my earliest experiences teaching *Dutchman* over a generation ago in African American literature surveys. I began with questions about passing raised by Charles W. Chesnutt's *The House Behind the Cedars* (1900), questions that reverberated in subsequent reading assignments, such as James Baldwin's "Sonny's Blues" (1957) and Toni Morrison's *The Bluest Eye* (1970). These texts highlight the perils of ancestrally determined identities and so looked ahead to the final reading assignment, *Dutchman*. Thus, chronologically, we began with a novel published as the Jim Crow system was erected and ended with a play that appeared as it was legally dismantled and as passing (as conventionally understood) ceased to be a widespread practice. In more recent years, however, I have paired *Dutchman* and Roth's novel *The Human Stain* (2000) to explore the transformations that passing underwent in the period after *Brown v. Board of Education*, when the social value of physical imposture seemed to diminish and the practice seemed more than ever like a morally abhorrent risk. Ultimately, we have focused on the role of place identification in racial identity construction.

As LeRoi Jones, Baraka began his literary career during this paradigm shift, as did fellow Newarker Roth. Like Baraka, Roth made his mark by making ethnicity a focal point in his writing. A fascination with passing also came to preoccupy Roth over the course his career (Rowe 189). While passing became a vexing preoccupation among African Americans, its conceptual counterpart, assimilation, became a greater concern among American Jews, who came to regard assimilation as both a disagreeable compromise and a remedy for past oppression (Jacobson 21, 128, 175, 278; Cooper 35). Michele Elam has argued that, while slowly expanding opportunities during the second of half of the twentieth century diminished the appeal of passing as a "historical practice and a literary trope," passing persists as "a mode of . . . social inquiry and literary analysis," as a challenge to "canards of identity formation" (750), and as an opportunity for generating new norms (763). Since Baraka and Roth skewered such norms and canards, and since both writers undertook the inquiry Elam describes, pairing them highlights for students an agenda that informs much ethnic American writing.

The Human Stain is Roth's most important effort to raise these questions. The novel's protagonist, a classics professor named Coleman Silk, was born into an African American family but successfully passed as white for his entire adult life. Late in the narrative, Silk's sister, Ernestine, emerges as a focal character and opens the kind of inquiry that Elam discusses. At Silk's funeral, Ernestine, a retired history teacher, explains passing and draws a "wider picture of what was going on back then," beginning in 1947, "before the civil rights movement": "the decision that he made, despite his Negro ancestry, to live as a member of another racial group—that was by no means an uncommon decision before the civil rights movement. . . . Changing your racial group. . . . [I]t fascinated people the way they are fascinated by a fairy tale" (323). Verbose and euphemistic, the repeated phrase "racial group" turns passing into a children's story, a "fairy tale," and implicitly questions the many other ways of neutralizing the sting of racism that made passing appealing.

Roth and Baraka both look beyond the familiar version of passing that Ernestine describes. Baraka calls a great deal of attention to the role of class in racial identity construction. In *Dutchman*, Lula mocks Clay more for his apparent class pretensions than for challenging the color line. Lula's emphasis on social status prompted one European critic to declare that, by the end of the play, "Lula's and Clay's 'color' becomes immaterial" (Ceynowa 18). Reviewing the New York premiere of *Dutchman* in 1964, Roth noted that "it is the Negro who is missing" from the play because Clay "is not Negro enough" ("Channel X" 11). Even Baraka once played down the play's racial politics, insisting that "*Dutchman* is about the difficulty of becoming a man in America" (*Home* [Morrow] 188).

It is also important to note that Baraka's discourse of racial identity construction often focuses on another ethnic minority group. For Baraka, Jews were a group with a history of oppression, but recently they had nearly disappeared into middle-class America, and their intellectuals had not mounted an effective cultural resistance on the group's behalf. Throughout much of *Dutchman*, Jewishness, instead of blackness, preoccupies Lula and Clay, each characterizing the other as an unacknowledged Jew. Soon after Lula compares Clay to "all those Jewish poets" whom she stereotypes as hapless neurotics, Clay chides her for confusing Nazi concentration camps and antebellum Southern plantations. Her reference to barbed wire prompts him to conclude, "[Y]ou must be Jewish" (29–30).

As Baraka's interest in "Jewish poets" begins to suggest, his discourse of racial identity construction is also a discourse on the intellectual. Lula's most emphatic attack on Clay's affectations targets his "middle-class" intellectual and artistic striving (31)—his "passing" as a "poet" (35). Clay's public persona, including his aspirational three-button suit (18), leads Lula to deprecate him for passing as a "well-known type" (12). Lula's sharpest barb ridicules Clay for representing himself as "the black Baudelaire" (19, 20), a poseur playing at being a cosmopolitan European.

With this reference to Baudelaire, Baraka establishes a pattern of references to European high culture that students may need to look into. The play's allusive density begins with its title, an allusion to Richard Wagner's opera *The Flying Dutchman* (1843). Once alerted to this reference, students might consider whether Baraka's shortening of the title dashes all hope of flying. A recurring metaphor for freedom, as in the hymn "I'll Fly Away" and in Ralph Ellison's story "Flying Home" (1944), flying implicitly speaks to the hope common among the oppressed and marginalized of transcending stifling origins. Thus, with his truncated ("flightless") Wagner allusion, Baraka casts aspiring poets like Clay not as bold Wagnerian voyagers but as, in James Baldwin's terms, downtrodden "bastards of the West" (*Notes* 6). Clay echoes Baldwin by dismissing his own writing as "bastard literature" (35).

Much like the speaker in Countee Cullen's "Heritage" (1925)—which ends by intimating that the poet's grasp of civilization endlessly eludes him despite his tour de force performance of well-wrought stanzaic English verse—Baraka and Clay seem to have found their European heritage both inescapable and alienating. Clay reaches the same impasse as Cullen's speaker by acknowledging Lula's declaration of his whiteness, his status as "a dirty white man" "full of white man's words" (31). Clay's performance as a "dirty white man" exemplifies the "striving to be European and black" that Paul Gilroy has characterized as "play[ing] occidental rationality at its own game." By confessing to being a "dirty white man," Clay identifies himself with the "aspirant intellectualism" that Baraka objected to in Richard Wright's work (Gilroy 1, 38, 173).

As students consider the overall effect of *Dutchman*'s allusive density, they might ask whether, in channeling Wagner and Baudelaire, Clay is really no more than a cultural "bastard" or even an impostor who continues to wear Paul Laurence Dunbar's famous mask. According to Elam, this sort of question has no definite answer. Instead of settling identity questions, passing, she argues, works as a heuristic that sets in motion an endlessly renewing "series of narrative acts" (756). Lula's stories about the various identities she sees Clay "playing at" (17), or passing as, constitute such a series: "All stories are whole stories. All of 'em. Nothing but change. How could things go on like that forever?" (28). Late in the play, Clay seizes on this insight. Aiming to win his conceptual "battle" with Lula (Ceynowa 16), he changes his "story." Recasting himself as a defiant artist and identifying with Bessie Smith and Charlie Parker, whose message he paraphrases as "kiss my black ass," Clay activates the kind of sequence Elam describes, only to interrupt his rhetorical flight into rage with a diminuendo shift to a "weary blues" stance (35). Prefacing Clay's renunciation of speaking for and avenging "[m]y people," who "don't need any defense," is the stage direction "*Suddenly weary*" (35, 36).

This view of passing as provisional and performative draws on Elam's reading of Roth's *The Human Stain*, particularly her reading of an exchange that speaks directly to Clay's role as "the black Baudelaire." In this exchange, Silk's girlfriend, a self-made "Village girl" from a black family, describes Greenwich Village as ground zero for American passing, racial and otherwise: "the four freest square miles in America," where a striver like Silk can launch his "trajectory outward" (136). Roth could also be describing Baraka's mid-century Greenwich Village milieu or "the atmosphere," the postracial utopia, that Lula sarcastically imagines enjoying at Warren Enright's party (22–23). Asad Haider has recently argued that for Baraka, at this point in his career, intellectual aspiration itself represented *"a kind of passing."*

Written for "an era in which," Henry Louis Gates argues, "the very notion of passing was beginning to seem less plangent than preposterous" (205), *The Human Stain* sustains an argument that *Dutchman* introduced a generation earlier and displaces the popular interest in color-centered passing. Roth focuses on how Coleman Silk's adopted identity rested on his cultural affiliations rather than on the genealogical dissembling that disturbed his siblings and still fascinates readers of such novels as Chesnutt's *House Beyond the Cedars* and Nella Larsen's *Passing* (1929). Roth reportedly based *The Human Stain* on Anatole Broyard's real-life passing story (Staples; Bloomgarden). The influential critic passed as a "mandarin" exemplar of "worldliness and high culture" (Gates 180). With "all western literature at his fingertips" (181), Broyard dazzled the artistic and intellectual Greenwich Village community in which Baraka moved during the late 1950s and early 1960s. Broyard exhibited the cultural aspirations that Lula attributes to Clay and appealed to the same cultural legacy. "Quoting Baudelaire turn[ed] out to be key" to Broyard's passing as well as to his wooing, Gates observes (191). Roth depicts Silk as another such cultural aspirant, an authority on Greek tragedy who is superlatively steeped in the European literary canon. By marriage, Silk becomes Jewish and thus appropriates one of the precarious identities Lula and Clay thrust on each other. Jewishness complements Silk's calling as a classicist, insofar as intellectual sophisticates have long been taught, by authorities ranging from Matthew Arnold to Erich Auerbach, that the European intellectual heritage rests on a union of Hellenism and Hebraism. Before his marriage, Silk's more formative Jewish connection was with the trainer who helped transform him into a teenage boxing champion.

A connoisseur of the "myriad subtleties" Dunbar acknowledged in "We Wear the Mask," this boxing mentor taught Silk to box artfully and "ignore his feelings, rather than explosively reacting and aiming for a knockout" (97, 90, 100; see also Ceynowa 16). Once, however, Silk flouted this subtle aesthetic. He knocked a white opponent "all over the place" before a crowd that saw only Silk's white appearance and knew nothing of his black heritage: "He threw a hook, one that seemed to go three-quarters of the way into the guy's body. . . . [T]he guy folded forward. . . . Coleman set himself to whack him with the right one more time—all he saw as this white guy was going down was somebody he wanted to beat the shit out of" (101). Elam describes Roth's account of Silk's teenage ring career as a reprise and reversal of "Ralph Ellison's excruciating

Battle Royale scene in *Invisible Man*" (757). Unlike the career of Ellison's narrator, Silk's triumphs in prizefighting set the stage for his lifelong battle against tyranny, which Silk expected to win by passing (Roth, *Human Stain* 108–09).

Mixing aggression and wiliness, Silk contains in one ambiguously dark body the warring ideals of violence and restraint. At the end of *Dutchman*, Clay moves between these poles in his climactic face-off with Lula. Clay's violent, mostly verbal explosion, his threat to "murder" her on the basis of "very rational explanations" (36), provokes her to murder him instead. Clay's failure to master violence and even his failure to become the "murderer" Lula accuses him of being (21) stand in sharp contrast to Silk's successes as both a physical and intellectual aggressor. Roth describes Silk as "something of an operator, something of a warrior" (4); "direct, frank, unacademically forceful" (4); "bulldozing" (9); a "barroom brawler" (23); and "a force" (82).

Depictions of Silk and Clay as amalgams of rage and refinement, cerebral sophistication and uneasily contained violence, speak to the question that reverberates throughout mid-century African American writing: Langston Hughes's much-anthologized "what becomes of a dream deferred?" ("Harlem"). Since Hughes's question and its threat also reverberate throughout work by twentieth-century white ethnic writers such as Mike Gold, James Farrell, and John Fante, comparisons between Clay and Silk allow students to reflect on the strategies deployed by American writers and the choices made by oppressed and marginalized Americans to resist the status quo.

Pairing Baraka and Roth will reveal passing as one such strategy. During the era of unprecedented social mobility in which Baraka and Roth came of age, passing became subtler as physical imposture became less expedient. Ernestine's disparagement of her brother's passing as an anachronistic "fairy tale" reinforces these views that passing encompasses far more than skin color. Fairy tales, Bruno Bettelheim has influentially argued, seek to solve life's problems and to furnish coping strategies (Acocella). Clay, too, invokes our shared fairy tale legacy and looks to the Brothers Grimm for such a social coping strategy. When Lula demands that Clay join her in "do[ing] the nasty" and "[r]ub[bing] bellies" and chants a ditty about "ten little niggers sitting on limb," Clay tries to placate her by comparing her to Snow White and praising her as "the fairest one of all" (30). The very name Snow White bespeaks coldness and purity, in sharp contrast to the overheated sexuality that Lula exudes and caricatures. Lula's resistance to Clay's rhetorical infantilizing meets with a peremptory response from Clay: "sit down. . . . Be cool" (31). Though the problems that fairy tales may solve seem universal and perennial, the stories seldom meet the needs of adult sense-making (Bettelheim 126–27). Thus, with Lula's next outburst, the failure of Clay's Snow White trope becomes unmistakable. Rising from her subway seat in order to dance herself into a murderous frenzy, Lula appears more akin to the wicked queen than to the heroine. This contrast underscores how much Clay has misread and misappropriated the Grimm story, and the play implicitly discredits popular views of fairy tales as coping strategies.

The crises of identity that *Dutchman* stages and the promise of social mobility that Lula disparages discredit the time-tested fairy-tale authority that Roth's Ernestine questions. The play thus undermines the claims of all supposedly time-tested narratives. In drawing a contrast between her brothers—the younger one who passed and the older one who didn't—Ernestine uses a metaphor that recalls Clay's effort to "cool" Lula and explains how the older brother, Walt, reacted to the younger's passing:

> Walt froze everything in time. And that is never a good idea. It wasn't going to be 1953 forever. People age. Nations age. *Problems* age. Of course if you look at it narrowly, simply from the point of view of social advantage, of course it was advantageous in the well-spoken Negro middle class to do it Coleman's way just as it's advantageous today not to dream of doing it that way. (326)

In *Dutchman*, Baraka positions Clay—and Lula pins him down—between these irreconcilable options. This endlessly liminal position, which Clay's subway ride evokes, becomes a space in which traditional passing no longer seems feasible and where ambiguous cultural masquerading displaces binary physical imposture.

Both these options, however, prove perilous for Clay and Silk. As color becomes increasingly fallible as an identity marker, geography maintains much of its traditional authority. According to Lisa Siraganian, Baraka's singular emphasis on place illustrates how an attachment to a distinctive locale can be a compelling measure of identity (162). Suggesting the same of himself, Roth summed up his "knowledge repertoire" as "family, family, family, Newark, Newark, Newark, Jew, Jew, Jew" (*Facts* 16). In *Dutchman*, Baraka looks, more broadly, to New Jersey as whole in introducing Clay's place-based identity. Thus, Lula's intended insult early in *Dutchman*, "You look like you live in New Jersey" (8), aligns outward appearance with geographical origins and implies that being from New Jersey resembles a racial or an ethnic attachment. Lula's put-down targets the place identification that Roth and Baraka share and prompts questions about "liv[ing] in New Jersey" as a distinct cultural identity.

The fascination with Newark's folkways and idioms that permeates Baraka's and Roth's work may help address these questions. Where Baraka cites its "street anthropology" and its "poetic" inventiveness (*Autobiography* [Lawrence Hill] 30, 17; Sollors 254), Roth stresses its "rivalrous ethnic" climate, its "self-defining heterogeneity" (*Facts* 37), and its "lyrical feeling" (*Zuckerman* 403). These evocations suggest that Baraka and Roth, in repeatedly writing about this city throughout their careers, were spurred by the same blend of curiosity and affection.

The title story of Roth's first book, "Goodbye, Columbus" (1959), locates Newark's poetic possibilities along its tenacious color line. Throughout "Goodbye, Columbus," the librarian narrator turns from his main plot, a Gatsbyesque poor-boy/rich-girl blighted-summer romance, to explore his relationship with the grade school African American library patron, a Gauguin enthusiast like Baraka, whom he tries to befriend (37, 47, 59; Baraka, *System* [Akashic] 73). In imagining the boy's life beyond the library, Roth looks to the same neighborhood in which Baraka lived as a child. What the narrator finds while passing through the "Negro section of Newark" ("*Goodbye*" 90), once "the old Jewish immigrant slum" (*I Married* 91), is a crucible of heritage narratives and a rich source of opportunities for historically informed lyricism. Roth's narrator pictures the "Kosher delicatessens" where his immigrant grandparents shopped and the streets where "the shouts of Negro children playing at Willie Mays with a broom handle and half a rubber ball" replace the grandparents' Yiddish ("*Goodbye*" 90). Then he mourns "the Old Jews" who "had struggled and died" and contrasts them with "their offspring [who] had struggled and prospered, and moved" beyond Newark's ghettos. Finally, the narrator observes that now "the Negroes were making the same migration" (90). While remaining within the city limits, Baraka's upwardly mobile family followed this demographic trajectory (*Autobiography* [Lawrence Hill] 7, 48, 53).

As a prominent Newarker, Baraka became a flashpoint in Roth's novels. In *American Pastoral* (1997), Roth's most sustained account of what it means to "live in New Jersey," Baraka figures as a scapegoat for the loss of Newark's rough charm and is vilified by an old Newarker as "that son of a bitch LeRoi Jones" (*Pastoral* 163; Schwartz). In *Zuckerman Unbound* (1981), an unhinged quiz-show champion, who boasts of being "a Newarker myself," denounces Baraka as a literary fraud, who writes "black propaganda" masquerading as "literature" (*Zuckerman* 193). Roth's persistent preoccupation with Baraka complements their shared geographic and historical preoccupations, which underscore the value of linking Baraka and Roth by shared origins and by the taboo-challenging depictions of identity formation—and deformation—that placed them both among the most influential writers of their generation.

Teaching *Dutchman* with *Chappelle's Show*: Arguments along the Color Line

Caleb Corkery

In my experience, student readers of *Dutchman* are typically filled with troubling questions about the play's representation of blackness and whiteness—questions that can distance them irretrievably from the text. Without adequate preparation, students may quickly dismiss the work as racial propaganda of a bygone era. To help my students engage both deeply and critically with the text, I try to raise their awareness of racial identities as they study the historic arguments that have more broadly defined race in American history.

Among other lessons, *Dutchman* can offer students a rhetorical moment when the color line was reimagined. Baraka's rhetoric presents blackness as being constructed through whiteness. As Nita Kumar observes, "*Dutchman* does not so much posit an authentic black sense of selfhood as explore the processes and modes of misrepresentation concerning it" (274). *Dutchman* presents blackness as a reaction to whiteness, exposing racial identity as being about a kind of power that allows the dominant group to determine the attributes of racial categories. In other words, we see Clay's black identity defined and redefined through Lula's manipulations. We are left with the overblown power of Lula's whiteness, which she uses to control black identity as she pleases. Baraka's depictions, though, invite critique rather than identification with either racial category. He allows his audience to see exaggerated, symbolic representations of both races. The characters provide insight through a distant perspective on the absurd history that creates such racialized beings.

Though Baraka's Clay and Lula ultimately play out a tragedy, these absurd portraits could just as easily be comic. Like Baraka, the comedian Dave Chappelle exaggerates racialized characters to reimagine the color line. And like Baraka, Chappelle allows his audience to observe racial categories objectively rather than personally. Analyzing *Chappelle's Show* (2003–06) skits for their critique of racial identity can help students observe the strategies by which *Dutchman* reveals the constructedness of American racial categories.

In developing my African American literature course materials, I followed Mary Louise Pratt's example of focusing on moments when social power has been asserted and defended and on moments when subordinate groups have demanded entry to dominant institutions (37). Pratt uses the term "contact zone" to describe a classroom world in which all students see "their roots traced back to legacies of both glory and shame" as they think through conflicts represented in the course material (39). In order to address the hurtful legacies of subordination, Pratt envisions a space where "[n]o one [is] excluded, and no one [is] safe" (39).

I appreciate Pratt's desire to disrupt student comfort and challenge them to face their individual connections to histories of oppression. I want my students to feel a broader context to their racial identities, recognizing that their senses of self are built on an inherited racist tradition. However, my pedagogy offers a safe space for students to develop a critical awareness they can use to understand the play and to consider its themes in relation to their personal racial identities. I contend that students need objective distance to handle the emotional sting and confusion that comes with critiquing one's race in a multiracial classroom.

Social identity research also supports giving students space to think about their racial identities. Charmaine Wijeyesinghe and Bailey Jackson, in their book on emerging frameworks of racial identity development, recognize intersectionality as a key to understanding how identity development in one area (such as race) occurs within development of other social identities (such as gender, class, faith tradition, etc.) (3). Intersectionality invites us to "take a more holistic and integrated approach in describing and representing the lived experience of individuals" (3). A fully intersectional approach examines race in the context of other social group memberships, encouraging us to consider how all social categories mutually shape each other. But, as Diane Goodman and Jackson point out, this approach is not equally effective at all stages in the process (217). Goodman and Jackson discuss situations in which focusing initially on racial identity is constructive and indeed necessary. The authors also describe strategies to do so. For instance, students might use timelines to track how their or others' racial identities have evolved, potentially exposing moments when one's sense of race has intersected with other societal forces (225). Goodman and Jackson's goal, like mine, is to help students recognize the significance of race and racism through "some reflection on their own and others' process of racial identity development" (226).

My approach does not challenge students to integrate different social identities. Instead, I direct them to face racist moments in United States history that may intersect with—and help them reflect on—their sense of being raced. I introduce the course by discussing the social construction of race and the arguments of racial dominance and racial resistance. Eighteenth- and nineteenth-century science set a basis for racial classifications that established whites as superior. Consequently, nonwhite groups had to counter the arguments defining them as inferior. The following passages from my class notes show how arguments are used to define a group's identity:

> In studying the history of race, one can see how racial categories developed to favor those possessing social power. Columbus's fleet sails into the Caribbean to encounter a "simple race" paddling naked in canoes. Ideas that establish one group as superior to another we might think of as racial dominance arguments. These arguments either promote the higher position of one group or assign a lower status to another. In either case, the division is set between an "in" group that deserves social power and an "out" group that doesn't. Correspondingly, we might think of challenges

> to the position of the dominant group as resistance arguments. These arguments typically either raise the value of their racial category or downgrade the supposedly superior race.
>
> The enslavement of black Africans in this country is an obvious example of social power's being organized by race. One can see how slavery and then segregation were held in place by racial dominance arguments. One can also see how racial resistance arguments succeeded in weakening the laws that restricted African Americans.

Our subsequent readings reveal moments in United States history when arguments have been made along the color line. The authors define blackness or whiteness either to justify or to challenge racial dominance. African American literature emerges from the exigency created by white supremacy and offers a discourse to redefine black identity. The course material, then, presents moments when racial definitions have been asserted. My goal is to reveal the situated, constructed nature of the racial identities we have inculcated as normal.

Here are some of the rhetorical moments we study:

- When Thomas Jefferson claimed that blacks are savages closely akin to animals, Benjamin Banneker replied that blacks, like himself, are capable of sophisticated intellectual work.
- Frederick Douglass's Fourth of July speech refutes arguments of black inferiority and asserts a heroic black American identity.
- During the post-Reconstruction nadir, when arguments for white supremacy were based on appeals to high culture and civility, Ida Wells exposed the barbarism of white lynch mobs by describing their gruesome acts and identifying their racist motives.
- When racial division and violence mounted during this period, Booker T. Washington recast African Americans as helpful servants willing to work their way up in United States capitalist society.

Students do weekly responsive writings on our readings, and questions prompt them to focus on the texts' rhetorical situations.

Observing Chappelle

Watch one of Dave Chappelle's pieces on race with a classroom full of students, and you will see the group assign new authority to students of color. The white students look for cues for when to laugh and how much. The skits begin to take on extra meaning.

Chappelle gets us laughing at our racialized selves, making us wonder, "At whom, exactly, we are laughing?" He invites us to shift perspectives as we watch him embody different racialized personae, "speaking to multiple constituencies in the process of articulating identity," as Bambi Haggins puts it (233). Chappelle's characters "embody an ambiguous and fragmented notion of blackness" and challenge the audience to grapple with racist thinking in various ways (233). On the one hand, whites may worry laughing at black stereotypes aligns them with a racist tradition. Chappelle sets up self-examination for whites, since much meaning is associated with their laughter. On the other hand, however, the absurdity of Chappelle's portraits invites a humorous outburst, relieving whites of racist culpability since they surely do not fit the overblown white stereotype. But, in the end, though white students may use laughter to distance themselves from the racist portrayals, they also must consider what initially produced the funny stereotypes.

Black people can laugh at Chappelle's brazen portrayal of racism and be relieved by his honesty in a culture that is reluctant to acknowledge its racist legacy. However, revisiting racist depictions can trigger the pain of our racist history. And some whites react defensively when facing exaggerated stereotypes. Our reactions to Chappelle's depictions stir us to notice our racial selves. Our laughter reveals the extent to which we understand black and white perspectives.

The following skits provoke viewers to confront offensive racial stereotypes:[1]

A white family named the Niggars is portrayed as a typical suburban family of the 1950s; however, they enjoy teasing each other about their "niggar lips" and being "niggar rich." Their black milkman also enjoys adding his own racist comments, calling the family members "niggars" and taking them to task for being late on their payments. ("The Ni**ar Family")

A blind black man raised in the Deep South has developed white supremacist views. Those around him have protected him from his own racial identity, and his outspoken racism makes him a leader of the white power movement. He taunts black people with stinging, stereotypical insults. Once his racial identity is revealed, he divorces his wife for being a "nigger lover." ("Clayton Bigsby")

A black drug addict, Tyrone, visits an elementary school classroom to give a talk on drugs. However, he talks about how to buy drugs and how to get high. He embodies many degrading stereotypes as he teaches the children how to follow his example. ("Tyrone's Intervention")

While Chappelle's skits draw on stereotypes, they also portray the absurdity of those who hold racist views. Both are uncomfortable: we don't like to accept that negative black stereotypes are played out around us or the fact that white people can be defined by racist thinking.

The day I present the Chappelle skits, I ask students to consider several questions after the screenings. First, how does Chappelle get away with such racist representations? Students typically answer, "Because Chappelle is black." He's making fun of his own race. When Chappelle's ridicule extends to whites, students claim he now seems to be making fun of everybody.

Second, why does it seem racist when white people embody similar racial stereotypes? Though some students may claim that a racial double-standard applies, others usually point out the history of the color line, a history during which whites have defined the meaning of blackness. And of course, the semester's readings evince African Americans challenging those definitions. I have heard Chappelle's skits compared to Chester Himes's *If He Hollers Let Him Go* (1945) and Alice Walker's "Everyday Use" (1973), narratives whose characters dramatize resistance to racial thinking in comic—and tragic—ways.

Third, at what, exactly, are we laughing? Are we all laughing at the same thing? Does our sense of racial identity affect how we react? Examining the skits can connect individual racial identity to cultural representations of race. Noticing how Chappelle's exaggeration elicits laughter or discomfort is worthwhile. I have heard white students claim that Chappelle is race baiting, exaggerating racial differences to fabricate a sense of racial injustice. Others respond that Chappelle is not exploitative since he makes fun of all our racial stereotypes. Articulating how they can and cannot identify with the characters facilitates exploration of Chappelle's technique and the students' different identifications with race.

Finally, to what extent are these stereotypes true? Though some students show disdain for Chappelle's racial representations, others admit that the skits reflect some truth about the racist attitudes in our culture. A discussion over these questions can help students recognize and critique American racial identities. However, applying that critique to one's own sense of being black or white may require more privacy. For example, students may feel freer to write, rather than speak, their response to a question like the following: "Does your sense of racial identity affect how you react to Chappelle's skits?" Students who are not accustomed to thinking of themselves in racial terms may not have considered the extent to which they embody and assign racial stereotypes. Conducting such exercises publicly and privately allows students to consider more deeply the power of Chappelle's critique—and Baraka's.

After working with Chappelle's skits and considering the source of their humor, I point out how such exaggerated depictions could just as easily be tragic. Introducing *Dutchman*, I show how both Chappelle and Baraka invite us to view their overblown portrayals of race objectively, not personally. My aim is to bring to our reading of the play a broader context of the characters' racial identities.

Responding to Dutchman

To help students engage with the play, I ask them the following questions. How does each character relate to racialized identities we have studied this term? How do the characters and their interactions amount to arguments along the color line? What connection do these characters and arguments have to our lives today? Their responses to these questions reveal how they perceive their constructed racial identities. The following excerpts are from students in my ENGL 334 African American Literature II course from the spring of 2011.[2]

Students' responses to the first question often connected Clay to racial uplift characters we had studied. Lula reminded many students of our readings' femme fatales, such as Madge from Himes's *If He Hollers Let Him Go* and Daphne in Walter Mosley's *Devil in a Blue Dress* (1990). More developed responses also connected social forces to characters' individual identities. The students' names below have been anonymized.

> ERICA: "Lula, like [other white female characters studied in the course], can exert the little power she has as a woman over a black man because she is white. Just like Chappelle making fun of how whites are 'proper' and uptight, [*Dutchman*] shows how quickly racial stereotypes can define a person."
>
> NICOLE: "[The play] suggests that [Clay's] upper-class status and his nice clothing and his reserved manner are all meaningless as he becomes powerless to her whiteness. Lula's repeated attacks cause Clay to question his [racial] 'uplift' identity."
>
> JOHN: "[Like other characters we have studied, Lula] exudes arrogance, power, and a complete control over [Clay]. Furthermore, she seems to enjoy using him to reinforce her sense of power. [Clay] is invisible and powerless beside her. When he realizes how she has controlled him, he is powerless again to stop it."

Each of these responses articulates the relation between race and power. The students define the characters' identities through their familiarity with the rhetorics of racial uplift and white supremacy. Students are picking up on the binary thinking that shapes black and white identities. Erica recognizes that Lula's sense of self is derived from the power she feels over black men. Nicole points out that Clay's drive for uplift is undermined by Lula's assertions of power. Likewise, John notices how Lula controls Clay "to reinforce her sense of power." In each case, the characters are primarily constituted by the historic power associated with race.

The second question allows students to treat race more abstractly. Common among these responses was the observation that Lula represents white oppression and Clay represents black repression. More developed responses reveal how the characters act in relation to arguments along the color line.

MARCUS: "Clay is working on becoming a white man with black skin. But Lula constantly reminds him that he can't cross the color line. Lula is the black man's forbidden fruit. She tempts him but because of race he can never have her. She is the voice in his head that he's not white and upper class."

EMILY: "Clay represents how reluctant blacks are to standing up against whites and their attempt to stay away from whites. In the end, the black man's power is suppressed as can be seen by Clay's death. [The play shows how] Clay is not able to overcome the restrictions of the color line. He is powerless and a victim to the color line."

These students describe the characters as representations of racial thinking. Marcus points out that Clay's effort to "become white" is impossible as long as black men are forbidden to succumb to the sexual temptations of white women. And Lula is "the voice inside [Clay's] head" that reminds Clay that he cannot assimilate into whiteness. She represents a central assumption behind color line distinctions. And, as Emily points out, Clay is "powerless" "to overcome the restrictions of the color line." Clay's sense of agency is an illusion, since the meaning of the color line dictates his ultimate fate.

The third prompt encourages private reflection on the subject, allowing students to talk about black and white identities from a safe, analytical distance. Though few explicitly put themselves into their comments, their insights could relate to their lived experiences.

FRANCIS: "Clay represents a victim of the color line. In my opinion, I almost feel as if the audience would most easily identify themselves with the bystanders. Conflict due to the color line is all around us, but we are just bystanders and a lot of the time are not sure how to react. You still see whites assuming they are more important. And the loss of a black man, no big deal."

DEREK: "The characters are exaggerated to show how small the issue of race really is or should be. Race is as big an issue as we make it. Someone like Clay finds out he has no control over himself because he lets race define him so much."

HILLARY: "Injustices like what happened to Clay still happen today, just like how the audience knows it is wrong. Black men get treated unfairly and no one does anything about it."

These responses show the critical distance students can assume when led to see Clay and Lula through a history of color line thinking. Instead of seeing the characters as personal assaults, these students contextualize the play more broadly to see the larger social relevance of Baraka's statement. Hillary and Francis focus on the bystanders in the train to examine the racial thinking represented by Lula and Clay. Francis points out that we are all bystanders to the conflicts of the color line around us. Likewise, Hillary notes how "no one does anything" about the unfair treatment of black men.

Derek's response is more personal, though, showing his skepticism toward the current power of color line thinking. In my comments on his paper, I asked whether segregation and other discriminatory practices of the play's era might make racial distinctions real for black men. I also asked, "If color line divisions were real then, what has happened to them today?" What has happened to change that influence on our identities? Rather than challenging him on his denial of racism or on his belief that our society should be color-blind, I ask him to reconcile privately the rhetorical history we have studied with his contemporary views of racial politics.

The earlier framing of Chappelle's exaggerated racial depictions prepares students to distinguish between personal attack and cultural critique. Despite the different interpretations, all these students position themselves as observers and critics. Their responses do not invoke their individual racial identities, yet their comments critique a racial world of which they are members.

In the open forum of the classroom, students can discuss the readings' historical contexts and rhetorical moves. However, students can confront their personal relation to and understanding of our racist history more privately through reflective writing responses. A student like Derek can express his skepticism about the significance of racial thinking today, a skepticism that might mark him as insensitive to issues of race in the context of the course, but through private written exchanges, I can help students figure out the extent to which racial thinking has defined them and their view of the world.

Teaching *Dutchman* in conjunction with Dave Chappelle's skits leads students away from identifying with *Dutchman*'s racialized characters and frees them to critique the play's depictions, allowing them to see the play's importance. Of course, my students possess racialized American identities, but Clay and Lula, like many of Chappelle's characters, offer students an opportunity to suspend identifications and observe the constructed racial selves present around us. Instead of becoming defensive, students can apply broader arguments of racial definition to Clay and Lula and integrate their understanding of the characters into their identities. Instead of sitting as an artifact of history, the play becomes a tool for excavating the sources of American racial identities.

NOTES

[1] The skits can be found in Chappelle, *The Best of Chappelle's Show Uncensored* (Comedy Central, 2007).

[2] I did not ask my students to identify themselves racially. The university student body is eight percent African American and seventy-five percent Caucasian ("Common Data Set").

NOTES ON CONTRIBUTORS

Andrew Ade, associate professor of English at Westminster College (PA), teaches dramatic literature and criticism, world fiction, film history, and playwriting. His research focuses on theater history and drama criticism. For his playwriting he has received the Arts & Letters Prize in Drama, several best play festival awards, the Kennedy Center National Teaching Artist Grant, and creative writing residency fellowships at the MacDowell Colony, the Ragdale Foundation, and the Hambidge Center.

James D. Bloom teaches at Muhlenberg College. His books include *Hollywood Intellect* (2009), *Gravity Fails* (2003), *The Literary Bent* (1997), *Left Letters* (1992), *The Stock of Available Reality* (1984), and *Reading the Male Gaze in Literature and Culture* (2017). He has published in *American Literary History*, *American Studies*, *American Quarterly*, *Chronicle of Higher Education*, *Contemporary Literature*, the *European Journal of American Culture*, *The New York Times Book Review*, the *Philadelphia Inquirer*, and *Style*.

Matthew Calihman, associate professor of English at Missouri State University, teaches African American and American literature. He has published "Black Power beyond Black Nationalism: John A. Williams, Cultural Pluralism, and the Popular Front" (*MELUS*) and "'Where Are the Italian Anarchists?' Amiri Baraka and the Usable Pasts of the Immigrant Left" (*Voices in Italian Americana*). With Tracy Floreani and A Yęmisi Jimoh, he coedited a special issue of *American Studies* on Ralph Ellison.

Tess Chakkalakal is associate professor of Africana studies and English at Bowdoin College. Her books include *Novel Bondage: Slavery, Marriage, and Freedom in Nineteenth-Century America* (2011) and *Literature, Jim Crow, and the Legacy of Sutton E. Griggs* (2013). She is currently at work on a biography of Charles Waddell Chesnutt and scholarly editions for undergraduates of works by Chesnutt and Griggs.

Jim Cocola is associate professor of literature, film, and media and associate head for the humanities in the Department of Humanities and Arts at Worcester Polytechnic Institute in Worcester, Massachusetts. His research interests focus on modern and contemporary American literatures and cultures. Recent publications include articles in *College Literature*, *The Explicator*, and *Studies in American Jewish Literature* and a book, *Places in the Making: A Cultural Geography of American Poetry* (2016).

Caleb Corkery teaches at Millersville University of Pennsylvania, where he is associate professor of English. His research focuses on intersections between race and rhetoric. His most recent publication was "What Paltry Learning in Dumb Books! Teaching the Power of Oral Narrative," which appeared in *Teaching Africa: A Guide for the Twenty-First-Century Classroom* (2013).

Gerald Early is Merle Kling Professor of Modern Letters, professor of English, and chair of the African and African American Studies Department at Washington University. Among his publications are *A Level Playing Field: African American Athletes and the Republic of Sports*; *This is Where I Came In: Black America in the 1960s*; *The*

Culture of Bruising: Essays on Prizefighting, Literature, and Modern American Culture; and *One Nation Under a Groove: Motown and American Culture.*

Kurt Hemmer is the editor of the *Encyclopedia of Beat Literature* (2007) and professor of English at Harper College. With the filmmaker Tom Knoff, he produced several award-winning films: *Janine Pommy Vega: As We Cover the Streets, Rebel Roar: The Sound of Michael McClure, Wow! Ted Joans Lives!, Keenan*, and *Love Janine Pommy Vega*. His essay on the beats appears in *A History of California Literature* (2015).

Molly Hiro is associate professor of English at the University of Portland, where she teaches American literature, African American literature, and protest literature. She has published articles in *Novel: A Forum on Fiction, Arizona Quarterly*, and *Pedagogy* and is currently at work on a study of the place of slavery in contemporary and early-twentieth-century accounts of African American history and identity. In 2014, she was a Fulbright lecturer at the University of Mysore, India.

Danny M. Hoey, Jr., is associate professor of English at Indian River State College. His first novel, *The Butterfly Lady*, won the Debut Fiction Award and the Bronze Award from the Foreword First Book of the Year Awards. His teaching and research focus on black males and their precarious relationship to society.

Katarzyna Jakubiak is associate professor of English at Millersville University of Pennsylvania. Her research and teaching interests focus on the intersections between African diaspora literature and translation and on the reception of African diaspora literature in Cold War–era Poland. Her publications include articles on Polish productions of *A Raisin in the Sun* (in *Theatre Journal*) and on Polish reception of *Uncle Tom's Cabin* (forthcoming in *Transnational Histories of* Uncle Tom's Cabin).

Jean-Philippe Marcoux is professor of American literature at Université Laval in Québec. He is the author of *Jazz Griots: Music as History in the 1960s African American Poem* (2012). He has published articles and book chapters on Langston Hughes, Sonia Sanchez, Gwendolyn Brooks, Carolyn Rodgers, David Henderson, and Amiri Baraka. He is currently working on a book-length study of the Umbra poets and workshops.

William Thomas McBride teaches film and drama at Illinois State University and is the author of *Stylized Moments: Turning Film Style into Meaning*. He has published on Hitchcock's "fathead" shot, online film pedagogy, techno-mediated modes of being in Jonze's *Her*, Scharf's apocalyptically fun paintings, New Orleans Indian masking and native funk, Beckett's *homo mensura*, midrash and circumcision in the Tanakh, Dracula's shyster vampires, chiasm, *lex talio* and money in Esther, and Bakhtin's Marxist formalism.

D. Quentin Miller is professor of English at Suffolk University. His publications include *"A Criminal Power": James Baldwin and the Law, Re-Viewing James Baldwin: Things Not Seen, The Routledge Introduction to African American Literature, Understanding John Edgar Wideman*, and *American Literature in Transition, 1980–1990.* His book *James Baldwin in Context* is fourthcoming. He teaches African American literature, contemporary American literature, and fiction writing.

Koritha Mitchell is associate professor of English at Ohio State University. Her study *Living with Lynching: African American Lynching Plays, Performance, and Citizen-*

ship won book awards from the American Theatre and Drama Society and the Society for the Study of American Women Writers. Her articles include "James Baldwin, Performance Theorist, Sings the *Blues for Mister Charlie*" (*American Quarterly*) and "Love in Action" (*Callaloo*), which draws parallels between lynching and anti-LGBT violence.

Deborah M. Mix is professor of English at Ball State University. Her publications include *"A Vocabulary of Thinking": Gertrude Stein and Contemporary North American Women's Experimental Writing* (2007) and articles in *Contemporary Women's Writing*, *American Literature*, and *The Cambridge History of Twentieth-Century American Women's Poetry*. With Logan Esdale, she is editing a volume on Gertrude Stein for the MLA series Approaches to Teaching World Literature.

Daniel Morris is professor of English at Purdue University, where he has taught since 1994. He is the author of *The Writings of William Carlos Williams* (1995), *Remarkable Modernisms* (2002), *The Poetry of Louise Glück* (2006), *After Weegee* (2012), *Lyric Encounters* (2013), and *Not Born Digital* (2016). He has also published poetry, most recently *If Not for the Courage* (2010) and *Hit Play* (2015).

Meenakshi Ponnuswami is associate professor of English at Bucknell University in Pennsylvania, where she teaches modern drama and theater history. Her scholarship focuses on postwar British theater, including New Left historical drama and the work of black British and British Asian playwrights. She is currently writing about contemporary British Muslim theater and comedy and about African American women playwrights of the 1960s and 1970s. She has taught African American drama, including *Dutchman*, for over twenty-five years.

Andrew Sargent is associate professor of English at West Chester University, where he teaches African American, American, and civil rights literature. His essays on authors such as Donald Goines, Chester Himes, James Weldon Johnson, and Katori Hall have appeared in *MELUS*, *College Literature*, *Great Lives from History: African Americans*, and *Critical Insights: Civil Rights Literature Past and Present*. He is currently working on a study of African American literature and the civil rights movement.

Richard Schur is professor of English and director of the honors program at Drury University in Springfield, Missouri. He is the author of *Parodies of Ownership: Hip-Hop Aesthetics and Intellectual Property Law* and coeditor of *African American Culture and Legal Discourse*. His research focuses on African American culture, popular music, and law. He cohosts the *New Books in Music Podcast* (newbooksnetwork.com/category/arts-letters-music/).

Roland Leander Williams, Jr., is the author of *Black Male Frames: African Americans in a Century of Hollywood Cinema, 1903–2003* (2015). He is professor of English at Temple University, where he teaches courses on African Americans in literature and cinema. His forthcoming book is entitled *Smooth Operating and Other Social Acts*.

SURVEY PARTICIPANTS

The following scholars responded to our survey on teaching Baraka's *Dutchman*. Their responses aided the editors as they conceived this volume's introductory essays. The institutional affiliations listed below are those that the survey participants provided at the time of their responses.

Lena Ampadu, *Towson University*
Robert Craig Baum, *River Valley Community College*
James D. Bloom, *Muhlenberg College*
Tess Chakkalakal, *Bowdoin College*
Jim Cocola, *Worcester Polytechnic Institute*
Caleb Corkery, *Millersville University of Pennsylvania*
Daniel Shank Cruz, *Northern Illinois University*
Babak Ebrahimian, *Queens College, City University of New York*
Maureen N. Eke, *Central Michigan University*
Danielle Glassmeyer, *Bradley University*
Jurgen E. Grandt, *Gainesville State College*
Kurt Hemmer, *Harper College*
Toru Kiuchi, *Nihon University*
Diane Krumrey, *University of Bridgeport*
William Lawlor, *University of Wisconsin, Stevens Point*
Monifa Love, *Morgan State University*
Christine Mazurkewycz, *University of Iowa*
William Thomas McBride, *Illinois State University*
L. Bailey McDaniel, *Oakland University*
James Mellis, *Temple University*
D. Quentin Miller, *Suffolk University*
Koritha Mitchell, *Ohio State University*
Deborah M. Mix, *Ball State University*
Daniel Morris, *Purdue University, West Lafayette*
A. Myrna Nurse, *Delaware State University*
Imafedia Okhamafe, *University of Nebraska*
James Braxton Peterson, *Bucknell University*
Elizabeth Pittman, *George Washington University*
Meenakshi Ponnuswami, *Bucknell University*
Marguerite Rippy, *Marymount University*
Gregory E. Rutledge, *University of Nebraska, Lincoln*
Metta Sama, *Goddard College*
Andrew Sargent, *West Chester University*
James Smethurst, *University of Massachusetts, Amherst*
Steve Tracy, *University of Massachusetts, Amherst*
Richard Trama, *Richard Stockton College of New Jersey*
Gayle Wald, *George Washington University*
Roland Leander Williams, Jr., *Temple University*
Richard Yarborough, *University of California, Los Angeles*
Vershawn Ashanti Young, *University of Kentucky*
Anthony Zias, *Coppin State University*

WORKS CITED

Acocella, Joan. "Once Upon a Time: The Lure of the Fairy Tale." *The New Yorker*, 23 July 2012, www.newyorker.com/magazine/2012/07/23/once-upon-a-time-3.

Albee, Edward. *The American Dream*. Coward-McCann, 1961.

———. *The Zoo Story*. The Zoo Story; The Death of Bessie Smith; The Sandbox, by Albee, Coward-McCann, 1960, pp. 8–62.

Alexander, Michelle. *The New Jim Crow: Mass Incarceration in the Age of Colorblindness*. The New Press, 2012.

Allen, Donald, editor. *The New American Poetry: 1945–1960*. U of California P, 1999.

Allen, James. *Without Sanctuary: Lynching Photography in America*. Twin Palms, 2000.

America and the Intellectuals: A Symposium. Partisan Review, 1953.

"Amiri Baraka." *Poetry Foundation*, www.poetryfoundation.org/poets/amiri-baraka.

Amour, Carol Ann. "StageWrite Is Right On." *Incite/Insight*, vol. 2, no. 5, 2010, pp. 5–7.

Anadolu-Okur, Nilgün. *Contemporary African American Theater: Afrocentricity in the Works of Larry Neal, Amiri Baraka, and Charles Fuller*. Garland, 1997.

———. "Drama and Performance from Civil Rights to Black Arts." *The Cambridge Companion to Civil Rights Literature*, edited by Julie Buckner Armstrong, Cambridge UP, 2015, pp. 65–84.

Anderson, Elliott, and Mary Kinzie, editors. *The Little Magazine in America: A Modern Documentary History*. Pushcart, 1978.

Andreas, James R. "Othello's African American Progeny." *South Atlantic Review*, vol. 57, no. 4, 1992, pp. 39–57.

Appiah, Kwame Anthony, editor. Narrative of the Life of Frederick Douglass, an American Slave *and* Incidents in the Life of a Slave Girl. Modern Library, 2000.

Arrabal, Fernando. *The Two Executioners*. *Four Plays*, translated by Barbara Wright, Calder, 1962, pp. 23–41.

Artaud, Antonin. *The Theater and Its Double*. *Antonin Artaud: Selected Writings*, edited by Susan Sontag, translated by Helen Weaver, U of California P, 1988, pp. 213–76.

———. *The Theater and Its Double*. Translated by Mary Caroline Richards. Grove, 1958.

Azouz, Samy. "Amiri Baraka's Participatory and Ceremonial Theatre: From Mimesis to Methexis." *Journal of Dramatic Theory and Criticism*, vol. 29, no. 2, 2015, pp. 25–41.

Baker, Christopher. "A Trip with the Strange Woman: Amiri Baraka's *Dutchman* and the Book of Proverbs." *South Atlantic Review*, vol. 78, no. 3–4, 2013, pp. 110–28.

Baker, Houston. *Blues, Ideology, and Afro-American Literature*. U of Chicago P, 1984.

———. *The Journey Back: Issues in Black Literature and Culture*. U of Chicago P, 1980.

Baldwin, James. *The Amen Corner: A Play*. Dial, 1968.

———. *Blues for Mister Charlie*. Dial, 1964.

———. *Blues for Mister Charlie*. Vintage, 1992.

———. *Collected Essays*. Edited by Toni Morrison, Library of America, 1992.

———. "The Discovery of What It Means to Be an American." Baldwin, *Collected Essays*, pp. 37–142.

———. "Many Thousands Gone." Baldwin, *Collected Essays*, pp. 19–34.

———. *Notes of a Native Son*. Beacon, 1985.

———. *Sonny's Blues*. Penguin, 1995.

———. "The Uses of the Blues." *The Cross of Redemption: Uncollected Writings*, edited by Randall Kenan, Pantheon, 2010, pp. 57–66.

———. "The White Man's Guilt." Baldwin, *Collected Essays*, pp. 722–27.

Bambara, Toni Cade. "Black Theater." Gayle, *Black Expression*, pp. 134–43.

Bamboozled. Directed by Spike Lee, performance by Damon Wayans, Jada Pinkett Smith, Savion Glover, Tommy Davidson, Michael Rappaport, Paul Mooney, and Mos Def, New Line Cinema, 2000.

Banes, Sally. *Greenwich Village 1963: Avant-Garde Performance and the Effervescent Body*. Duke UP, 1993.

Bank, Rosemarie K. *Theatre Culture in America, 1825–1860*. Cambridge UP, 1997.

Baraka, Amiri. "*An Agony. As Now.*" Baraka, *Dead Lecturer*, pp. 15–16.

———. "American Sexual Reference: Black Male." Baraka, *Home* [Akashic], pp. 216–33.

———. "Amiri Baraka." *PennSound*, writing.upenn.edu/pennsound/x/Baraka.php. Accessed 23 Oct. 2015.

———. *The Autobiography of LeRoi Jones*. Freundlich, 1984.

———. *The Autobiography of LeRoi Jones*. Rev. ed., Lawrence Hill, 1997.

———. *The Baptism*. Baraka, The Baptism *and* The Toilet, pp. 7–32.

———. The Baptism *and* The Toilet. Grove, 1967.

———. "The Beat Generation." *The Partisan Review*, vol. 25, no. 3, 1958, pp. 472–73.

———. "Black Art." Gates and Smith, vol. 2, pp. 703–04.

———. "Black Art." *Anthology of Contemporary American Poetry*, edited by Cary Nelson, 2nd ed., vol. 2, Oxford UP, 2014, pp. 427–29.

———. "The Black Arts Movement." Baraka, *LeRoi Jones/Amiri Baraka Reader*, pp. 495–506.

———. "Black Dada Nihilismus." Baraka, *Dead Lecturer*, pp. 61–64.

———. *Black Magic: Collected Poetry, 1961–1967*. Bobbs-Merrill, 1969.

———. *Black Music*. Morrow, 1967.

———. "Black Writing." Baraka, *Home* [Morrow], pp. 161–65.

———. *Blues People: Negro Music in White America*. Morrow, 1963.

———. "The Changing Same (R&B and New Black Music)." 1968. Gayle, *Black Aesthetic*, pp. 118–31.

———. "Channel X." Reply to Philip Roth. *New York Review of Books*, 9 July 1964, www.nybooks.com/articles/1964/07/09/channel-x-1/.

———. "Confessions of a Former Anti-Semite." *Village Voice*, 17–23 Dec. 1980, pp. 1+.

———. *Conversations with Amiri Baraka*. Edited by Charlie Reilly, U of Mississippi P, 1994.

———. "Cuba Libre." Baraka, *Home* [Akashic], pp. 11–62.

———. *The Dead Lecturer: Poems*. Grove, 1964.

———. *Dutchman*. Baraka, Dutchman *and* The Slave, pp. 1–38.

———. *Dutchman*. Parone, pp. 190–214.

———. Dutchman *and* The Slave. HarperCollins, 2001.

———. *The Eighth Ditch*. Di Prima and Jones, pp. 81–87.

———. *Experimental Death Unit #1*. *Four Black Revolutionary Plays*, Bobbs-Merrill, 1969, pp. 1–15.

———. *The Fiction of LeRoi Jones/Amiri Baraka*. Lawrence Hill, 2000.

———. *Home: Social Essays*. Akashic, 2009.

———. *Home: Social Essays*. Morrow, 1966.

———. "How You Sound??" *The New American Poetry*, edited by Donald M. Allen, Grove, 1960, pp. 424–25.

———. "Hunting Is Not Those Heads on the Wall." Baraka, *Home* [Morrow], pp. 173–78.

———. Introduction. Baraka, *Home* [Akashic], pp. 15–20.

———. "Jazz and the White Critic." *Black Music*, Morrow, 1967, pp. 11–20.

———. *Jello*. Third World, 1970.

———. *The LeRoi Jones/Amiri Baraka Reader*. Edited by William J. Harris, 2nd ed., Thunder's Mouth, 1999.

———. "LeRoi Jones Talking." Baraka, *Home* [Morrow], pp. 179–88.

———, editor. *The Moderns: An Anthology of New Writing in America*. Corinth, 1963.

———. "Notes for a Speech." Baraka, *Preface*, p. 47.

———. "Philistinism and the Negro Writer." *Anger, and Beyond: The Negro Writer in the United States*, edited by Herbert Hill, Harper and Row, 1966, pp. 51–61.

———. *Preface to a Twenty Volume Suicide Note*. Totem/Corinth, 1961.

———. "The Revolutionary Theatre." Baraka, *Home* [Akashic], pp. 236–41.

———. "The Revolutionary Theatre." Baraka, *Home* [Morrow], pp. 210–15.

———. "The Revolutionary Theatre." *The Making of African American Identity, Volume 3: 1917–68*, National Humanities Center, nationalhumanitiescenter.org/pds/maai3/protest/text12/barakatheatre.pdf.

———. "The Screamers." Baraka, *Tales*, pp. 71–80.

———. "Short Speech to My Friends." Baraka, *Dead Lecturer*, pp. 29–30.

———. *The Slave*. Baraka, Dutchman *and* The Slave, pp. 39–88.

———. *SOS: Poems, 1961–2013*. Edited by Paul Vangelisti, Grove, 2014.

———. *The System of Dante's Hell*. Akashic, 2016.

———. *The System of Dante's Hell*. Grove, 1965.

———. *Tales*. Grove, 1967.

———. *The Toilet*. Baraka, The Baptism *and* The Toilet, pp. 33–62.

———. "Uncle Udom's Cabin." *Kulchur*, vol. 3, no. 11, 1963, pp. 88–90.

———. "What Does Nonviolence Mean?" Baraka, *Home* [Morrow], pp. 133–54.

Baraka, Amiri, and Edward Dorn. *Amiri Baraka and Edward Dorn: The Collected Letters*. Edited by Claudia Moreno Pisano, U of New Mexico P, 2013.

Baraka, Amiri, and Duma Ndlovu. "An Adaptation of Amiri Baraka/LeRoi Jones's *Dutchman*." N.d.T.S. Amiri Baraka Papers, Rare Book and Manuscript Library, Columbia University, New York.

Baraka, Amiri, and Larry Neal, editors. *Black Fire: An Anthology of Afro-American Writing*. Morrow, 1968.

Barrios, Olga. *The Black Theatre Movement in the United States and in South Africa*. U of València P, 2008.

Barry, Peter. *Beginning Theory: An Introduction to Literary and Cultural Theory*. Manchester UP, 2009.

Barzun, Jacques. *The House of Intellect*. Harper, 1959.

Bean, Annemarie, editor. *A Sourcebook of African-American Performance: Plays, People, Movements*. Routledge, 1999.

Beckett, Samuel. *Play*. Play *and Two Short Pieces for Radio*, Faber, 1964, pp. 7–24.

Belasco, Susan, and Linck Johnson, editors. *The Bedford Anthology of American Literature*, vol. 2, Bedford, 2008.

Benston, Kimberly W. *Baraka: The Renegade and the Mask*. Yale UP, 1976.

———, editor. *Imamu Amiri Baraka (LeRoi Jones): A Collection of Critical Essays*. Prentice-Hall, 1978.

———. *Performing Blackness: Enactments of African-American Modernism*. Routledge, 2000.

Bergé, Carol, et al. *Four Young Lady Poets: Carol Bergé, Barbara Moraff, Rochelle Owens, Diane Wakoski*. Totem/Corinth, 1962.

Bernstein, Rosemary E., et al. "Piloting PlayWrite: Feasibility and Efficacy of a Playwriting Intervention for At-Risk Adolescents." *Journal of Creativity in Mental Health*, vol. 9, no. 4, 2014, pp. 446–67.

Bettelheim, Bruno. *The Uses of Enchantment: The Meaning and Importance of Fairy Tales*. Knopf, 1976.

A Black Quartet: Four New Black Plays. New American Library, 1970.

Bloomgarden, Karen. "Broyard's Daughter Responds to Roth." *New York Observer*, 20 Sept. 2012, observer.com/2012/09/philip-roth-gets-response/.

Boal, Augusto. *Theatre of the Oppressed*. Translated by Charles A. McBride and Maria-Odilia McBride, Theatre Communications Group, 1985.

Bobo, Lawrence D. "Somewhere between Jim Crow and Post-Racialism: Reflections on the Racial Divide in America Today." *Daedalus*, vol. 140, no. 2, 2011, pp. 11–36.

Bottoms, Stephen J. *Playing Underground: A Critical History of the 1960s Off-Off-Broadway Movement*. U of Michigan P, 2004.

Boucicault, Dion. *The Octoroon; or, Life in Louisiana: A Play, in Four Acts*. French, 1859.

Bourne, St. Clair, director. *In Motion: Amiri Baraka*. First Run/Icarus, 1983.

———. "Interview with Allen Ginsberg." Gwynne, pp. 76–83.

Bracey, John H., Jr., et al., editors. *SOS—Calling All Black People: A Black Arts Movement Reader*. U of Massachusetts P, 2014.

Bradley, Adam, and Andrew DuBois, editors. *The Anthology of Rap*. Yale UP, 2010.

Breton, André. "Second Manifesto of Surrealism." *Manifestoes of Surrealism*, translated by Richard Seaver and Helen R. Lane, U of Michigan P, 1972, pp. 117–87.

Brewer, Mary F. *Staging Whiteness*. Wesleyan UP, 2005.

Brooker, Peter, and Andrew Thacker. *The Oxford Critical and Cultural History of Modernist Magazines*. Vol. 2, Oxford UP, 2012.

Brown, Kenneth H. *The Brig: A Concept for Theatre or Film*. Hill and Wang, 1965.

Brown, Lloyd W. *Amiri Baraka*. Twayne, 1980.

Brown, Sterling. "Negro Characters as Seen by White Authors." *Journal of Negro Education*, vol. 2, 1933, pp. 179–203.

Brown, William Wells. *The Escape; or, A Leap for Freedom*. Hatch and Shine, pp. 35–60.

Buckley-Marudas, Mary Frances, and Joshua Block. "Putting Research on Stage: Playwriting in the English Classroom." *English Journal*, vol. 105, no. 2, 2015, pp. 102–07.

Bullins, Ed, editor. *New Plays from the Black Theatre: An Anthology*. Bantam, 1969.

———. "The So-Called Western Avant-Garde Drama." *Liberator*, vol. 7, no. 12, 1967, pp. 16–17.

Burgie, Irving, and Loften Mitchell. *Ballad for Bimshire*. London, 1963.

Butler, Octavia E. *Kindred*. Doubleday, 1979.

Calihman, Matthew. "'Where Are the Italian Anarchists?' Amiri Baraka and the Usable Pasts of the Immigrant Left." *VIA: Voices in Italian Americana*, vol. 18, no. 2, 2007, pp. 64–78.

Campbell, Lindsey. "Shirley Knight and the Performance of Gendered Race in *Dutchman*." *Offscreen*, vol. 19, no. 1, Jan. 2015, offscreen.com/view/shirley-knight-and-the-performance-of-gendered-race-in-_dutchman_.

Cardullo, Robert. "Names and Titles in Amiri Baraka's *Dutchman*." *ANQ: A Quarterly Journal of Short Articles, Notes, and Reviews*, vol. 22, no. 3, 2009, pp. 51–56.

Carroll, Vinnette, and James Weldon Johnson. *Trumpets of the Lord*. Directed by Donald McKayle, Astor Place Theatre, New York, 1963–64.

Cash, W. J. *The Mind of the South*. 1941. Vintage, 1991.

Ceynowa, Andrzej. "The Dramatic Structure of *Dutchman*." *Black American Literature Forum*, vol. 17, no. 1, 1983, pp. 15–18.

Chappelle, Dave, et al., creators. *The Best of Chappelle's Show Uncensored*. Comedy Central, 2007.

Chesnutt, Charles W. *Stories, Novels, and Essays*. Library of America, 2002.

Chielens, Edward E. *American Literary Magazines: The Twentieth Century*. Greenwood, 1992.

Chinitz, David E. *Which Sin to Bear? Authenticity and Compromise in Langston Hughes*. Oxford UP, 2013.

Chizhik, Alexander Williams. "Literacy for Playwriting or Playwriting for Literacy." *Education and Urban Society*, vol. 41, no. 3, 2009, pp. 387–409.

Clay, Steven, and Rodney Phillips. *A Secret Location on the Lower East Side: Adventures in Writing, 1960–1980: A Sourcebook of Information*. New York Public Library/Granary, 1998.

Cleaver, Eldridge. "Psychology: The Black Bible." *Post-Prison Writings and Speeches*, edited by Robert Scheer, Random House, 1969, pp. 18–20.

———. *Soul on Ice*. Dell, 1999.

Coates, Ta-Nehisi. "The Case for Reparations." *The Atlantic*, June 2014, www.theatlantic.com/magazine/archive/2014/06/the-case-for-reparations/361631/.

Cockrell, Dale. *Demons of Disorder: Early Blackface Minstrels and Their World*. Cambridge UP, 1997.

Colbert, Soyica Diggs. *The African American Theatrical Body: Reception, Performance, and the Stage*. Cambridge UP, 2011.

Coleman, Ornette. *Free Jazz: A Collective Improvisation*. Atlantic, 1961.

Coleridge, Samuel Taylor. *Biographia Literaria: The Collected Works of Samuel Taylor Coleridge, Biographical Sketches of My Literary Life and Opinions*. Edited by James Engell and W. Jackson Bate, vol. 7, Princeton UP, 1985.

Collins, Lisa Gail, and Margo Natalie Crawford, editors. *New Thoughts on the Black Arts Movement*. Rutgers UP, 2006.

Collins, Patricia Hill. *Black Sexual Politics: African Americans, Gender, and the New Racism*. Routledge, 2004.

"Common Data Set 2016–2017." *Millersville University*, Millersville University Department of Institutional Research, www.millersville.edu/iea/ir/files/CDS201617MI.pdf.

Cone, James H. *The Spirituals and the Blues*. Orbis, 1991.

Cooper, Alan. *Philip Roth and the Jews*. State U of New York P, 1996.

Copeland, Charlton. "'Fists and the Voices of Sorrowful Women': Race, Gender, Violence, and the Reconstruction of the Word in Toni Morrison's *Jazz*." *African American Culture and Legal Discourse*, edited by Lovalerie King and Richard Schur, Palgrave, 2008, pp. 131–58.

Coser, Lewis A. *Men of Ideas: A Sociologist's View*. Free, 1965.

Crespy, David A. "A Paradigm for New Play Development: The Albee-Barr-Wilder Playwrights Unit." *Theatre History Studies*, vol. 26, 2006, pp. 31–51.

———. *Richard Barr: The Playwright's Producer*. Southern Illinois UP, 2013.

Cruse, Harold. *The Crisis of the Negro Intellectual*. Morrow, 1967.

Cubria, Kaitlin. "Four Theories That'll Change the Way You Look at *101 Dalmations*." *Clevver*, 7 Nov. 2014, www.clevver.com/101-dalmatians-theories-hidden-messages/.

Cullen, Countee. "Heritage." *Color*, by Cullen, Harper, 1925, pp. 36–41.

Curti, Merle. *American Paradox: The Conflict of Thought and Action*. Rutgers UP, 1956.

Dace, Letitia. *LeRoi Jones (Imamu Amiri Baraka): A Checklist of Works by and about Him*. Nether, 1971.

"Dancing in the Street." Written by Marvin Gaye et al., performed by Martha and the Vandellas. *Sixteen Original Big Hits*, vol. 3, Motown Records, 1964.

Davidoff, Paula, and Carolyn Hunt. "Raising Voices: Teaching Teen Girls to Speak Out." *Teaching Artist Journal*, vol. 13, no. 4, 2015, pp. 218–26.

Davis, Angela Y. *Blues Legacies and Black Feminism: Gertrude "Ma" Rainey, Bessie Smith, and Billie Holiday*. Pantheon, 1998.

Davis, Carol Bunch. *Prefiguring Postblackness: Cultural Memory, Drama, and the African American Freedom Struggle of the 1960s*. UP of Mississippi, 2015.

Davis, Ossie. *Purlie Victorious: A Comedy in Three Acts*. French, 1961.

Decker, Jeffrey Louis, editor. *The Black Aesthetic Movement*. Gale, 1991. Vol. 8 of *The Dictionary of Literary Biography Documentary Series*.

Dent, Tom. "Umbra Days." *Black American Literature Forum*, vol. 14, no. 3, 1980, pp. 105–08.

di Prima, Diane. *Recollections of My Life as a Woman, the New York Years: A Memoir*. Viking, 2001.

di Prima, Diane, and LeRoi Jones, editors. *The Floating Bear: A Newsletter*. McGilvery, 1973.

Dixon, Melvin. *Ride Out the Wilderness: Geography and Identity in Afro-American Literature*. U of Illinois P, 1987.

Dorn, Edward. "Non-Review: Dutchman *and* The Slave." *Wild Dog*, vol. 2, no. 2, 1964, pp. 3–7.

Duberman, Martin B. *In White America: A Documentary Play*. Houghton Mifflin, 1964.

Du Bois, W. E. B. *The Souls of Black Folk: Essays and Sketches*. McClurg, 1903.

Duke, Vernon, et al. *Cabin in the Sky: A Musical Fable*. ICM, 1985.

Dunbar, Paul Laurence. "We Wear the Mask." *Poetry Foundation*, www.poetryfoundation.org/poems/44203/we-wear-the-mask.

Dutchman. Directed by Mark Clayton Southers, performance by Tami Dixon and Jonathan Berry, Bricolage Production Company, Pittsburgh, PA, 11 May 2012.

Early, Gerald. "The Case of LeRoi Jones / Amiri Baraka." *Salmagundi*, vol. 70–71, 1986, pp. 343–52.

Eberstadt, Isabel. "King of the East Village." *New York Herald Tribune*, Sunday magazine section, 13 Dec. 1964, pp. 13+.

Eisler, Jerzy. "Marzec 1968." *PRL od lipca 44 do grudnia 70*, edited by Krzysztof Persak and Paweł Machcewicz, Bellona, 2010, pp. 321–49.

Elam, Harry J., Jr. "Post–World War II African American Theatre." *The Oxford Handbook of American Drama*, edited by Jeffrey H. Richards and Heather S. Nathans, Oxford UP, 2014, pp. 375–91.

———. *Taking It to the Streets: The Social Protest Theater of Luis Valdez and Amiri Baraka*. U of Michigan P, 1997.

———. "The *TDR* Black Theatre Issue: Refiguring the Avant-Garde." *Not the Other Avant-Garde: The Transnational Foundations of Avant-Garde Performance*, U of Michigan P, 2006, pp. 41–66.

Elam, Harry J., Jr., and David Krasner. *African-American Performance and Theater History: A Critical Reader*. Oxford UP, 2001.

Elam, Michele. "Passing in the Post-Race Era: Danzy Senna, Philip Roth, and Colson Whitehead." *African American Review*, vol. 41, no. 4, 2007, pp. 749–68.

Eliot, T. S. "The Love Song of J. Alfred Prufrock." Belasco and Johnson, pp. 672–76.

———. "*Ulysses*, Order, and Myth." *Selected Prose of T. S. Eliot*, edited by Frank Kermode, Harcourt Brace, 1975, pp. 175–78.

———. *The Waste Land*. Belasco and Johnson, pp. 678–96.

Ellison, Ralph. *"Flying Home" and Other Stories*. Random House, 1996.

———. *Invisible Man*. Vintage, 1995.

———. *Shadow and Act*. Random House, 1964.

Englert, Maciej. Interview with Katarzyna Jakubiak. 9 Mar. 2011.

Epstein, Andrew. *Beautiful Enemies: Friendship and Postwar American Poetry*. Oxford UP, 2006.

Ernest, John. *Chaotic Justice: Rethinking African American Literary History*. U of North Carolina P, 2009.

Essien-Udom, E. U. *Black Nationalism: A Search for an Identity in America*. U of Chicago P, 1962.

Esslin, Martin. *The Theatre of the Absurd*. Vintage, 2004.

Estes, Steve. *I Am a Man! Race, Manhood, and the Civil Rights Movement*. U of North Carolina P, 2005.

Ethnic Notions: Black People in White Minds. Directed by Marlon Riggs, California Newsreel, 1987.

Eversley, Shelly. *The Real Negro: The Question of Authenticity in Twentieth-Century African American Literature*. Routledge, 2004.

Fabre, Geneviève. *Drumbeats, Masks, and Metaphor: Contemporary Afro-American Theatre*. Harvard UP, 1983.

Fanon, Frantz. *The Wretched of the Earth*. Translated by Constance Farrington, Grove, 1963.

"Flare Festival." *Artslink.co.za*, 30 Apr. 2008, www.artlink.co.za/news_article.htm?contentID=5480.

"Flying Dutchman." *Encyclopedia of Myths*, www.mythencyclopedia.com/Fi-Go/Flying-Dutchman.html. Accessed 29 Oct. 2015.

Frazier, E. Franklin. *Black Bourgeoisie: The Rise of a New Middle Class in the United States*. Free, 1957.

Frick, John W. Uncle Tom's Cabin *on the American Stage and Screen*. Palgrave Macmillan, 2012.

Fugard, Athol. *Blood Knot*. French, 1964.

Fuller, Hoyt W. "Up in Harlem: New Hope." *Negro Digest*, vol. 14, no. 12, 1965, pp. 49+.

Gardiner, Paul, and Michael Anderson. "Can You Read That Again? Playwriting, Literacy and Reading the 'Spoken' Word." *English in Australia*, vol. 47, no. 2, 2012, pp. 80–89.

Gates, Henry Louis, Jr. *Thirteen Ways of Looking at a Black Man*. Random House, 1997.

Gates, Henry Louis, Jr., and Nellie Y. McKay. "Introduction: Talking Books." Gates and McKay, *Norton Anthology*, pp. xxvii–xlvii.

———, eds. *The Norton Anthology of African American Literature*. 2nd ed., W. W. Norton, 2003.

———. "The Vernacular Tradition." Gates and McKay, *Norton Anthology*, pp. 3–8.

Gates, Henry Louis, Jr., and Valerie Smith, editors. *The Norton Anthology of African American Literature*. 3rd ed., W. W. Norton, 2014. 2 vols.

Gayle, Addison, Jr., editor. *The Black Aesthetic*. Doubleday, 1971.

———, editor. *Black Expression: Essays by and about Black Americans in the Creative Arts*. Weybright and Talley, 1969.

———. Introduction. Gayle, *Black Aesthetic*, pp. xv–xxiv.

Genet, Jean. *The Blacks: A Clown Show*. Translated by Bernard Frechtman, Grove, 1960.

Gennari, John. *Blowin' Hot and Cool: Jazz and Its Critics*. U of Chicago P, 2006.

Gilroy, Paul. *The Black Atlantic: Modernity and Double Consciousness*. Harvard UP, 1993.

Ginsberg, Allen. "Howl." *"Howl" and Other Poems*, City Lights, 1993, pp. 9–20.

———. *The Letters of Allen Ginsberg*. Edited by Bill Morgan, Perseus, 2008.

———. *Spontaneous Mind: Selected Interviews, 1958–1996*. Edited by David Carter, HarperCollins, 2001.

Giovanni, Nikki. "For Saundra." Gates and Smith, vol. 2, pp. 880–81.

Godard, Jean-Luc, director. *Masculin Féminin*. Criterion, 2005.

Goodman, Diane J., and Bailey W. Jackson III. "Pedagogical Approaches to Teaching about Racial Identity from an Intersectional Perspective." Wijeyesinghe and Jackson, pp. 216–39.

Gossett, Thomas. Uncle Tom's Cabin *and American Culture*. Southern Methodist UP, 1985.

Graff, Gerald, and James Phelan. "Writing about Critical Controversy and *The Tempest*." *William Shakespeare: The Tempest: A Case Study in Critical Controversy*, 2nd ed., Bedford, 2009, pp. 413–18.

Griffin, John Howard. *Black Like Me*. Signet, 2010.

Griffith, D. W., director. *Birth of a Nation*. Griffith, 1915.

Grimké, Angelina Weld. *Rachel*. Hatch and Shine, pp. 133–68.

Gruen, John. *The New Bohemia*. A Cappella, 1990.

Guess Who's Coming to Dinner. Directed by Stanley Kramer, performance by Sidney Poitier and Spencer Tracy, Sony Pictures, 2004.

Gwynne, James B., editor. *Amiri Baraka: The Kaleidoscopic Torch: A Literary Tribute*. Steppingstones, 1985.

Haft, Adele J. "Outlining Your Own Greek Drama: A Creative Project." *Approaches to Teaching the Dramas of Euripides*, edited by Robin Mitchell-Boyask, Modern Language Association of America, 2002, pp. 95–102.

Haggins, Bambi. *Laughing Mad: The Black Comic Persona in Post-Soul America*. Rutgers UP, 2007.

Haider, Asad. "Passing for Politics." *Medium*, 15 June 2016, medium.com/@ahaider/passing-for-politics-559e14c813f7.

Hairston, William, and Hans Habe. *Walk in Darkness: A Play in Three Acts*. Studio Duplicating Service, 1963.

Hanley, William. *Slow Dance on the Killing Ground: A New Play*. Random House, 1964.

Hansberry, Lorraine. *A Raisin in the Sun*. Vintage, 1995.

———. *A Raisin in the Sun: A Drama in Three Acts*. Random House, 1959.

———. *The Sign in Sidney Brustein's Window: A Drama in Three Acts*. Random House, 1965.

Harris, William J. "Amiri Baraka's Adventures with the Out and the Gone." *Callaloo*, vol. 37, no. 3, 2014, pp. 483–85.

———. "Chronology." Baraka, *LeRoi Jones/Amiri Baraka Reader*, pp. xxxi–xxxiii.

———. Introduction. Baraka, *LeRoi Jones/Amiri Baraka Reader*, pp. xvii–xxx.

———. *The Poetry and Poetics of Amiri Baraka: The Jazz Aesthetic*. U of Missouri P, 1985.

Harrison, Paul Carter. *The Drama of Nommo*. Grove, 1972.

Harvey, Anthony, director. *Dutchman*. Kaitlin, 1994.

Hatch, James V., and Ted Shine, editors. *Black Theatre U.S.A.* Rev. ed., vol. 1, Free, 1996. 2 vols.

The Heath Anthology of American Literature. Edited by Paul Lauter et al., 7th ed., Wadsworth Cengage, 2014. 5 vols.

Heble, Ajay. "The Poetics of Jazz: From Symbolic to Semiotic." *Textual Practice*, vol. 2, no. 1, 1988, pp. 51–68.

Henderson, Stephen E., editor. *Understanding the New Black Poetry: Black Speech and Black Music as Poetic References*. Morrow, 1973.

Hernton, Calvin. *Sex and Racism in America*. Anchor, 1992.

Hill, Errol, editor. *The Theatre of Black Americans: A Collection of Critical Essays*. Prentice-Hall, 1980.

Hill, Errol G., and James V. Hatch. *A History of African American Theatre*. Cambridge UP, 2003.

Himes, Chester. *If He Hollers Let Him Go*. Thunder's Mouth, 2002.

Hitchcock, Alfred, director. *Vertigo*. Paramount, 1958.

Hofstadter, Richard. *Anti-Intellectualism in American Life*. Knopf, 1963.

Hopkins, Pauline. *Peculiar Sam; or, The Underground Railroad*. *The Roots of African American Drama*, edited by Leo Hamalian and James Vernon Hatch, Wayne State UP, 1991, pp. 100–23.

Houen, Alex. *Powers of Possibility: Experimental American Writing since the 1960s*. Oxford UP, 2012.

Hudson, Theodore R. *From LeRoi Jones to Amiri Baraka: The Literary Works*. Duke UP, 1973.

Hughes, Langston. "Harlem." *The Collected Poems of Langston Hughes*, edited by Arnold Rampersad and David Roessel, Vintage, 1994, p. 426.

———. *Jerico-Jim Crow*. Folkways, 1964.

———. "The Negro Artist and the Racial Mountain." Belasco and Johnson, pp. 557–61.

———. "The Negro Artist and the Racial Mountain." Gates and Smith, vol. 1, pp. 1320–24.

———. "The Negro Artist and the Racial Mountain." *The Portable Harlem Renaissance Reader*, edited by David Levering Lewis, Penguin, 1994, pp. 91–95.

———. *Tambourines to Glory*. *Five Plays*, edited by Webster Smalley, Indiana UP, 1963, pp. 183–258.

Hurston, Zora Neale. "How It Feels to Be Colored Me." Gates and Smith, vol. 1, pp. 1040–42.

Imbrie, Ann E. "An Archetypal Approach." *Approaches to Teaching Shakespeare's* King Lear, edited by Robert H. Ray, Modern Language Association of America, 1986, pp. 69–74.

Jackson, Blanche M. "Doubtful 'Dutchman.'" *Village Voice*, 14 May 1964, pp. 4+.

Jacobson, Matthew Frye. *Roots Too: White Ethnic Revival in Post–Civil Rights America*. Harvard UP, 2006.

Jan. 1st 1959: Fidel Castro. Totem, 1959.

Jarrett, Gene Andrew. *Representing the Race: A New Political History of African American Literature*. New York UP, 2011.

Jeffers, Lance. "Afroamerican Literature: The Conscience of Man." *New Black Voices*, edited by Abraham Chapman, New American Library, 1972, pp. 506–13.

Jester, Caroline, and Claire Stoneman. *Playwriting across the Curriculum*. Routledge, 2011.

Jimoh, A Yẹmisi. *Spiritual, Blues, and Jazz People in African American Fiction: Living in Paradox*. U of Tennessee P, 2002.

Johnson, Abby Arthur, and Ronald Maberry Johnson. *Propaganda and Aesthetics: The Literary Politics of Afro-American Magazines in the Twentieth Century*. U of Massachusetts P, 1979.

Johnson, E. Patrick. *Appropriating Blackness: Performance and the Politics of Authenticity*. Duke UP, 2003.

Johnson, James Weldon. *The Autobiography of an Ex-Coloured Man*. Vintage, 1989.

Jones, Hettie. *How I Became Hettie Jones*. Dutton, 1990.

Jones, LeRoi (*see also* Baraka, Amiri). Dutchman *and* The *Slave: Two New Plays*. Morrow, 1964.

Jones, Meta DuEwa. "Jazz Prosodies: Orality and Textuality." *Callaloo*, vol. 25, no.1, 2002, pp. 66–91.

Joseph, Peniel. "Our National Postracial Hangover." *Chronicle of Higher Education*, 27 July 2009, www.chronicle.com/article/Our-National-Postracial/47462.

Kane, Daniel. *All Poets Welcome: The Lower East Side Poetry Scene in the 1960s*. U of California P, 2003.

Karenga, Ron. "Black Cultural Nationalism." Gayle, *Black Aesthetic*, pp. 32–38.

Katznelson, Ira. *When Affirmative Action Was White: An Untold History of Racial Inequality in Twentieth-Century America*. W. W. Norton, 2005.

Kennedy, Adrienne. *Funnyhouse of a Negro*. French, 1969.

Kennedy, Randall. *Race, Crime, and the Law*. Vintage, 1997.

Kerouac, Jack. "Beatific: The Origins of the Beat Generation." *The Portable Jack Kerouac*, edited by Ann Charters, Viking, 1995, pp. 565–73.

———. *The Dharma Bums*. Penguin, 2006.

———. *On the Road*. Penguin, 2003.

———. "239th Chorus." *Mexico City Blues*, Grove Weidenfeld, 1990.

King, Woodie, Jr., director. *Black Theatre: The Making of a Movement*. California Newsreel, 1978.

Knox, George. "The 'Mythology' of LeRoi Jones's *Dutchman*." *Interculture: A Collection of Essays and Creative Writing Commemorating the Twentieth Anniversary of the Fulbright Program at the Institute of Translation and Interpretation University of Vienna, 1955–1974*, edited by Sy M. Kahn and Martha Raetz, Braumüller, 1975, pp. 243–51.

Kornweibel, Theodore. *Railroads in the African American Experience*. Johns Hopkins UP, 2010.

Kumar, Nita N. "The Logic of Retribution: Amiri Baraka's *Dutchman*." *African American Review*, vol. 37, nos. 2–3, 2003, pp. 271–79.

Lacey, Henry C. *To Raise, Destroy, and Create: The Poetry, Drama, and Fiction of Imamu Amiri Baraka (Le Roi Jones)*. Whitston, 1981.

Larsen, Nella. *Passing*. Knopf, 1929.

———. *Quicksand*. Penguin, 1987.

Lasch, Christopher. *The New Radicalism in America, 1889–1963: The Intellectual as a Social Type*. Knopf, 1965.

Lee, Harper. *To Kill a Mockingbird*. HarperCollins, 2002.

Lee, Young Jean. Songs of the Dragon Flying to Heaven *and Other Plays*. Theatre Communications Group, 2009.

Leeming, David. *James Baldwin*. Knopf, 1994.

Lennon, Mary Ellen. "A Question of Relevancy: New York Museums and the Black Arts Movement, 1968–1971." Collins and Crawford, pp. 92–116.

"LeRoi Jones to Give a Course on Playwriting at Columbia." *The New York Times*, 22 June 1964, p. 22.

Levesque, George A. "LeRoi Jones' *Dutchman*: Myth and Allegory." *Obsidian*, vol. 5, no. 3, 1979, pp. 33–40.

Levine, Lawrence W. *Black Culture and Black Consciousness: Afro-American Folk Thought from Slavery to Freedom*. Oxford UP, 1978.

Lewis, Leslie W. "Naming the Problem Embedded in the Problem That Led to the Question 'Who Shall Teach African American Literature?'; or, Are We Ready to Discard the Concept of Authenticity Altogether?" *White Scholars / African American Texts*, edited by Lisa A. Long, Rutgers UP, 2005, pp. 52–67.

Lhamon, W. T., Jr. *Raising Cain: Blackface Performance from Jim Crow to Hip Hop*. Harvard UP, 1998.

Li, Stephanie. *Playing in the White: Black Writers, White Subjects*. Oxford UP, 2015.

———. *Signifying without Specifying: Racial Discourse in the Age of Obama*. Rutgers UP, 2011.

Lindberg, John. "*Dutchman* and *The Slave*: Comparisons in Revolution." Benston, *Imamu Amiri Baraka*, pp. 141–47.

Lindfors, Bernth, editor. *Africans on Stage: Studies in Ethnological Show Business*. Indiana UP, 1999.

Lipsitz, George. *The Possessive Investment in Whiteness: How White People Profit from Identity Politics*. Rev. and expanded ed., Temple UP, 2006.

Little, Stuart W. *Off-Broadway: The Prophetic Theater*. Coward, McCann, and Geoghegan, 1972.

Locke, Alain. "The New Negro." *The New Negro*, edited by Locke, Simon and Schuster, 1992, pp. 3–16.

Löfgren, Lotta M. "Clay and Clara: Baraka's *Dutchman*, Kennedy's *The Owl Answers*, and the Black Arts Movement." *Modern Drama*, vol. 46, no. 3, 2003, pp. 424–49.

Lorde, Audre. "The Master's Tools Will Never Dismantle the Master's House." *Sister Outsider*, Crossing, 1984, pp. 110–13.

———. "Poetry Is Not a Luxury." Gates and Smith, vol. 2, pp. 643–46.

———. "Uses of the Erotic." *Sister Outsider*, by Lorde, Crossing, 1984, pp. 53–59.

Lott, Eric. *Love and Theft: Blackface Minstrelsy and the American Working Class*. Oxford UP, 1993.

"(Love Is Like a) Heat Wave." Written by Lamont Dozier et al., performed by Martha and the Vandellas. *Heat Wave*, Motown Records, 1963.

Lowell, Robert. *Benito Cereno*. *The Old Glory*, Farrar, Straus and Giroux, 1965, pp. 135–214.

Luter, Matthew. "Dutchman's Signifyin(g) Subway: How Amiri Baraka Takes Ralph Ellison Underground." *Reading Contemporary African American Drama: Fragments of History, Fragments of Self*, edited by Trudier Harris and Jennifer Larson, Peter Lang, 2007, pp. 21–38.

MacAdams, Lewis, and John Dorr, directors. *Amiri Baraka*. Lannan Foundation, 1991.

Mackey, Nathaniel. *Discrepant Engagement: Dissonance, Cross-Culturality, and Experimental Writing*. Cambridge UP, 1993.

Mahar, William J. *Behind the Burnt Cork Mask: Early Blackface Minstrelsy in Antebellum American Culture*. U of Illinois P, 1999.

Major, Clarence, editor. *The New Black Poetry*. International, 1969.

Malcolm X. *The Autobiography of Malcolm X*. With Alex Haley. Ballantine, 1992.

———. "The Ballot or the Bullet." *Malcolm X Speaks: Selected Speeches and Statements*, edited by George Breitman, Grove, 1965, 23–44.

Marinetti, F. T. "Initial Manifesto of Futurism." *Futurism*. Joshua C. Taylor, Museum of Modern Art, 1961, pp. 124–25.

Marlowe, Christopher. *The Tragical History of Doctor Faustus. The Harvard Classics*, edited by Charles W. Eliot, vol. 19, Collier, 1909, pp. 205–50.

Martin, Michael T., and David C. Wall. "'Where Are You From': Performing Race in the Art of Jefferson Pinder." *Black Camera*, vol. 2, no. 1, 2010, pp. 72–105.

Matlin, Daniel. *On the Corner: African American Intellectuals and the Urban Crisis*. Harvard UP, 2013.

Maxwell, William J. *F.B. Eyes: How J. Edgar Hoover's Ghostreaders Framed African American Literature*. Princeton UP, 2015.

McDarrah, Fred W. *Greenwich Village*. Corinth, 1963.

McGee, Celia. "A Return to Rage, Played Out in Black and White." *The New York Times*, 14 Jan. 2007, pp. A4, A7.

Meer, Sarah. *Uncle Tom Mania: Slavery, Minstrelsy, and Transatlantic Culture in the 1850s*. U of Georgia P, 2005.

Miller, Arthur. *A View from the Bridge: A Play in Two Acts*. Penguin, 2009.

Miller, D. Quentin. "Using the Blues." *A Historical Guide to James Baldwin*, edited by Douglas Field, Oxford UP, 2009, pp. 83–110.

Miller, Monica. *Slaves to Fashion: Black Dandyism and the Styling of Black Diasporic Identity*. Duke UP, 2009.

Mills, C. Wright. *Power, Politics, and People: The Collected Essays of C. Wright Mills*, edited by Irving Louis Horowitz, Ballantine, 1963.

———. "The Social Role of the Intellectual." Mills, pp. 292–304.

Miłosz, Czesław. *The Captive Mind*. Random House, 1990.

Mitchell, Koritha. "James Baldwin, Performance Theorist, Sings the *Blues for Mister Charlie. American Quarterly*, vol. 54, no. 1, 2012, pp. 33–60.

———. "Supreme Court Agrees with Michigan Voters: Affirmative Action Must Remain for Whites Only." *Huffington Post*, 23 Apr. 2014, www.huffingtonpost.com/entry/supreme-court-agrees-with_b_5200809.html.

Mitchell, Loften. "LeRoi Jones Brings 'Dutchman' to Harlem." *N.Y. Amsterdam News*, 3 July 1965, p. 37.

Morrison, Toni. *The Bluest Eye*. Plume, 1993.

———. *Sula*. Knopf, 1973.

Mosley, Walter. *Devil in a Blue Dress*. Norton, 1990.

Moten, Fred. *In the Break: The Aesthetics of the Black Radical Tradition*. U of Minnesota P, 2003.

Motherwell, Robert, editor. *Dada Painters and Poets.* Wittenborn and Schultz, 1951.

Moyers, Bill D., director. *Sounds of Poetry with Bill Moyers: Amiri Baraka.* Films Media, 1999.

"'The Names We Give': Events in Arts, Culture, and Society, 13–15 May 2011." *University of Cape Town*, www.uct.ac.za/usr/calendar/2011/names_we_give.pdf. Accessed 31 Oct. 2017.

Ndlovu, Duma. "Re: Seeking Research Help." E-mail message received by Mbongiseni Magagula and Katarzyna Jakubiak, 2 Nov. 2017.

Neal, Larry. "The Black Arts Movement." Gayle, *Black Aesthetic*, pp. 272–90.

———. "The Black Arts Movement." *The Drama Review*, vol. 12, no. 4, 1968, pp. 29–39.

———. "The Black Arts Movement." Gates and McKay, *Norton Anthology*, pp. 2039–50.

Nelson, Cary. "Multiculturalism without Guarantees: From Anthologies to the Social Text." *The Journal of the Midwest Modern Language Association*, vol. 26, no. 1, 1993, pp. 47–57.

Nelson, Hugh. "LeRoi Jones' *Dutchman*: A Brief Ride on a Doomed Ship." *Educational Theatre Journal*, vol. 20, no. 1, 1968, pp. 53–59.

Nelson, Scott. *Steel Drivin' Man: The Untold Story of an American Legend.* Oxford UP, 2006.

nhlanhla. "dutchman . . . #5–9." 75, 15–27 May 2009, 75.co.za/kool_one_ebony/2009/05/15.

Nichols, Mike, director. *Who's Afraid of Virginia Woolf?* Warner Brothers, 1966.

Nielsen, Aldon Lynn. *Black Chant: Languages of African-American Postmodernism.* Cambridge UP, 1997.

———. *Integral Music: Languages of African American Innovation.* U of Alabama P, 2004.

———. *Writing between the Lines: Race and Intertextuality.* U of Georgia P, 1994.

Olaniyan, Tejumola. *Scars of Conquest / Masks of Resistance: The Invention of Cultural Identities in African, African-American, and Caribbean Drama.* Oxford UP, 1995.

Ongiri, Amy Abugo. *Spectacular Blackness: The Cultural Politics of the Black Power Movement and the Search for a Black Aesthetic.* U of Virginia P, 2010.

Osęka, Piotr. *Marzec'68.* Znak, 2008.

Panish, Jon. *The Color of Jazz: Race and Representation in Postwar American Culture.* UP of Mississippi, 1997.

———. "Kerouac's *The Subterraneans*: A Study of 'Romantic Primitivism.'" *MELUS*, vol. 19, no. 3, 1994, pp. 107–23.

Parks, Suzan-Lori. *The Death of the Last Black Man in the Whole Entire World.* The America Play *and Other Works*, by Parks, Theatre Communications Group, 1995, pp. 99–132.

Parone, Edward, editor. *New Theatre in America.* Dell, 1965.

Paton, Alan, and Krishna Shah. *Sponono: A Play in Three Acts.* Scribner, 1965.

Patterson, Charles. *Black-Ice: A Play in One Act*. Baraka and Neal, pp. 559–65.

Perry, Mia, et al. "From Playbuilding to Devising in Literacy Education: Aesthetic and Pedagogical Approaches." *Journal of Adolescent and Adult Literacy*, vol. 56, no. 8, 2013, pp. 649–58.

Peterson, Louis. *Take a Giant Step: A Drama in Two Acts*. French, 1954.

Piggford, George. "Looking into Black Skulls: Amiri Baraka's *Dutchman* and the Psychology of Race." *Modern Drama*, vol. 40, no. 1, 1997, pp. 74–85.

Podhoretz, Norman. "The Know-Nothing Bohemians." *The Partisan Review*, vol. 25, no. 2, 1958, pp. 305–18.

———. "My Negro Problem—and Ours." *Commentary*, 1 Feb. 1963, www.commentarymagazine.com/articles/my-negro-problem-and-ours/.

Poggioli, Renato. *The Theory of the Avant-Garde*. Translated by Gerald Fitzgerald, Harvard UP, 1968.

Pratt, Mary Louise. "Arts of the Contact Zone." *Profession*, vol. 91, 1991, pp. 33–40.

Rambsy, Howard II. *The Black Arts Enterprise and the Production of African American Poetry*. U of Michigan P, 2011.

Ramey, Lauri. *Slave Songs and the Birth of African American Poetry*. Palgrave Macmillan, 2008.

Rawson, Christopher. "*Dutchman* Talk-Backs Go 'Between the Lines.'" *Pittsburgh Post-Gazette*, 3 May 2012, www.post-gazette.com/ae/theater-dance/2012/05/02/Dutchman-talk-backs-go-Between-the-Lines/stories/201205020220.

Rebhorn, Matthew. "Flaying Dutchman: Masochism, Minstrelsy, and the Gender Politics of Amiri Baraka's *Dutchman*." *Callaloo*, vol. 26, no. 3, 2003, pp. 796–812.

Reck, Tom S. "Archetypes in LeRoi Jones' *Dutchman*." *Studies in Black Literature*, vol. 1, no. 1, 1970, pp. 66–68.

Reed, Ishmael. *Flight to Canada*. Scribner, 1998.

Rembrandt. *Sampling Officials of the Drapers' Guild* [*De Staalmeesters*]. 1662. *Rijksmuseum*, www.rijksmuseum.nl/en/collection/SK-C-6.

Retman, Sonnet H. "Langston Hughes's 'Rejuvenation through Joy': Passing, Racial Performance, and the Marketplace." *African American Review*, vol. 45, no. 4, 2012, pp. 593–602.

Riley, Clayton. "On Black Theater." Gayle, *Black Aesthetic*, pp. 313–30.

Rose, Tricia. *Black Noise: Rap Music and Black Culture in Contemporary America*. UP of New England, 1994.

Ross, Marlon B. "Camping the Dirty Dozens: The Queer Resources of Black Nationalist Invective." *Callaloo*, vol. 23, no. 1, 2000, pp. 290–312.

Roszkowski, Wojciech. *Historia Polski, 1914–2005*. Wydawnictwo Naukowe PWN, 2009.

Roth, Philip. *American Pastoral*. Random House, 1997.

———. "Channel X: Two Plays on the Race Conflict." *New York Review of Books*, 28 May 1964, pp. 10–12.

———. *The Facts*. Random House, 1997.

———. *"Goodbye, Columbus" and Five Short Stories*. Random House, 1993.

———. *The Human Stain*. Random House, 2001.

———. *I Married a Communist*. Random House, 1999.

———. *Zuckerman Bound: A Trilogy and an Epilogue*. Farrar, Straus, and Giroux, 1985.

Rowe, John Carlos. *Afterlives of Modernism: Liberalism, Transnationalism, and Political Critique*. Dartmouth College P, 2011.

Russell, Charlie L. "LeRoi Jones Will Get Us All in Trouble." *Liberator*, vol. 4, no. 6, 1964, pp. 10–11.

Russell, Ross. "Bebop." *The Art of Jazz: Essays on the Nature and Development of Jazz*, edited by Martin Williams, Oxford UP, 1959, pp. 187–213.

Sanders, Leslie Catherine. *The Development of Black Theater in America: From Shadows to Selves*. Louisiana State UP, 1988.

Saroyan, William. *An Armenian Trilogy*. California State UP, 1986.

Saul, Scott. *Freedom Is, Freedom Ain't: Jazz and the Making of the Sixties*. Harvard UP, 2003.

Saunders, James. Neighbours *and Other Plays*. Heinemann, 1968.

Schur, Richard. "The Crisis of Authenticity in Contemporary African American Literature." *Contemporary African American Literature: The Living Canon*, edited by Lovalerie King and Shirley Moody-Turner, Indiana UP, 2013, pp. 235–54.

Schwartz, Larry. "Roth, Race, and Newark." *Cultural Logic*, vol. 8, 2005, clogic.eserver.org/2005/schwartz.

Scottsboro: An American Tragedy. Directed by Daniel Anker and Barak Goodman, PBS Home Video, 2005.

Sell, Mike. *Avant-Garde Performance and the Limits of Criticism: Approaching the Living Theatre, Happenings/Fluxus, and the Black Arts Movement*. U of Michigan P, 2005.

———. "The Drama of the Black Arts Movement." *A Companion to Twentieth-Century American Drama*, edited by David Krasner, Blackwell, 2004, pp. 263–84.

Shakespeare, William. *Othello*. Norton, 2003.

Shange, Ntozake. *Spell #7. Nine Plays by Black Women*, edited by Margaret B. Wilkerson, Penguin, 1986, pp. 239–91.

Simanga, Michael. *Amiri Baraka and the Congress of African People: History and Memory*. Palgrave Macmillan, 2015.

Simone, Nina. *Nina Simone in Concert*. Philips, 1964.

Siraganian, Lisa. *Modernism's Other Work: The Art Object's Political Life*. Oxford UP, 2012.

Smethurst, James Edward. *The Black Arts Movement: Literary Nationalism in the 1960s and 1970s*. U of North Carolina P, 2005.

Smith, Anna Deavere. *Twilight: Los Angeles, 1992*. New Dramatists Play Service, 2003.

Smith, David Lionel. "What Is Black Culture?" *The House That Race Built: Black Americans, U.S. Terrain*, Pantheon, 1997, pp. 178–94.

Smith, Michael. "Theatre: Three at the Cherry Lane." *Village Voice*, 2 Apr. 1964, pp. 17–18.

Smith, Suzanne E. *"Dancing in the Street": Motown and the Cultural Politics of Detroit*. Harvard UP, 1999.

Sollors, Werner. *Amiri Baraka/LeRoi Jones: The Quest for a "Populist Modernism."* Columbia UP, 1978.

Southerne, Thomas. *Oroonoko*. U of Nebraska P, 2003.

Soyinka, Wole. *Death and the King's Horseman*. Edited by Simon Gikandi, Norton, 2003.

———. *Kongi's Harvest*. Oxford UP, 1967.

Stam, Robert, and Louise Spence. "Colonialism, Racism, and Representation: An Introduction." *Screen*, vol. 24, no. 2, 1983, pp. 2–20.

Staples, Brent. "Back When Skin Color Was Destiny." *The New York Times*, 7 Sept. 2003, p. 1.

Stowe, Harriet Beecher. *The Christian Slave: A Drama: Founded on a Portion of Uncle Tom's Cabin*. Philips, Sampson, 1855.

———. *Uncle Tom's Cabin*. Norton, 1994.

Stuckey, Sterling. *Slave Culture: Nationalist Theory and the Foundations of Black America*. Oxford UP, 1998.

Sukenick, Ronald. *Down and In: Life in the Underground*. Morrow, 1987.

Tanner, Samuel Jaye. "Accounting for Whiteness through Collaborative Fiction." *Research in Drama Education*, vol. 21, no. 2, 2016, pp. 183–95.

Tate, Greg. "How We Talk about Race: *Dutchman* and *White People* Take a Stab at Truth-Telling." *American Theatre*, May–June 2000, pp. 44–46.

Taubman, Howard. "The Theater: 'Dutchman.'" *The New York Times*, 25 Mar. 1964, p. 46.

Taylor, Diana. *The Archive and the Repertoire: Performing Cultural Memory in the Americas*. Duke UP, 2003.

Taylor, Willene P. "The Fall of Man Theme in Imamu Amiri Baraka's [LeRoi Jones'] *Dutchman*." *Negro American Literature Forum*, vol. 7, no. 4, 1973, pp. 127–31.

"Theater." *Playboy*, Oct. 1964, p. 51.

Thom, Jennifer S., and David Blades. "Exploring the Issues of Incorporating Cultural Differences in Education: A Curriculum Journey in Playwriting." *Educational Studies*, vol. 50, no. 5, 2014, pp. 498–513.

Thomas, Lorenzo. "Black Art/Handbills." *Callaloo*, vol. 4, 1978, pp. 73–76.

———. *Extraordinary Measures: Afrocentric Modernism and Twentieth-Century American Poetry*. U of Alabama P, 2000.

Thompson, Jack. "'Play' Tops New Bill." *New York Journal-American*, 25 Mar. 1964, p. 23.

Toll, Robert C. *Blacking Up: The Minstrel Show in Nineteenth-Century America*. Oxford UP, 1974.

Turner, Darwin T. "Visions of Love and Manliness in a Blackening World: Dramas of Black Life since 1953." *The Black Scholar*, vol. 25, no. 2, 1995, pp. 2–12.

Tzara, Tristan. "Dada Manifesto 1918." Motherwell, pp. 76–82.

"Uncle Tom." *Oxford English Dictionary*, Oxford UP, 2017, www.oed.com/view/Entry/210446?.

"Uncle Tomism." *Dictionary.com*, 2017, www.dictionary.com/browse/uncle-tomism.

"Underground Fury." *Newsweek*, 13 Apr. 1964, p. 60.

Valdez, Luis. Zoot Suit *and Other Plays*. Arte Publico, 1992.

Van Deburg, William. *New Day in Babylon: The Black Power Movement and American Culture, 1965–1975*. U of Chicago P, 1993.

Vangelisti, Paul, director. *Dutchman*. Pacifica Radio, KPFK, Los Angeles, 12 Jan. 1982.

Von Eschen, Penny M. *Satchmo Blows Up the World: Jazz Ambassadors Play the Cold War*. Harvard UP, 2004.

The Wadsworth Anthology of Drama. Edited by W. B. Worthen, 6th ed., Cengage, 2011.

Wagner, Richard. *The Flying Dutchman*. Edited by Felix Weingartner, Dover, 1988.

Wakefield, Dan. *New York in the Fifties*. Houghton Mifflin/Seymour Lawrence, 1992.

Walker, Alice. "Advancing Luna—and Ida B. Wells." *You Can't Keep a Good Woman Down*, by Walker, Harcourt, 2003, pp. 85–104.

———. "Everyday Use." *In Love and Trouble: Stories of Black Women*, by Walker, Harcourt, 1973, pp. 47–59.

Walker, Victor Leo II. "Archetype and Masking in LeRoi Jones/Amiri Baraka's *Dutchman*." *Black Theatre: Ritual Performance in the African Diaspora*, edited by Paul Carter Harrison, Gus Edwards, and Walker, Temple UP, 2002, pp. 236–43.

Warren, Kenneth W. *What Was African American Literature?* Harvard UP, 2011.

Watkins, Mel. *On the Real Side: A History of African American Comedy*. Lawrence Hill, 1999.

Watson, Veronica T. *The Souls of White Folk: African American Writers Theorize Whiteness*. UP of Mississippi, 2013.

Watts, Jerry Gafio. *Amiri Baraka: The Politics and Art of a Black Intellectual*. New York UP, 2001.

Werner, Craig. *A Change Is Gonna Come: Music, Race, and the Soul of America*. Rev. ed., U of Michigan P, 2006.

Whitehead, Colson. "The Year of Living Postracially." *The New York Times*, 4 Nov. 2009, p. A31.

Wiegman, Robyn. *American Anatomies: Theorizing Race and Gender*. Duke UP, 1995.

Wijeyesinghe, Charmaine, and Bailey W. Jackson III. Introduction. *New Perspectives on Racial Identity Development: Integrating Emerging Frameworks*, edited by Wijeyesinghe and Jackson, New York UP, 2012, pp. 1–7.

Williams, Mance. *Black Theatre in the 1960s and 1970s: A Historical-Critical Analysis of the Movement*. Greenwood, 1985.

Williams, Robert F. *Negroes with Guns*. Edited by Marc Schleifer, Marzani and Munsell, 1962.

Williams, Sherley Anne. *Give Birth to Brightness: A Thematic Study in Neo-Black Literature.* Dial, 1972.

Willis, John, editor. *Theatre World.* Vol. 21, Crown, 1965.

Wilson, August. *Two Trains Running.* Plume, 1993.

Winn, Maisha T. "'Our Side of the Story': Moving Incarcerated Youth Voices from Margins to Center." *Race, Ethnicity and Education*, vol. 13, no. 3, 2010, pp. 313–25.

Woodard, Komozi. *A Nation within a Nation: Amiri Baraka (LeRoi Jones) and Black Power Politics.* U of North Carolina P, 1999.

Woodard, Komozi, et al., editors. *The Black Power Movement, Part 1: Amiri Baraka from Black Arts to Black Radicalism.* University Publications of America, 2000.

Woolland, Brian. *Pupils as Playwrights: Drama, Literacy and Playwriting.* Trentham, 2008.

Wright, Richard. "Big Boy Leaves Home." *Uncle Tom's Children*, by Wright, HarperCollins, 1989, pp. 16–61.

———. *Black Boy.* Harper, 1945.

———. "The Man Who Lived Underground." *Cross-Section: A Collection of New American Writing*, edited by Edwin Seaver, Fischer, 1944, pp. 58–102.

———. *Native Son.* HarperCollins, 1989.

———. *The Outsider.* Harper, 1953.

Ząbek, Maciej. *Biali i czarni. Postawy Polaków wobec Afryki i Afrykanów.* DiG, 2007.

Zangwill, Israel. *The Melting Pot: Drama in Four Acts.* Macmillan, 1912.

Zygmonski, Aimee. "Amiri Baraka and the Black Arts Movement." *The Cambridge Companion to African American Theatre*, edited by Harvey Young, Cambridge UP, 2013, pp. 137–54.

INDEX